Securing India

Assessment of the Defence and Security Capabilities

Col. (Retd.) S. C. Narang

PRASHANT PUBLISHING HOUSE
DELHI-110094

Published by :
PRASHANT PUBLISHING HOUSE
C-34, 28 Foota Road, Gali-3,
West Karwal Nagar, Delhi-110094
Phone : 011-22963970, Mob. : 9810396373
e-mail.: prashantpublishinghouse@gmail.com

Securing India : Assessment of the Defence and Security Capabilities

First Published 2017

ISBN : 978-81-934253-3-6

PRINTED IN INDIA
Published by Mr. R.K. Jha M/s Prashant Publishing House and Published at H.S. Offset House Press, Delhi.

Securing India : Assessment of the Defence and Security Capabilities

Contents

Preface

National security issues have hardly been discussed by political parties during Defence budget debates in Parliament. The parliamentary attendance then presents a sorry spectacle. Yet when grave national crises occur every second politician becomes a master strategist or tactician minus the grasp of the essentials of strategy and the intricacies of military operations and oblivious to the fact that the parliamentarians own strategic incompetence brought about the military aggression in the first place.

India's security needs are expanding to the full range of the spectrum of conflict, from lone wolf to nuclear attacks. The present force structure and strategy essentially cater for a defensive policy with limited offensive capability, and separate strategies for Pakistan and China. The need for a proactive strategy is a fundamental requirement in a fast changing world, where reaction is prone to delayed actions as well as loss of escalation dominance. In conventional non-nuclear operations, the shift from the attritional style of warfare to mobile operations provides greater flexibility to planners and policy-makers. Not only does it release troops from fixed areas, it also creates an offensive approach and attitude in the forces. The centre of gravity for future wars will also include the political, population, and psychological domains. Hence, wars will be fought across the length of the nation, on many planes, besides the military, such as cyber, population, or infrastructure. Technology must play a critical role in addressing threats and in the conduct of war as a force multiplier. In any security facet, human resources will remain a paramount requirement and should be trained to the highest standards in all fields i.e. political, diplomatic, military and technical.

Security and geopolitical considerations are, naturally, threaded through these economic engagements. Since Atal Bihari Vajpayee revitalized ties with GCC states, New Delhi has shown an admirable pragmatism, juggling its relationships with competing power centres like Riyadh and Tehran—even in light of the witches' cauldron of proxy struggles and sectarian conflicts that is currently West Asia. This is the hallmark of mature diplomacy. The pay-off has been visible, from Saudi Arabia extraditing terror suspects to India to Qatari aid when Indian nationals have been endangered by the Islamic State and in Afghanistan.

This book fulfills the long felt necessity of a text dealing with concepts of this subject. It can also prove to be a worthy companion and guide for the students, users and researchers. This book is a modest attempt to fill this gap by placing in perspective the policy on defence and security by the security establishment and its manifestation into capabilities to meet the current and emerging challenges.

—*Editor*

1

Introduction

CHANGES IN INDIA'S SECURITY

India has been ruled since the end of the Cold War mainly by the Indian National Congress (INC, or Congress Party) government led by Narasimha Rao (June 1991 to May 1996); the United Front governments led successively by Janata Dal's Deve Gowda (June 1996 to April 1997) and I. K. Gujral, and supported by the INC and its allies; the National Democratic Alliance government led by the BJP and Atal Bihari Vajpayee (March 1998 to May 2004); and the United Progressive Alliance government led by the INC and Manmohan Singh (May 2004 to the present). The author considers India's security concept to have been through two phases of change over this period: the March 1998 assumption of office by the BJP, and the successful nuclear detonation in May of the same year. The collapse in 1998 of the Vajpayee government's ruling coalition and its subsequent fall from power left the prime minister and other leaders of the caretaker government no time that year to attend to foreign affairs. When the BJP again won the national elections in 1999, Vajpayee organized a stable coalition government that enabled the new leadership to act on its ambitions in the domestic, diplomatic and security spheres.

India's Post-Cold War Security Concept

India Believes the Security Environment is Still Grim, not Because of any Military Threat but Rather One Consisting in Politics and Economics; Specifically the Threat of its Marginalization within the International Community. The strategic thinking of Prime Minister Indira Gandhi, who held office for a total of 17 years (1966–1977 and 1980–1984), was India's dominant and representative security concept from 1962 to the closing years of the Cold War. In her view, India's security environment was problematic because of the serious military threats it faced from all directions. Foremost was the two-front Chinese and Pakistani threat. India believed that Sino–Indian hostilities faced the point of no return after the Sino–Indian armed conflict of 1962, and that China and Pakistan stood together as its main enemies. The situation the Nehru government had sought to avoid during the early 1950s—that of simultaneously facing enemies to the east and west—had become a reality. It was a threat that appeared to intensify from the mid-1960s onwards as China and Pakistan became ever closer.

The second threat comprised American military support for Pakistan during the 1950s and 1960s, US strategic cooperation with China during the 1970s and US coordination with both Pakistan and China on the Afghan crisis during the 1980s, all of which made the Indian government extremely uneasy.

The third was constituted by the fact that small South Asian states such as Bangladesh, Nepal and Sri Lanka sought political and military cooperation with the United States and China at various times and on the basis of different considerations. India interpreted this as a threat to its status as leading regional power as well as to its national security.

The end of the Cold War did not bring India any sense of security. In the words of the Rao's Foreign Secretary, J. N. Dixit, even though it brought no real threat to India's territory or national security, potential threats nevertheless existed. First, having stood with the Soviet Union during the Cold War, India felt a sense of loss; the break-up of the USSR left the subcontinent stranded within the new world order. Second, India's international influence suffered a serious setback after the rapid post-Cold War cooling-off of the non-aligned movement. Third, the external payments crisis from 1990 to 1991 pushed the Indian economy to the point of collapse. And last, India faced growing international pressure in the areas of non-proliferation, human rights and economics. The indefinite extension of the Nuclear Non-Proliferation Treaty in the mid-1990s and the opening of talks on the Comprehensive Nuclear Test Ban Treaty made apparent to the Indian government the growing global pressure that the international non-proliferation mechanism exerted on its nuclear options and guided missile programme. It also interpreted Western nations' complaints about India's economic reforms and criticisms of its human rights record as interference in Indian domestic affairs. These circumstances implied to the Indian government that the greatest threat the nation faced in the aftermath of the Cold War was marginalization within the international community, or in other words, India's being regarded as a regional power of a similar order to Pakistan.

India's Understanding of Strength Changes

Having reckoned its failure in the 1962 Sino–Indian conflict as due to a lack of military preparedness, India placed unprecedented emphasis on military strength to maintain national security. Nehru wrote an article in 1963 calling on India to strengthen its army and expand production of arms and equipment. It was further suggested after Indira Gandhi took office that the nation's strength be visible and tangible through expansion of its military power. She believed that protecting national interests relied primarily on India's self-reliance and strengthening, or in other words, that India's security could be guaranteed only by a fortified military.

The military reforms begun in 1962 gathered momentum during her term, and India's conventional force was greatly enhanced. The sub-continent's military expenditure increased from 1962 to the years towards the end of the Cold War from the 1.8% of GDP of the early 1950s to more than 3%. India's leaders demonstrated on several occasions during this period both their resolve and desire to use military force to preserve national security, waging war with Pakistan in 1965 and 1971, and carrying out its first underground nuclear test in 1974. Rajiv Gandhi's government also deployed troops in the late 1980s to deal with domestic conflicts in Sri Lanka and the Maldives. The external payments crisis of 1990–1991, however, compelled India to carry out economic reforms, and gradually shift from the nationalized, domestically oriented economic policy that had prevailed since independence to one that is more open and liberal. As earlier mentioned, economic weakness aggravated India's unease as the Cold War drew to its conclusion.

The Soviet Union's disintegration made plain to Indian leaders that blindly seeking military supremacy was no certain guarantee of national security, particularly as it was economics that eventually defeated the USSR, even though it had prepared adequately during the Cold War for all manner of armed conflict with NATO. China's successful economic reforms at the same time demonstrated to India's leaders that China had, by engaging in foreign trade and attracting foreign investment, offset political hostilities with the United States and other Western nations and expanded its political influence in the Asia-Pacific region. Even though India's political leaders never publicly discussed the strategic value of economic strength during this period, economic development and the opening of Indian markets became an important aspect of India's post-Cold War security strategy, as well as a means of warding off international isolation and marginalization. India hence improved and strengthened its relations with European, Southeast Asian and neighbouring countries while at the same time making an economic recovery and expanding its foreign commercial contacts.

Maintaining National Security

As mentioned earlier, India maintained national security after 1962 by expanding military strength and supplementing it through the initiation of alliances. Although India's foreign policy emphasized non-alignment as a basic principle, this creed was challenged for the better part of the Cold War because India began seeking military aid from the USSR, United States and United Kingdom around the time of the 1962 Sino–Indian conflict. Its reliance on the Soviet Union deepened with the suspension in 1965 of American and British military aid, and the Soviet Union became India's de facto military and political ally in 1971 when the two nations signed the Treaty of Peace and Friendship and Cooperation. But the end of the Cold War and the disintegration of the Soviet Union left India marooned within the international community. Cold War after-effects made improving historically frigid relations with other powers difficult, even when the power in question was the USSR's successor; India's relationship with Russia needed redefinition. The security of alliances, therefore, was already history, regardless of the desires of Indian leaders at the time. India could now rely only on itself. But India's new-found independent security differed from that it had possessed during the Cold War. As mentioned, India's gradual recognition of the vital influence of economic factors on national security had motivated its concentration of energies into restoring the domestic economy. As regards foreign policy, India's main objective was to create a friendly environment for its economic recovery.

The Second Change in India's post-Cold War Security Concept

India restored its good relations with many nations at the turn of the millennium in spite of international sanctions after its nuclear tests of 1998, and its security environment was the best it had ever been since independence, the main reason being the expansion of India's own strength. Economic reforms that began with the Rao government resuscitated India's economy and put it on the developmental fast-track. India's international image consequently experienced a leap from that of a poor and backward developing nation to a main economic power and leader in technology, human resource development and the service industries. The nuclear tests of 1998 also attained for India the status of a nuclear power, thus expanding its strategic space.

The second main reason for India's upgraded security environment was the changed balance of international power at the turn of the century. China's rapid rise brought major adjustments to Asia's power structure, accentuating differences between the United States and China. Against this background, India began to receive more attention and to be entrusted with the important new role of acting as a'swing state in the global balance of power'. In other words, the major powers compete to have India on their sides in the process of the construction of a new world order. As Prime Minister Manmohan Singh said in August 2007, while celebrating the 60th anniversary of Indian independence, ' the world today wants India to do well. The world community wishes us well. Our external situation is benign and favourable.'

India Formally Introduces a Comprehensive Security Concept

The contribution of India's economic rise to improvements in its security environment during the 1990s, combined with the role the country had achieved within the new world order, spurred India's leaders to pursue a systematic assessment and revision of its traditional security concept and strategy. A special task force composed of the ministers of home affairs, external affairs, defence and finance ministries hence submitted a report stating: 'The traditional concept of national security has undergone fundamental changes over the years. It is no longer synonymous with sufficient military strength to defend the nation and its interests. In today's world, military might alone does not guarantee either sovereignty or security. The more realistic and comprehensive approach to national security also includes economic strength, internal cohesion and technological prowess.' This was the first time since the end of the Cold War that India's government had formally proposed a comprehensive security concept. As the INC stated in its campaign programme of 2004, 'The Congress perceives the national security not within the narrow prism of the purely military context. It has political, economic, social and developmental dimensions.' This statement demonstrates continuity in the accord of the two major political parties on the issue of a comprehensive security concept.

Post-Cold War India Sees Security Dialogue

India's acknowledgement of non-traditional security issues became more profound at the turn of the millennium. The Indian government considered that international terrorism, proliferation of weapons of mass destruction (WMD), compromised sea-lanes, trans-national organized crime and other non-traditional threats, 'have also served to bring countries closer and cooperate for their mutual security'. It consequently began expanding and strengthening its dialogue and cooperation with governments of other nations. India has so far established bilateral security dialogues and cooperation mechanisms with the United States, Russia, the United Kingdom, France, China, Italy, South Africa, Vietnam, Myanmar and Sri Lanka, and commenced both regular and extemporaneous exchanges of military personnel, joint military exercises and naval port-calls with many nations. India and Pakistan's 1999 armed conflict in Kargil notwithstanding, the momentum of dialogue between the two nations has grown rather than diminished. The composite dialogue initiated in September 1998 had by January 2004 formally developed into an Indo–Pakistani peace process. Although progress has been slow, the two nations' strengthened, systematic dialogue has played an important role in reducing misunderstandings and dissolving tensions.

INDIA'S SECURITY CHALLENGES

The profound changes in the world wrought about by the end of the Cold War have made for a fundamental restructuring of international relations. The end of ideological rivalry provided an objective opportunity for evolving a better security environment. However, there is a great deal of uncertainty and fluidity all around, as the new global equilibrium gets in place. Two or three factors would deserve attention in this regard.

The Cold War bipolar structure has been replaced by a "polycentric" world with the United States, Japan, China, the European Union and Russia emerging as the main partners in power.

Technology and economic power has moved to the forefront of international relations, emerging as a crucial factor in global realignments in the new setting.

The near symmetry in power capabilities and global reach between the two superpowers in a tightly bipolar world has given way to a certain disaggregation in the levels of power and capabilities among the new centres of power, given their uneven spread of techno-economic power, military capabilities and political influence. Even the United States, the most powerful nation today, has neither the will nor the capability to play a global role of the earlier order and magnitude. China, Japan, the European Union and Russia are in a process of defining their role in the new world order. Relationships between and among these centres of power are increasingly marked by elements of both engagement and containment.

Notwithstanding a broad shift from confrontation to conciliation at the global and regional levels, new points of pressures are unfolding themselves even as some old conflicts remain unresolved. For the developing countries, there is also evidence of new concerted pressures in economic, security and nuclear fields.

It is clear that there are manifold pressures emanating from the international environment which make for a complex and multilayered set of challenges and opportunities for India in the changed world order. India would have to respond to, if not anticipate, the new challenges and maximise its strategic political options, drawing essentially from its own power potential and bargaining leverages. This would at the least call for proactive strategies in terms of both restructuring old ties and forging new relationships at the regional and global levels.

India's security perspectives would inevitably be governed by the interplay of its domestic imperatives, regional balance of forces and the global challenges which impinge on its role and capabilities. India with its size, resource potential and strategic location is being increasingly seen as a regional influential poised on the threshold of emerging as a centre of power in the new international order. This is as much a recognition of its credible democratic functioning as the potential of its vast economic resources and political clout. India is a large multiplural society which has been able to successfully manage the challenges emanating from regional, linguistic and religious diversities without damaging its national cohesiveness. The remarkable resilience of its democratic functioning in a secular federal framework, despite some distortions, has continued to bely the scepticism of its worst critics. India's democracy remains fundamentally secure, underpinned as it is by an active judiciary, free media and a functioning and vigilant Opposition. India's economic development has also remained steady over the years. In the last couple of years, the Indian economy has registered an impressive growth rate of 7 per cent. The expansion and diversification of its industrial capacity have made important strides. Currently India ranks among the topmost industrialised nations of the world. It has the distinction of having the third largest pool of trained and scientific manpower in the world. Agricultural production has also shown substantial growth resulting in not only self-sufficiency in food grains but also reserves of impressive buffer stocks. Today with its burgeoning middle class, huge untapped markets for trade and industry, and large scale foreign investments, India has emerged as an economic power of some significance on the global scene. India has also built an impressive level defence capability. It has the fourth largest Army in the world with an impeccable professional record. It has a credible and self-reliant defence structure which has been built assiduously over the past three decades.

India's missile development programme has also grown apace underlining its indigenous technological capabilities.

It is clear that India is slated to play an increasingly larger role in the coming decades. Its future as a credible power would, however, depend as much on its ability to manage the present stage of transition as on the projection of its strategic perspectives and policy options for the future. Two or three points deserve mention in this regard. First, India's status and power projections remain essentially contingent on its national security in terms of political stability, economic development and military strength. Second, although the asymmetrical power structure in South Asia ensures India's centrality, its regional power and influence tends to get circumscribed by the neighbouring countries' sustained pressure to counter its pre-eminence.

In particular, Pakistan's unceasing search for parity with India makes for a deep-rooted strategic dissonance in the region which effectively reduces its capacity to shape or influence events in its neighbourhood. Third, continued involvement of external powers in the region remains an integral part of South Asian geo-political realities. The end of the Cold War has weakened the inevitable link up between regional conflict and Great Power rivalry. However, the inability of the states of the region to evolve a credible bilateral and regional framework for cooperation would continue to play an important role in reinforcing the pattern of external involvement—primarily in pursuance of their own stategic interests—in the region. This is bound to impinge on India's security perspectives, both short-term and long-term.

An overarching framework of India's national security has to take cognisance of military and non-military dimensions in terms of both external threats and internal challenges to its territorial integrity and national unity. Threats to a nation emanate as much from external aggression as from internal strife but at times internal factors can erode national security more critically than any external danger. National power based on political stability, societal cohesion and economic development would thus remain central to the future of India's national security.

India is passing though a crucial period of its post-independence history. Successively fragile coalition governments at both the central and state levels are affecting India's political, social and economic stability at a time when it is facing major challenges to its unity and integrity as a nation. The Indian political system is being subjected to manifold pressures from the progressive collapse of political and public institutions; incipient erosion of democratic norms; social unrest and corruption underlining a growing malaise in Indian polity. Increasing demands for power by more and more socio-economic groups, on the one hand, and limited resources and capabilities for redistribution of wealth, on the other, make for growing political and social turmoil. Widening economic disparities and growing rate of unemployment pose a major challenge for India's economic development notwithstanding a credible economic performance. It is estimated that by the year 2000, the total number of people living below the poverty line will more than the entire Indian population at the time of independence.

India's growing inability to manage political and economic challenges on the domestic front is a cause of deep concern. Although India's national integrity remains fundamentally secure, pressures from fissiparous cleavages in growing challenges of communalism and religious fanaticism have acquired disturbing dimensions. Political manipulation of religious sentiments for narrow political ends has long-term implications for the future of India's secular federal framework. The incipient threats to Indian federal polity in many parts of the country are putting growing strains on the political structure. Although India has been so far able to manage these challenges with a certain skill and patience, there is growing anxiety about the pressures getting intensified at a time when there is a steady erosion in the state's role in resolving conflict and bringing about social transformation. This is accompanied by a decline in the mediating role of the governing elite and party system. Decline in the state's order and authority has led to greater violence outside the established political channels, compounding the general law and order situation.

Continuing civil strife and incipient secessionism poses a major problem for India's national security. The northeast continues to be characterised by an uneasy peace. Although there is no full scale armed insurrection for secessionism as resorted to by the Nagas and Mizos in the Sixties, the problem of insurgency in Tripura, Manipur and Nagaland continues. Assam which had settled to a period of normal political functioning after the volatile agitation on the influx of foreign nationals in the early Eighties, is once again going although the fire of violence perpetrated by the United Liberation Front of Assam (ULFA) which is committed to armed struggle for the formation of a sovereign "ASOM". Punjab went through the unfortunate agony of sustained armed violence for over a decade before normal political processes were restored after heavy-handed crushing of Khalistan terrorists. The people of the state have, however, paid a heavy price for the then government's short-sighted policies for narrow political ends which changed what was essentially a party agitation to a Sikh movement encompassing divergent orientation and rationales. This has important lessons for the future of Indian federal polity which can only be ignored at one's own peril. The situation in Kashmir remains a cause for deep and continuing concern. Mishandling of a brewing political crisis brought about by the state government's dismal performance, marked by rampant corruption and inefficiency, led to an explosive situation in the sensitive valley.

The eruption of violence in 1990 served to underline the appalling failure of the intelligence agencies and the complete isolation of the political and administrative machinery from the ground realities. In the event, alienation of large sections of the civil population and their growing sympathy for the militants left little meeting ground between the people and the government. The recent restoration of political processes in the state following Parliamentary and Assembly elections and the increased weariness of the people with economic dislocation and high-handed intrusion of outside militants is leading to a slow change in the equation of forces on the ground.

But the overall situation remains precarious. The process of rebuilding the sundered economic and political fabric in the state and winning over the confidence of its people for any worthwhile and lasting solution continues to remain in uphill task. There is no gainsaying that the problems facing Indian polity are enormous as evidenced by the persistence of insurgency and slow entrenchment of terrorism in several parts of the country. If left unresolved, these could critically jeopardise India's national sovereignty and territorial integrity from within.

It is self-evident that the foremost task for India is to overcome the challenge to its nation building and national security. India's real autonomy in working out its destiny as an independent centre of power would lie in its internal strength and cohesion.

There is no getting away from the urgent task of upholding its unity and integrity as a nation state through a credible framework of secular federal democracy. The need for reinvigorating its democratic functioning and strengthening the role and efficiency of the state remains imperative in this regard.

India would also have make sustained efforts to vitalise its economy through optimisation of its vast resources, manpower and technical know-how. The need for redefining the role of the state in terms of eradication of poverty and greater economic equity remains self-evident. At the same time, India would have to raise itself to a new level of efficiency and competitiveness to acquire necessary leverages to stand up to growing global pressures and to hold its own in a friendly competitive world.

India can also not afford to drop its guard on building an adequate defence capability to counter any vulnerabilities which can be manipulated by external forces. There is some concern regarding growing deficiencies in India's conventional capability due to reduced defence expenditure in recent years. The need for adequate defence expenditure and defence allocation, constant modernisation and updating of its defence acquisitions for its defence preparedness remains imperative in this regard. A credible defence capability would provide an effective guarantee for maintaining its territorial integrity in the face of both external aggression and also externally engineered internal subversion that has emerged as a primary threat in recent years.

In the final analysis, it is only a politically stable, economically prosperous and militarily strong India which can seek to play its legitimate role in the world community, commensurate with its size and vast power potential.

Issues of regional peace and stability continue to loom large on India's strategic horizon. South Asia is today on the threshold of a new era of democratisation as the process of evolving democratic structure is under way in almost all the countries of the region.

The peaceful electoral transfer of power in Pakistan four times in a brief span of nine years reflects a growing commitment to democratic norms in that country. Bangladesh is firmly back on the track of democratic functioning after a long paralytic spell of negative agitational politics. Notwithstanding ups and downs, Nepal also continues to manage its democratic experiment credibly.

At the same time, there are vested and deeply entrenched authoritarian interests in all these states, particularly the ones which have been under military rule for long years. For instance, the continued dominance of bureaucratic military oligarchy in the political set-up in Pakistan makes for a fundamental dysjunctive in its policy. Given the fragile democratic institutions in all these countries, the democratic process itself is releasing new pressures. It is thus that the domestic environment in South Asia continues to remain generally characterised by political unrest and regime instability. Pressures from ethno-sectarian conflicts and religious fundamentalism are also rising in all countries of South Asia.

Pakistan is sitting atop an ethnic cauldron as pressures simmer, threatening to tear apart the fabric of Islamic identity from below. The challenge in Sindh underscores the disturbing dimensions of large scale violence between ethnic groups. The continued Punjabi domination in the power structure spells a certain uncertainty for the future of Pakistani federal polity. Running feuds between Shias and Sunnis in various parts of Pakistan have become a common feature on the Pakistani scene. Sri Lanka remains mired in prolonged ethnic conflict as the continued intransigence of the Liberation Tigers of Tamil Eelam (LTTE) makes for a virtual civil war in the strife-torn island. Sinhalese resistance to grant of effective and substantive devolution power to the Tamils only queers the pitch of ethnic politics in the multi-ethnic society of Sri Lanka. Even Bangladesh which has a relatively homogeneous society is facing problems in overcoming difficulties in integrating its small tribal minority. The likelihood of the region remaining in a state of crisis due to rising scale of political and social discontent is thus going to be a part of South Asian realities for quite some time. This not only poses a threat to state structures within these countries but also has an adverse impact on the matrix of inter-state relationships in the region.

The overlap of a large number of ethnic, linguistic and religious groups across essentially porous borders in South Asia makes for a cross-border spill-over movement of refugees, guns and drugs which generates inter-state tensions. The steady movement of refugees, following prolonged domestic conflict in the countries of origin, has emerged as a multi-dimensional problem which affects regional security. Refugees who tend to settle down in the host countries, given the intractable nature of ethnic conflict, put an intolerable burden on the demographic, financial and social sectors which has long-term implications for national security of the host country. Pakistan is still reeling under the impact of 3.5 million Afghan refugees who sought refuge following the Afghanistan crisis in the Eighties. Thousands of refugees are living in camps in Nepal as a result of ethnic conflict in Bhutan. Bangladesh has also had to cope with the Rohingyyas fleeing from Myanmar.

For India particularly, which has been the host to the largest inflow of refugees with practically no outflow, the magnitude and frequency of refugee movement has been a vexing problem. This has particularly grave implications for the social, economic and political stability of the sensitive northeast. The presence of a large number of Chakmas in Tripura is intensifying tensions among the local inhabitants who are resenting encroachment on limited jobs and resources and scarce land.

Thousands of Sri Lankans who sought refuge in Tamil Nadu in the Eighties are continuing to stay on, creating pressures with the attendant problem of anti-social and criminal activities. Induction of arms and anarchy with refugees is becoming a growing political liability. Internecine conflict among militant refugees groups and their continued links with trans-border militant groups intensifies social unrest and level of violence with grave implications for the future of civil society in these regions.

Growing linkages between drug trafficking and organised violence and the magnitude of the proliferation of small arms are also becoming major sources of instability in the region. In India there is growing concern regarding inter-state linkages between militant organisations, on the one hand, and between states and militant organisations on the other, adding to the complexity of secessionist movements. The crucial link-up between hostile external forces and domestic forces of political subversion poses a serious challenge to India's national security by giving impetus to secessionist forces. Terrorism in Kashmir since the Nineties, and earlier in Punjab in the Eighties, has acquired disturbing proportions with Pakistan's unabashed manipulation and support through planning and coordination, training of militants, and unlimited supply of arms and finances. The supply of sophisticated weaponry in particular—including rockets and explosive devices—has undeniably helped to raise the level of conflict to a new high.

By some accounts, the number of men lost in combatting the low intensity conflict in the sensitive state of Kashmir has outstripped the number of casualties in all the full scale Indo-Pak Wars put together. It may be mentioned here that internal political dynamics in Pakistan would continue to make for increasing domestic compulsions to keep the pot boiling in Kashmir, both in terms of diverting attention from pressing domestic problems as well as the inherent stakes of the military establishment in retaining the primacy of calling the shots in Pakistan.

In the strategic northeast ringed as it is by Myanmar, China and Bangladesh, incipient secessionism remains vulnerable to external manipulation. Although China which had offered arms and sanctuaries in the Sixties is no longer doing so, its unchanged stand on recognising the grant of statehood to Arunachal Pradesh and its military presence in Myanmar underscores its potential to foment trouble at a time of its own choosing. Bangladesh's involvement—albeit low key—is well-documented. Pakistan's Inter-Services Intelligence (ISI) is also carrying out anti-India activities from Nepal and Bangladesh adding to India's security concerns in view of persistently unsettled conditions in the northeast.

Today the growing incidence of insurgency, fomented and abetted by hostile external forces has in some way emerged as a major problem for India's security establishment. The statement of the former Chief of Army, terming the low-intensity conflict as the foremost challenge for India's national security only serves to underline the growing intensity of the problem.

Proliferation of small arms in the region is yet another disturbing dimension of cross-border terrorism. The inflow of weapons is a direct fallout of the Afghan conflict and the siphoning of major chunks of arms sent by the US, China and Saudi Arabia for onward transmission to the Afghan Mujahideen. It bears pointing out that "small" arms is a mere euphemism for progressively more sophisticated and lethal weapons.

The weapons circulating in the region include automatic rifles, machine guns as also landmines, sophisticated explosive devices, and communication systems. Even more worrisome in the fact that these lethal devices are finding their way to non-state actors and terrorist groups. This has significantly altered the level of internal conflict in India's troubled regions, making for deep concern for the inevitably long-drawn and prolonged conflict in sensitive border states with major implications for the deployment and engagement of security forces.

Unwholesome linkages between the drug barons and arms dealers comprise yet another cause for concern. The enormous funds generated by drug sales are being increasingly used to finance purchase of sophisticated weaponry by terrorist groups in South Asia. South Asia is abutted by two of the largest drug producing areas on its western and eastern flanks.

The growth of narcotics trade has been exponential in Pakistan, with the presence of a reported 1.5 to 2 billion heroin addicts. Infiltration of drug money into the Pakistan economy and political system is now well documented. There are also growing reports of significant penetration by the narcotics network in Pakistan's law enforcement agencies and military intelligence.

The widespread Kalashnikov culture in Pakistan is a function of the mutually supportive phenomenon of drugs and weapons. Vast quantities of these arms have found their way to Punjab and Kashmir. These weapons have also been used to create internal unrest in urban centres as evident by the vicious bomb blasts in Bombay in 1993. India is also fast emerging as a transit route for the narcotics trade, given its strategic location between two major narcotics producing areas. Drugs from Pakistan and Myanmar are being transmited from India for onward transmission to European markets. It is no mere coincidence that the most critical challenges of insurgency in India are located in the sensitive border states in the northwest and northeast which adjoin the drug generating regions. More important, the growth of a flourishing criminal underworld underpinned by a nexus between illegal traders, drug peddlars, and gun dealers in tandem with internal security forces and law enforcement agencies is a cause for increasing concern. The enormous toll in human and economic terms as a consequence of mindless violence and narco-terrorism getting entrenched in civil society has implications which have yet to be comprehended fully.

The complexity of these transnational problems defies strictly national solutions. The urgency for building bilateral cooperative relationships and promoting a coordinated regional perspective on these critical developments which are cutting across the sanctity of national borders, remains, if anything, self-evident. The South Asian Association for Regional Cooperation (SAARC) Conventions on curbing drug trafficking and terrorism in the region are important steps forward in evolving suitable regional mechanisms to tackle the twin menace. The conventions, however, remain presently at odds with the ground realities. The political push to add substance to declarations of intent obviously awaits a qualitative improvement in the political climate in South Asia. Till such time, the challenges of narco-terrorism would call for sustained vigilance on India's part to counter the insidious threat to its national security.

South Asia has been generally characterised by a great deal of political and strategic complexity. To understand the complex South Asian phenomenon, one or two factors deserve special attention. First, India with its undeniably greater power potential and centrality looms large on the South Asian scene. Second, the legacy of common civilisational heritage has lent a sharper edge to neighbouring countries' sensitivities regarding their national identity in a clearly uneven setting. India with its looming presence and power potential is often projected as a core threat by these countries.

India's relations with practically all its neighbours have been strained over a whole range of issues be they of trade, or water sharing or migration or ethnic sensitivities. At the same time, there have been no even patterns of relationships in the region. India's relations with Bhutan and Maldives have been generally smooth and rancour-free. India's relations with Bangladesh, Nepal and Sri Lanka have witnessed significant ups and downs over the years but have never been allowed to dip to an unmanageable low. Indo-Bangladesh relations which had become extremely strained over the Farakka issue and the Tin Bigha controversy have witnessed a dramatic improvement with the signing of the historic agreement on sharing of Ganga waters. India and Nepal have also been able to put the unfortunate events of the Eighties behind them. Today they are set for a qualitatively improved relationship with closer economic ties and better political understanding. The signing of the Mahakali Treaty and grant of overland transit route for its trade with Bangladesh by India underlines the positive shift. The Indo-Sri Lankan relationship today is a far cry from the palpable antagonism of the Eighties.

However, the Indo-Pak relationship has been characterised by a virtually unbroken record of sustained hostility. Indo-Pak discord which to some extent has been rooted in the bitter legacy of partition became more sharp with the conflicting national interests and ideologies of the two states. Pakistan's inability to work out a viable form of nationalism and its eternal quest for achieving parity with its larger neighbour remains at the core of Pakistan's hostility towards India. The three Indo-Pak Wars—the only intra-regional wars in South Asia—were all motivated by Pakistan's desire to alter the status quo. Pakistan's military relationship with the United States in the Fifties was also directed to counter-balance India and erode its prominence in the region. This not only brought Cold War politics to the region, irretrievably puncturing the area of peace that Nehru had sought to build, but also considerably aggravated India's security concerns. Pakistan's continued overtures to external powers, particularly the United States and China, for diplomatic backing and augmentation of defence capabilities remains directed towards eroding India's pre-eminence and power. It is not necessary here to go into the details of unresolved issues between India and Pakistan except to mention that Indo-Pak relations have remained lockjammed over a wide range of issues—Kashmir, Siachin, the Afghanistan crisis and the nuclear issue. For the past five decades, Kashmir has, however, remained the central and overriding concern for Pakistan. Pakistan sees Kashmir as an unfinished agenda of partition which must be resolved on the basis of the UN Resolutions which have long been overtaken by the realities on the ground. India has made it clear that Kashmir is an integral part on which it can countenance no compromise. This is so not only for obvious strategic considerations but also because it would deal a blow to India's secular framework and open the floodgate to demands for separation. India, however, remains willing to discuss Kashmir and all other outstanding issues on the basis of the Simla Agreement which expressly enjoins bilateralism and non-recourse to force by both countries which is not what is on the Pakistani mind.

Meanwhile, Pakistan's continued support—money, training and sophisticated weaponry—to secessionists in Kashmir makes for grave tensions for India. This is not to underestimate the urgent need for India to take steps to put its own house in order but to point out that Pakistan's proxy war in Kashmir represents a direct and immediate threat to India's security. It is also important to bear in mind that Pakistan has never given up the option of going to war with India to get back Kashmir. This has its own implications for India's security planning notwithstanding a growing recognition in both countries that the realities of a crumbling economy and sustained international pressure would militate against a full-fledged war. The world opinion has also decisively veered towards a peaceful solution of the Kashmir problem, with both the

United States and China recognising the inevitability of a bilateral negotiated settlement. There is also a section of opinion which considers nuclear deterrence itself as a stabilising factor in Indo-Pak relations. Nevertheless, Pakistan's declared nuclear capability makes for India's heightened security concern, given Pakistan's less than peaceful intentions towards India. There is no gainsaying that India is faced with Pakistan's nuclear challenges at a time when the absence of a credible Russian nuclear guarantee in the post-Cold War world makes it more vulnerable than at any time before.

This also aggravates the existing pressures emanating from Chinese nuclear might and United States' insidious nuclear presence in the region. Although India has made it abundantly clear that it has the capability to respond effectively to any nuclear misadventure by Pakistan, India's security perspectives would have to reckon with a nuclearised subcontinent in all its future calculations. It also needs to be borne in mind that while the Indo-Pak Agreement on not attacking each other's nuclear facilities is a positive step foward in confidence-building, this or any other such confidence-building measure would remain essentially meaningless unless simultaneous exploration is made of the ways and means to resolve the underlying problems between India and Pakistan.

It is thus that the recent resumption of Indo-Pak dialogue at the Foreign Secretary level, after a long period of tense silence, is a welcome development for the future of Indo-Pak relations. However, even as New Delhi's call for initiating a qualitatively new chapter of amity underlines its sincere desire for a more forward looking and constructive approach, Pakistan's usual style of blowing hot and cold and its recent efforts to militarily activate the ceasefire line do not at present give much cause for optimism for Pakistan's similar response. There is, however, no denying that it is in India's long-term interests to reduce hostility with its important South Asian neighbour. This would at the least call for proactive strategies to build greater trust and cooperation with Pakistan in a framework of mutual goodwill.

India's long-term security hinges perhaps in a larger measure on the future of Sino-Indian relations. It is, therefore, in India's abiding interest to work for peaceful and cooperative relations with its most powerful neighbour with whom it shares a long disputed border. A stalemate in Sino-Indian relations during the Sixties and Seventies only served to limit India's diplomatic manoeuvrability and potential role in the region.

Rajiv Gandhi's visit to China in 1988 marked a significant breakthrough in thawing the stalemate between the two countries. The agreement signed during the visit on maintaining peace and tranquillity on the Line of Actual

Control (LAC), pending a final solution of the border dispute, was a momentous step forward in normalisation of ties between the two neighbours. Re-emphasis on Panchsheel and the decision to initiate confidence-building measures to reduce tensions on the borders underlined a new forward looking approach on the part of both countries. The formation of a joint Working Group at the level of Ministers to carry forward negotiations on the boundary question reflected the new political thrust at the highest level. The process of normalisation has been since carried foward by a number of steps. Agreements have been signed to re-establish the Consulate General in Shanghai and Bombay and to resume border trade across specified points along the Tibet border. A set of confidence-building measures have been set in motion: agreeing on joint verification of the LAC, meetings between the local commanders, mutually agreed pull-back of troops from forward areas and prevention of aerial violations. These measures have not only helped to effectively defuse tensions on the borders but have also considerably eased India's defence burdens. More important, for the first time since the Sixties, India does not have to reckon with the nightmarish prospects of a two-war front with China and Pakistan.

At the same time, India can ill afford to have a let up in its defence preparedness to meet the long-term Chinese challenge. Although China would be hard put to challenge India a la 1992 because of changed correlation of forces on the ground, there is no underestimating the challenge of China's emergence as a formidable power in conventional as well as nuclear capabilities which has resulted in a vast power gap between the two countries. China's defence modernisation is continuing to move apace. China also continues to be engaged in augmenting its nuclear arsenal as its launching of inter-continental ballistic missiles and underground nuclear tests amply underline. Notwithstanding China's foreswearing of "first use," India can hardly ignore the implications of a total nuclear asymmetry with China. China's major military build up in Tibet—reportedly deploying ballistic missiles of medium and intermediate range—makes for long-term strategic concerns for India's security.

It may be pertinent to note here that China's remarkably growing economy, which has received additional boost with the reversion of Hong Kong in July 1997 also gives it a definite leverage in international affairs as underlined by its manoeuvrability in its relations with the US. It has been in recent years showing greater willingness to assert its power in pursuance of its interests in the adjacent regions. China's flexing of muscles in the South China Sea and its increasing assertiveness vis-a-vis Taiwan illustrate this. Although at present

China has great stakes in not upsetting its carefully structured political and economic equilibrium or aggravating tensions in its neighbourhood, given its growing economic and military power there would be continuing uncertainty regarding its future moves and projections. In recent years, more than posing a direct military threat, China continues to represent a challenge to India's role in South Asia.

China has, of course, visibly refrained from engaging in anti-Indian rhetoric in terms of its relations with its neighbours. It has also apparently softened its stand on Kashmir, urging Pakistan to virtually shelve the issue while working for improvement of relations with India in other areas. At the same time, it has remained committed to strengthening its political relations with all of India's neighbours. It continues to sell arms to Bangladesh, Pakistan, Sri Lanka and Burma which tends to hem India in a subtle way. In particular, its politico-strategic collaboration with Pakistan shows no appreciable change. China's help to Pakistan in developing its nuclear weapon capability is well-documented. Its recent supply of ring magnets and M-11 missiles has disturbing implications for India, seeking to threaten as it does the present balance of power in the region. China's supply of arms worth 1.6 billion dollars to Burma and its help in construction of naval and electronics facilities, and modernisation of its naval bases are also of concern to India in its strategic northeast and the adjacent seas.

China has, of course, come a long way since the Sixties in its national perspectives and world view, engaged as it is in consolidating its economic development, promoting regional peace and establishing a "just" new world order. This has led to a growing convergence of views with India which remains committed to world peace and a just and equitable world order. They have mutually shared perceptions on the need to preserve national territorial integrity and combatting challenges of fundamentalism, ethnic separatism and cross-border terrorism. There is also a broad understanding between the two countries on global trade issues and the pressures emanating from the industrialised world on human rights and good governance. All this augurs well for a more relaxed and cooperative relationship between India and China. It would, however, need to be clearly borne in mind for India's long-term projections that relations between the two Asian giants are bound to be marked by undercurrents of competition and contest, inherent in the logic of geo-political proximity and national rivalry. It also needs to be borne in mind that the border question has been shelved but not resolved. India has vital stakes in consolidating the process of normalisation with China but as long as the dynamics of military competition remains unchanged, a durable framework of Sino-Indian friendship would have to be underpinned by an overall balance of strength and a clear recognition of their mutual power status and stakes in the region.

It is clear from the foregoing that India has an abiding stake in peace and stability in its neighbourhood for its long-term security. India is going through a phase of rapid economic transformation and is poised to play a significant role in the global stage in the coming century. There is no gainsaying that India's projection on the world scene would depend in no small measure on its effective and constructive neighbourhood diplomacy. This would at the least call for evolving a framework of cooperative security in its neighbourhood. This would essentially mean striving to reduce tensions with China and Pakistan, its two powerful neighbours, without compromising on its core national strategic interests.

This is so not only because they separately and together constitute a long-term threat to its security but also because stable peace in this region hinges on India's friendly ties with these two countries. India's recent agreement with China offers ground for finding a viable basis of confidence on which to build cooperative relationships. India's offer of several confidence-building measures to Pakistan is also a step in the same direction. These include the agreement on prohibition of nuclear attack on population centres and economic targets; the agreement on "no first use" of nuclear weapons; and upgrading of communication links between DGMO of both sides. In some ways, the Simla Agreement itself provides for an effective mechanism for confidence-building between the two nations to build durable peace in the subcontinent. Sustained efforts to initiate new confidence-building measures and strengthen the existing mechanisms would remain imperative for building a credible framework of cooperative security in the region.

India would also need to take a lead in setting the tone for a framework of relations with its smaller neighbours. New Delhi is today committed to evolve a fresh perspective on its relations with its neighbours in a framework of positive asymmetry. There is no doubt that in the short run, anti-Indian rhetoric would continue to be manipulated at will by these countries, depending on their domestic compulsions, but in the long run, deft handling of the neighbours with flexibility and sensitivity is bound to lead to a more relaxed political environment. This itself would lend a great credibility to India's role as a regional influential. Peace and development in the region is in the long term a sine qua non for India's long-term security perspectives in South Asia which is facing staggering problems of poverty, illiteracy, malnutrition and under-development.

The biggest challenge to regional peace and security emanates from its poverty and the under-utilisation of its vast resources to address the socio-economic needs of its teeming millions. Pressures of endemic poverty and population explosion are becoming critical in the region. South Asia has sunk to the bottom rung in terms of the number of its people living below the line of poverty. SAARC provides an effective regional institutional arrangement for South Asia to optimise its regional resources and capabilities to promote the welfare of its peoples and a cooperative framework for the socio-economic development of the entire region. India as the largest South Asian power has a special responsibility to give a visible push to SAARC and invest in policies which are informed by a larger and long-term vision of a cooperative and stable South Asia.

An important challenge to India's security lies in the unfolding security environment in its adjacent neighbourhood which has a vital bearing on its geo-political interests. The volatile situation in Afghanistan is of major concern to India. Afghanistan seems set to witness a fierce and long drawn struggle among the main contenders for power which, if unresolved, will lead to grave destabilisation in the trouble-torn country.

Although India does not share any borders with Afghanistan, it has fundamental geo-political stakes in the unfolding events there which can be detrimental to its own long-term security interests in the region. India, therefore, has a major stake in any outcome of the protracted Afghanistan crisis. India rightly views any fundamentalist regime in Afghanistan as an insidious threat to its own secularism as well as a potentially destabilising factor in the region. An important dimension of Indian policy is the inevitable antagonism of such a regime to India which has traditionally enjoyed close links with Afghanistan based on a shared perception of regional interests. The possible spillover of a Taliban style fundamentalist regime, in terms of impact of ideology, violence and narco-terrorism, into Kashmir makes for deep concern for India's internal security. India has, therefore, a stake in seeing the evolution of a broad based government in Afghanistan which takes care of the legitimate interests of all major groups to enable it to emerge as a stable and non- fundamentalist nation. It is in this context that India is keeping contacts with major groups within Afghanistan and supporting all broad regional initiatives from outside to solve the problem. A growing understanding with Iran and other likeminded countries is emerging as an important dimension of India's policy not only towards Afghanistan but also the politically sensitive Central Asia.

Of late, Central Asia has emerged as an area of major concern for India in view of India's long-term interest in this strategic area. This is because the situation in the region which continues to be fluid because of political instability and challenges of Islamic fundamentalism has wider implications for India's own vicinity. Central Asia has also emerged as a major strategic region in view of its vast untapped reserves of oil, natural gas and other precious resources. This has made the region a focus of sharp interest and struggle among most major powers, notably the United States, Russia, China, Iran and Turkey, who want to exploit the tremendous economic potential of the area. Although India can do little to influence the interplay of Great Power rivalry in the region, it has a stake in deepening and broadening its own interaction with the region. This would call for a more energised policy in building upon existing economic and cultural ties with the Central Asian countries making for its reinforced presence in this vital area. India is already engaged in an exercise of exploring the avenues for extending support in the field of infrastructure and technology. India has to continue to take into account in its larger security perspectives the region's great strategic, economic and political importance in terms of its energy reserves, strategic location and emerging political dynamics that are attracting wide attention and will have major implications for this whole region.

India also has vital interests in the emerging political and strategic dynamics in the Indian Ocean region. This is so because of its vital need for uninterrupted energy supplies and maritime trade through its strategic waterways. India is vitally interested in keeping the major sea lanes of communication in the Indian Ocean free for the movement of substantial portion of its trade, particularly in terms of access to vital oil supplies. Its objections to superpower presence in the Indian Ocean in the Cold War days was also a function of its concerns over escalation of tensions in its vital strategic vicinity. India's positive role in the newly formed Indian Ocean Rim Community also underlines its desire to evolve a cooperative framework of relations among the littoral countries of the Indian Ocean without undue interference of outside powers.

India's demand for oil supplies is slated to grow very steeply in the coming decades. Till such time that Central Asian vast reserves are fully exploited, the Persian Gulf which is currently accounting for 60 per cent of world's energy resources, would hold the key to global energy security. The potential of the South China Sea remains as yet largely untapped. West Asia and the Persian Gulf in particular would thus continue to remain a region of great strategic concern for all major powers, including some of the erstwhile self-sufficient countries like Russia, China and Indonesia whose reserves are getting fast depleted. Given India's strategic location to the area, India's has abiding interests in long-term stability and peace in the area because any potential destabilisation or conflict would lead to insecurity in India's strategic neighbourhood. Given the external powers' continued quest for power and influence in the South Asian region, the need for diversification of strategic political options remains imperative for India as there is also evidence of new pressures in economic, security and nuclear fields. This calls for both restructuring the old ties and forging new relationships. India's policy towards the United States, Russia and China would have to be thus increasingly informed by the changing needs of national security and economic development as also the logic of its own role in the region.

Strategic and geo-political considerations had been critical for Indo-Soviet ties in the Cold War period. But it was essentially the mutuality of interests that sustained those ties lending them a certain autonomous structure, irrespective of extraneous inputs. Mutual convergence between the two countries rested on the basic premise of Soviet endorsement of India's pre-eminence in the region.

The Soviet support was critical for India in coping with its problems with both Pakistan and China, singly and together. More important, it helped India to build a credible and self-sufficient defence structure at a time when there was visible reluctance from the West to do so. In the post-Cold War world, India and Russia have been able to credibly rework their relationship despite the initial hitches in the transitional phase in a qualitatively altered framework.

Although there has been some reduction in the volume of trade and economic interaction between the two countries, the question of repayment of loan and currency adjustment has been settled to mutual satisfaction. The new treaty of friendship and cooperation between the two countries is a reaffirmation of the abiding mutuality of the interests between them. India and Russia would continue to have a convergence of interests in the developments in their proximate regions—Afghanistan and Central Asia—where both have vital geo-political interests in promoting peace and stability. There is also mutuality of interest on the need of averting internal destabilisation from ethnic conflict and trans-border terrorism in large multiplural societies.

This has particular significance for India which faces a simmering problem in the sensitive state of Kashmir. India also has a continued stake in strengthened defence relations with Russia, given its large scale dependence for Russian modern military hardware—at reasonable prices—and advanced civilian technology in space and nuclear fields.

India has been able to procure military equipment with provision for technology transfer, joint production and export to third countries. Recently,

India and Russia have set up a joint working group to address the operative elements of a long-term military technological programme—the only such programme Russia has signed with any foreign country—which has been extended for another ten years beyond 2000. Russia has also offered to India the latest and advanced technology in all areas of the defence field.

At the same time, any talk of "strategic partnership" is still premature, given Russia's strategic alliance with China and its continued dependence on the West. There are also difficulties in the supply of sensitive technology—underlined by the problems in the cyrogenic deal and differences over nuclear disarmament, particularly after Russia's signing of the Comprehensive Test Ban Treaty (CTBT) and India's own position on it.

There is, of course, some satisfaction in India that Russia has now re-endorsed its stand on India's pre-eminence in South Asia and moved back from the projection of equidistance between India and Pakistan. Moscow has now reaffirmed its support for India's stand on Kashmir and its firm commitment not to supply arms to Pakistan. Indo-Russian relations, although qualitatively altered in the changed world context, would have continued relevance for India's long-term strategic perspectives.

In the post-Cold War world, maintaining friendly and close relations with the United States, the only superpower today, which is capable of shaping the regional environment, would need to receive the highest priority in India's larger strategic calculations.

Indo-US relations have remained generally lukewarm over the years essentially for the United States' non-recognition of India as a power of consequence in the region. There has been no effort by the US to develop an autonomous approach to South Asia except in relationship to its broader global objectives. Shared democratic values have failed to provide a firm basis for understanding between the two countries whose divergent security interests lay at the root of the indifferent state of relations. This has remained so notwithstanding India's need and desire for improved relations with the United States, albeit on its own terms and from its own long-term security perspectives. The United States is seen in India as displaying singular insensitivity and disregard for India's vital security concerns in the region.

An important Indian objection to US policy in South Asia has been its commitment to the parity syndrome between India and Pakistan—including equating Indian and Pakistani nuclear policy—which India sees as not only immeasurably intensifying its security problems but also eroding India's pre-eminence in the natural balance of power in South Asia.

Notwithstanding an improved phase of relationship in recent years, the United States' continued reluctance to deliver sensitive technology to India only serves to underline its disregard for India's sensitivities to the qualitative alteration of the military balance of the region over the years.

There are today greater opportunities for developing understanding between the two countries on promoting peace and stability in both South Asia as also the neighbouring strategic regions of the Persian Gulf and the Indian Ocean. Although differences persist over a range of issues—nuclear proliferation, Kashmir, trade related issues and restructuring of the Security Council—all of which have a vital bearing on India's larger security concerns there are some positive indications of Indo-US relations acquiring greater depth with evidence of more intense economic interaction and the evolution of a strategic dialogue between the two countries.

The United States which has emerged as India's single largest trading partner and investor, has an abiding interest in India's vast economy and burgeoning markets. India, of course, would need the US capital, technology and markets which remain crucial to India's future economic development. India has welcomed the recent US declaration—although belated—formally designating the Pakistan-sponsored organisation Harkat-ul-Ansar, operating in Kashmir, as a terrorist outfit.

There is also some satisfaction with the US' full-hearted endorsement of the current Indo-Pak dialogue and its reaffirmation that it has no desire to intervene in Indo-Pak problems. All these would underline a growing US desire to build an independent relationship with India, notwithstanding Pakistan's continued relevance to its broader regional objectives. At the same time, a qualitative improvement in Indo-US relations would, in the long run, continue to remain contingent on the United States' recognition of India's regional pre-eminence in the building up of an independent policy towards India.

Given the inevitability of India's search for its own place in the global community, in view of its large size and power potential, and the growing complexity of its security challenges, India's nuclear policy would continue to have primacy in its national security agenda in the new world order. While nuclear disarmament must needs be India's long-term security goal, its nuclear policy has to take into account the given realities of the nuclear weapons having come to stay as an important bargaining leverage in international relations.

There is a growing recognition in India that given the current international realities and the situation of nuclear asymmetry in the region, mere retention of the nuclear option may not hold unconditionally in the altered scenario. India would have to give more sustained and serious thought to the timing of the exercise or non-exercise of its option in the days ahead. Developing a full-fledged nuclear weapon capability while continuing to press for total elimination of nuclear weapons will, of course, be the foremost challenge for India's future security perspectives.

Three or four factors deserve attention in this regard. First, time remains of the essence for India as domestic costs grow and international pressures mount on India to abandon its nuclear option and missile programme at a time when the nuclear powers are engaged in updating and refining their capabilities.

Second, India has to reckon with the prospects of undeniable pressures from the US, China and Russia, should it operationalise its nuclear option. It may also find itself under increased Chinese nuclear threat in view of its unquestioned nuclear might today.

Third, exercise of the nuclear option would bring to the fore the classic dilemma of development versus defence at a time when India's developmental goals require the greatest attention for sustaining its economic growth. Fourth, the goals of national security, short-term, as well as India's own aspirations, in the long-term, to play a global role of some significance, remain compelling for India's strategic perspectives. Last, can India afford to remain locked in continued confrontation with the nuclear powers—in the post-CTBT phase—and pay the inevitably high costs—economic, technological and political—without having actually exercised its nuclear option?

It is clear that the whole range of possibilities—retaining the present ambiguity, opting for recessed nuclear deterrence and operationalising its nuclear option—would hold the centre-stage of the national security agenda demanding a well coordinated and well thought out nuclear strategy that would sustain India's long-term security projections.

It is clear from the foregoing that India has to resolutely address itself to the emerging set of challenges and opportunities in the changed world order in a coordinated and comprehensive framework of paramount importance would be its ability to project its (long-term strategic perspectives and interests in responding to the interplay of domestic imperatives, regional balance of forces and global dynamics in the coming decades.

The overarching reality of India as a large independent nation which is destined to play an important role on the global stage would undoubtedly prevail over the present difficulties and obstacles.

The need for India to come to grips with the complexities of the rapidly changing configuration of forces at the domestic, regional and global levels, however, remains self-evident. India's long-term strategic perspectives would have to show greater dynamism and flexibility in responding to the increasingly complex demands of national security, regional aspirations and global commitments. This would at the least call for clearly defining India's security interests and evolving a coherent and multi-layered framework of its security policy and perspectives. In the final analysis, India's own strengths and capabilities—political, economic and military—would alone add substance to India's future projections as a power of some consequence in the emerging global order.

2

India's National Security Strategy

National interests lead to the drawing up of national security objectives and the formulation of national security policies. India's national security objectives have been adequately stated in the MEA Annual Report of 1998-99, reproduced above. The only aspect that really needs to be added is to strive to weaken the China-Pakistan collusive nexus in nuclear and missile technology and military hardware. It should be India's objective to marginalise Pakistan's military power by 2010-15 and eliminate its interference in India's internal affairs.

India's national security policies must be so formulated that India is in a position to provide leadership to other countries in the Southern Asian region so as to be able to exercise a reasonable degree of influence over their policies and actions to further its own security interests. India's security lies in establishing a confrontation free external environment. For this, India must be prepared to use all elements and instruments of national power to influence the actions of countries that follow policies and initiate measures inimical to India's national interests. Such policies would require matching strategies backed by necessary resources being devoted to diplomatic, military, intelligence and other efforts to achieve the desired objectives.

India's strategic frontiers extend to Tibet in the north, the Central Asian region, including Afghanistan, in the northwest, include the Saudi Peninsula in the west, extend to Mauritius and Diego Garcia in the Indian Ocean and the ASEAN countries in the east, including the Malacca Straits. India's national security strategy must reflect India's strategic interests in these regions. In the prevailing uncertain geo-strategic environment and unstable world order, with the primacy of the nation-state being gradually eroded, no country can afford to "go it alone" in organising its national security.

Even the US, the world's only remaining superpower, has formulated a well-crafted strategy of alliances to further its wide-ranging security interests. In this age of globalisation and trade blocks, the trend is inexorably towards collective security. India too needs to form strategic partnerships with countries sharing a mutuality of interests to countervail its adversaries. India's abhorrence for military alliances and its efforts towards pursuing a fiercely independent foreign policy have been well founded. However, India has found it difficult to single-handedly eliminate or even reduce the external threats and foreign-sponsored internal security challenges. India needs to establish strategic linkages with the US, Russia (as it will once again rise from the quagmire it is in at present to become a major power), Israel, Iran, Myanmar, Vietnam, Taiwan, Japan and South Korea to counter-balance China's growing power and influence.

One of the major reasons for the continuing violation of India's borders and the destabilisation of India through proxy wars is the prevalent perception of India as a soft state that is if not unmindful at least not adequately concerned about its external and internal security. This perception is founded on India's failure to exploit the advantages gained during the 1947-48, 1965 and 1971 conflicts with Pakistan and on its purely reactive handling of Pakistan's proxy war over the decade of the 1990s. India's continuously reducing defence expenditure throughout the period 1985-1999, even as the threats to its security increased manifold due to Pakistan's nuclearisation in 1987 and its proxy war against India from 1989-90 onwards, also sent a message of being relatively unconcerned. Inimical neighbours have always exploited such weaknesses to their advantage and so has been the case with India. Quite clearly, India now has no option but to adopt pro-active strategies to deal firmly with the threats confronting its security.

While India's nuclear doctrine of no first use and a credible minimum deterrent has been clearly stated, the strategies to be followed to give effect to this doctrine have not been spelt out except in passing in the recommendations of the National Security Advisory Board (NSAB) while formulating a draft Nuclear Doctrine. In fact, till the time of writing, the issue is yet to be debated in Parliament. The first inescapable ingredient of India's nuclear strategy would be overt signs of weaponisation - mere declaratory statements are not enough. If India's "nuclear capability is to become a source of power and influence during crises rather than only a strategic deterrent to total war... (a) public stance on the actual nuclear capability, the range and accuracy of delivery systems, the kilotonnage of warheads... the authorisation (procedures) for launch, and the custody of codes and interlocks for authorising a launch..." will be necessary. Having consciously abjured a first use doctrine, India's retaliatory strike strategy has to be based on destroying the adversary's large industrial and population centres if deterrence is to be successfully maintained. Only if the adversary's political and military leadership is convinced that the cost of a first strike would prove to be unbearably high, will it be deterred from doing the unthinkable. If India's retaliatory response strategy lacks credibility and the adversary is convinced that he can bank on an ambivalent Indian response, he may be tempted to risk a first strike. Deterrence is ultimately a mind game and turns on credibility.

Some other aspects that would enhance the credibility of India's nuclear deterrence include the establishment of a viable command and control system with well publicised procedures for nuclear decision-making, a clearly enunciated chain of succession, at least the partial transfer of the custody of nuclear warheads to the armed forces units designated to launch them and a well-conceived targeting philosophy. However, real credibility will stem from a demonstrated delivery system capability and an established programme for building the required number of missiles. While India's delivery systems are adequate to retaliate against nuclear threats from Pakistan, India is yet to develop a 5,000 km class missile to retaliate against a Chinese threat and other threats that may manifest themselves in future.

In fact, unless the N-5 agree quickly to adopt a time bound nuclear disarmament programme, only a remote possibility at present, India has no option but to develop an inter-continental ballistic missile (ICBM). Some commentators have written about such a programme named Surya but there has been no official confirmation. The status of the advanced technology vehicle (ATV) project for a nuclear powered submarine is also not clear. Unless India demonstrates the will to develop the required delivery systems and commits sufficient funds and efforts to their development, India's nuclear deterrence will continue to lack credibility.

In view of the doubts expressed by leading Indian nuclear scientists like Dr. P. K. Iyengar regarding the viability of the thermonuclear test carried out in May 199842 and the need for more tests if weapons in the megaton class or even 200 kiloton (kt) fusion warheads are to be developed, India will have to develop a suitable strategy to find a way around the CTBT to enable further testing without inviting a fresh round of sanctions and international opprobrium. In case India's nuclear warhead capability remains confined to

15 to 30 kt fission warheads, it will lead to the sub-optimal utilisation of India's meagre fissile material stockpile. With negotiations for the FMCT staring it in the face and the likelihood of an early agreement being reached, India would be hard put to stockpile adequate fissile stockpile for the total number of warheads that its retaliatory strategy and targeting philosophy may require. These are the tough issues confronting the development of a potent nuclear strategy. While there are no easy answers, a determined diplomatic stance and a tough negotiating position with some hard bargaining can achieve the desired results. The world is gradually getting used to the idea that a "cap, reduce, eliminate" policy is no longer feasible and that India's nuclear weapons, born primarily out of the need to safeguard national security, cannot now be rolled back.

Simultaneously with developing a credible nuclear deterrent, India must continue to pursue its nuclear disarmament efforts. The best nuclear strategy would undoubtedly be the total elimination of nuclear weapons from the face of the earth. However, this is one aspect in the affairs of mankind where progress will continue to be excruciatingly slow. This will have to be vectored into India's nuclear calculations. India must also seek to discuss and agree upon mutual nuclear risk reduction measures (NRRMs), particularly with China and Pakistan. Since neither China nor Pakistan is willing to negotiate a mutual no-first-use treaty with India, it would be in the interest of all the protagonists to ensure that sufficient safety checks are mutually in place to reduce the risk of knee-jerk responses in situations of panic and accidental nuclear war. The holding of discussions for NRRMs need not be linked to the lack of progress on other issues of concern such as a halt to Pakistan's sponsorship of terrorism in India. The possibility of the unleashing of nuclear weapons, even if unintended, is too horrific to make its reduction contingent upon other political and diplomatic considerations, no matter how deeply vexatious the issues concerned might be. The first aim of a well-rounded nuclear strategy should be to ensure that deterrence does not fail, whether by design or by default, and that the nuclear genie remains tightly bottled up - as it has been since August 1945.

It is apparent that India's world view has changed since Pokhran-II to one that is more assertive and more willing to reach out to safeguard national security, even if the new thinking is not very clearly and lucidly articulated officially. Indian defence analysts are becoming increasingly more forthright in spelling out specific policies and actions to reduce and gradually eliminate the manifold threats and challenges to national security. Bharat Karnad strongly advocates that Vietnam should be propped up as a nuclear counter to China to ensure the same level of discomfiture to China as China's collusion with Pakistan is causing to India. He rationalises that India would not be violating any international treaties in offering nuclear know-how to Vietnam and the international opprobrium that is bound to result would be justified in terms of India's larger security interests. He recommends that India must exploit the growing anti-Pakistan sentiments in Pakistan Occupied Kashmir (POK) and the Northern Areas of Gilgit and Baltistan and that India should sponsor and support an Azad Kashmir Liberation Front and provide its members "diplomatic, political and moral support" exactly like Pakistan claims to do to Kashmiri militants.

Bharat Karnad is also of the view that India's special operations capability needs to be increased to about a division worth of Special Forces troops to sustain covert special operations inside POK on a long-term basis to counter Pakistan's proxy war through pro-active trans-LoC operations. Appearing as a defence analyst on a TV programme, Lieutenant General Satish Nambiar (Retd.), Director, United Service Institution of India, New Delhi, recommended that trans-LoC operations be launched by the Indian army to raise the cost for Pakistan to sponsor foreign mercenary terrorists for operations in J&K. Mulayam Singh Yadav, a former Defence Minister and a member of Parliament, has publicly demanded "hot pursuit" operations across the LoC to stop Pakistan's trans-LoC terrorism. Ever since Lashkar-e-Toiba's brutal massacres in J&K on the night of August 1, 2000, in which 100 innocent people were killed, there has been a spate of editorials and opinion pieces in leading Indian dailies demanding hot pursuit and other trans-LoC operations. Leading Indian analysts like Brahma Chellaney have questioned whether a strong, stable and prosperous Pakistan is in India's interest.

It is emerging quite clearly that the limit of tolerance of the Indian people has been crossed and there will be greater demands on the government in future to adopt pro-active trans-LoC measures to put an end to Pakistan's proxy war against India. "... India will have to exploit Pakistan's weaknesses with a strategic blueprint that incorporates military, political and unorthodox elements. The main aim should be to start hitting Pakistan wherever it will hurt and whenever it least expects such counteraction." Since it is necessary to raise the ante on the LoC, India will have to be prepared for a larger conventional conflict with Pakistan that may not remain confined to the LoC and may spill over to the international border. Hence, India's strategy must be to further develop its conventional superiority to fight and win a limited war with Pakistan in a nuclear environment. Victory in such a limited war should be measured not through inflicting a comprehensive military defeat on Pakistan, as that in any case is not possible below the nuclear threshold, but by destroying a substantial portion of Pakistan's war waging potential so as to marginalise the Pakistan army as the force majeure in Pakistan's polity. It should be clear to all perceptive observers that the real problem between India and Pakistan is not the Kashmir issue or any other issue but the Pakistan army that drives Pakistan's foreign policy and is the progenitor of Pakistan's proxy war strategy to "bleed India through a thousand cuts". The early marginalisation of the Pakistan army should be a major national priority.

With China India faces a "capabilities-intentions" dilemma. While China has systematically resolved its long-standing, complex and seemingly intractable territorial and boundary disputes with Russia, Vietnam and the Central Asian Republics through protracted negotiations in a spirit of mutual accommodation and there is peace on these borders, it has shown remarkable intransigence in following the same approach with India. China continues to profess its willingness to resolve its territorial and boundary dispute with India through peaceful negotiations. Despite the Border Peace and Tranquillity Agreement signed in 1993 and the Confidence Building Measures in the military field mutually negotiated in 1996, there has been little change in the ground situation. China either fails to or does not deliberately wish to accept that the best confidence building measure would be to first delineate on the map and ground the Line of Actual Control (LAC). As long as the LAC is not clearly demarcated, border clashes can occur between the two opposing armies at any time in the disputed areas and these can lead to another border conflict. Though there is a fair possibility of such a conflict between the two nuclear-armed adversaries being fought below the nuclear threshold, it could rapidly escalate to nuclear exchanges that may not remain limited to battlefield targets. China is known to be engaged in modernising its armed forces and acquiring offensive conventional capabilities, including the creation of rapid reaction forces based on strategic airlift. It is also engaged in developing information warfare capabilities. Since China has successfully resolved its territorial disputes and boundary problems with most other neighbours, the new capabilities would be available to be used against India.

The only deduction that can reasonably be drawn is that China wishes to put its territorial dispute with India on the back burner for the time being, while it consolidates its economic and military power and is engaged in resolving the Taiwan dispute and in settling its claims to various islands in the South China Sea. Michael D. Swaine and Ashley J. Tellis have written that the basic logic underlying China's "indefinite postponement" approach has been to "steadfastly avoid conceding any Chinese claims with respect to the dispute, while simultaneously seeking to prevent the dispute from vitiating the pacific environment that China needs to complete its internal transformation successfully." Swaine and Tellis list several advantages of this approach:

- It positions China as a conciliatory state seeking to resolve all outstanding disputes peacefully.
- It does not increase the demands on China's military's forces at a time when the PLA is relatively weak and when the Chinese economy needs all the breathing room it can get.
- It prevents balancing coalitions from arising against China in the event Beijing pursued more coercive strategies.
- And, it delays the resolution of these disputes at least until the balance of power changes substantially in favour of China. At that time, both simple usurpation and coercive bargaining might become more attractive, although it is unclear today whether the Chinese leadership would conclude that the benefits of such actions easily exceed the costs.

China may choose to settle the territorial dispute with India at a time of its own choosing when it is militarily far more powerful. It may opt to do this either through coercive diplomacy or even by seeking a military solution. It is in India's interest to strive towards an early resolution of the territorial dispute with China so that India has only one major military adversary to worry about. India would also be able to re-deploy at least some of the 10 to 12 mountain divisions and perhaps four to six squadrons of the Indian Air Force from the Tibetan border in the east and the northeast to the western border to gain a decisive military edge against Pakistan.

India may even be able to "downsize" a few army divisions and utilise the savings that will accrue for the long-overdue qualitative upgradation of the army. Perhaps these are the real reasons that compel China to drag its feet in resolving its territorial and boundary dispute with India so that it can support Pakistan, its friend and ally, to continue to destabilise India through its proxy war without fear of major military retaliation. India's strategy should be to develop adequately powerful leverages to make it incumbent on China to act quickly to resolve the territorial dispute between the two countries. Developing the strategic linkages mentioned above could do this. There would be immense advantages in commencing the sale of modern military hardware to Vietnam, including some quantities of Prithvi missiles with launchers under government-to-government soft loans. The Defence Research and Development Organisation (DRDO) could provide technical know-how to Vietnam's nascent armament industry. If it becomes necessary, India should also be ready to play the Tibet card, something it has consciously avoided doing for almost half a century since China launched its brutal suppression of the human rights of the Tibetan people. The Chinese people's latent yearning for democracy could also be discreetly encouraged. The large number of multinational companies (MNCs) that are unhappy with their business ventures in China could be persuaded to invest in India instead through attractive offers. This would make both business as well as strategic sense.

Attempts to ensure a stable and peaceful external security environment would be meaningful only if internal security was first ensured. Throughout the last two decades of the 20th century, India's handling of militancy has lacked a firm and well-coordinated approach. India's reactive strategy of fighting Pakistan's proxy war through security forces' operations limited within its own territory has not produced the desired results. In addition to the trans-LoC pro-active measures mentioned above, India's internal security strategy needs to follow a three-pronged approach. Firstly, all security forces' operations in the states affected by armed militancy should be conducted in a comprehensively coordinated manner with well-streamlined procedures for the acquisition and sharing of intelligence. Secondly, there is an inescapable need to organise a national level para-military counter-insurgency force with the army's ethos and standards of training and, at least initially, army leadership. Such a force could be based on an existing police force like the CRPF that could be designated as the Central Government's primary counter-insurgency strike force. Its charter will have to be modified accordingly to relieve it of other law and order duties. Or, a new elite force could be raised from scratch for the purpose. The haphazard raising of additional police force battalions, guided more by turf battles rather than hard-nosed national security considerations, must stop.

It is also imperative that the army's involvement in counter-insurgency operations must be reduced gradually from the peak level of approximately 120,000 (six divisions equivalent) in 199849 as it is by now well recognised that the prolonged employment of the army for such tasks hampers its training and operational preparedness for conventional military operations. Ideally, internal security problems should be handled by the Ministry of Home Affairs without seeking the army's help. However, in proxy war situations involving well-trained foreign mercenary terrorists equipped with sophisticated weapons, it may become necessary to deploy the army. Such deployment should be for short-duration surgical operations only and even then, the army's specialised counter-insurgency strike forces like the Rashtriya Rifles (RR) should be employed and not regular infantry battalions.

If the present level of Pakistan-sponsored militancy is not rapidly reduced to more manageable levels by trans-LoC pro-active operations, it will be necessary to increase the number of RR battalions to between 75 to 80 to reduce the involvement of regular infantry battalions. Finally, armed militancy can never be eliminated only through security forces' operations. Ultimately it is a battle of hearts and minds and only a political solution can eliminate the root causes of militancy and assuage the feelings of hurt of the alienated people. The government must initiate a political dialogue with all parties concerned to find a lasting solution to the complex problems confronting the nation in J&K and the northeastern states while simultaneously expediting developmental activities. Good governance is also an important ingredient of a successful internal security strategy.

Effective border management strategies go hand in hand with well-conceived internal security strategies. The infiltration of well-armed mercenary terrorists from Pakistan, mass migrations from Bangladesh into lower Assam, narcotics and small arms trafficking across India's vast land borders and long coastline, the smuggling of consumer goods and fake Indian currency from Nepal, the operations of ULFA militants from safe hideouts in Bhutan and the sanctuaries available to the insurgent groups of the northeastern states in Myanmar and Bangladesh, have all added to India's border security challenges.

While the BSF should be responsible for manning all settled borders, the responsibility for unsettled and disputed borders, such as the LoC in J&K and the LAC on the Indo-Tibetan border, should be that of the army. The principle of 'single point control' must be followed if the borders are to be effectively managed. Divided responsibilities never result in effective control. While full operational control on the LoC is already with the army, it is not the case on the LAC with China. On the LAC, the ITBP, which is under the Ministry of Home Affairs (MHA), is responsible for the Ladakh, Himachal Pradesh and the Uttar Pradesh segments while the army is deployed in Sikkim.

The Assam Rifles, another MHA force but under the army's operational control, manages the LAC in Arunachal Pradesh. On the other hand, on the Tibetan side, Border Guards divisions of the Chinese army under a single commander manage the entire LAC. The BSF must be withdrawn from its internal security commitments and reverted to border management that is its primary role. Ad hoc measures in utilising police forces for operational tasks for which they are not trained, invariably leads to the lack of a cohesive response to critical situations affecting national security and further complicates the resolution of existing problems.

Achieving self-reliance in critical weapons technologies is another important ingredient of India's national security strategy. Stringent technology control regimes have been applied by the western powers as a consequence to India's independent line on nuclear weapons even though India has behaved extremely responsibly as a nuclear power and has refrained from proliferating nuclear weapons and ballistic missile technologies, unlike China that is a signatory to the NPT and the MTCR.

Though such technology denial regimes have only slowed down India's quest for self-reliance and not stopped it altogether, the present dependence on imports for major defence equipment needs to be reduced quickly and eliminated by 2020-25. The efforts already underway in indigenous weapons research and development need to be further stepped up. At the same time, India should establish closer strategic ties with countries like France and Israel that may be willing to enter into joint weapons development agreements with India. The leverages provided by India's weapons procurement programmes should be exploited to gain access to cutting edge defence technologies. Defence cooperation programmes need to be made more meaningful to establish strategic linkages with countries of consequence. The full importance of military diplomacy and its vast potential in furthering national security is yet to be realised in India. Other important national security strategies that need to be instituted include those for maritime and energy security, food, water and environmental security and for security against organised crime and cyber terrorism.

INDIA'S NATIONAL INTERESTS AND OBJECTIVES

National interests and objectives establish a nation's strategic requirements. Policies provide the guiding rules for satisfying them. National strategy integrates all elements of national power to achieve national interests and objectives, both during peace and war.

National strategy includes a political strategy, that addresses internal as well as international issues, an economic strategy, a national security strategy and so on. National security strategies together constitute "grand strategy" that is "the art and science of employing national power under all circumstances to exert desired degrees and types of control over the opposition through threats, force, indirect pressures, diplomacy, subterfuge and other imaginative means, thereby satisfying national security interests and objectives."

However, unlike solitaire, grand strategy is not a game that a nation can play all by itself. Actions and reactions of adversaries who will invariably seek to promote their own national interests and further their own objectives must always be vectored in, in as much as this grand strategy must be flexible and adaptable to emerging situations.

The four basic national interests of nation states are the defence of the homeland, economic well being, the creation of a favourable world order or external environment and the promotion of values. These national interests are generally graded on a four-tiered scale of priorities or intensities. The foremost among these are survival interests which deal with the very existence of a nation and are of broad, overriding importance to the survival, safety and vitality of a nation. There can be no compromises with survival interests, no matter what the diplomatic, political or financial cost because the survival of the nation cannot be imperilled under any circumstances. Vital interests are those which if not duly safeguarded, have the potential to result in serious harm to the security and well being of the nation. The next in the order of priority are major interests with a much reduced potential for serious harm than vital interests and at the lower end of the scale are peripheral or minor interests that are unlikely to require precipitate action. The time dimension provides another yardstick for measuring the intensity of an interest. Survival interests invariably require immediate attention. For example, the Japanese bombing of Pearl Harbour in 1941 had directly threatened the survival of the US and an immediate US reaction was necessary to ward off the threat. Vital interests require urgent planning and preparation to meet threats to national security, particularly if they have the potential to approach the survival level. Major interests require a serious approach but are generally those that can be handled through negotiations and an accommodative attitude based on give and take. In the case of peripheral interests, a wait and watch policy normally suffices.

The most basic national interest is the survival of the state. A state must ensure its survival "with an 'acceptable' degree of independence, territorial integrity, traditional life styles, fundamental institutions, values and honour intact. Nothing else matters if the country is exterminated as a sovereign entity. No other end is worth risking national extinction to attain." Post-World War II, the Cuban missile crisis was the most challenging example of the survival of the US being at stake. It is the survival instinct that will keep the Pakistan leadership, military or civilian, from launching a nuclear first strike on India knowing full well that Pakistan will cease to exist as a viable nation state after massive punitive Indian nuclear strikes in retaliation. No matter how irrational the Pakistani leaders make themselves out to be, India knows that they cannot afford to act irrationally as far as the very survival of their country is concerned.

It has been said that nations have no permanent friends or permanent enemies - they have only permanent interests. This is not really true. National survival is the only abiding national interest. All other interests can and do change from time to time. Vital interests include the physical security of territory, the safety of citizens, the economic well-being of society and the protection of critical national infrastructures from paralysing attack, both physical and cyber attack. These include banking, finance and stock markets, energy, telecommunications, transportation systems (roads and railways, airports and air traffic controls and shipping and inland waterways), water supply systems and emergency services. Threats to vital interests pose potential rather than imminent dangers and hence allow policymakers time to resolve those threats through diplomatic means and to convince an adversary that confrontation would prove extremely costly. A recent example of military action to safeguard a vital interest is that of the Coalition Forces campaign to evict Iraqi troops from Kuwait during the 1990-91 Gulf War.

India's foremost national interest is India's survival as a nation state. Despite several wars and low intensity conflicts having been thrust on it by inimical external powers, India has successfully survived the first half-century after independence. It is well known that India has no claims or territorial ambitions beyond its borders. Ample proof of this was provided after the 1971 war with Pakistan when India declared a unilateral cease-fire on the western border despite being in a position of immense military superiority after the Pakistani forces in East Pakistan (now Bangladesh) surrendered at Dacca. The Indian armed forces also vacated all Bangladesh territories by March 1972. However, Indian territory remains under the occupation of its adversaries. Pakistan is in occupation of approximately 80,000 square km of the state of J&K since 1947-48 despite a United Nations resolution calling upon it to vacate. China is in occupation of about 38,000 square km of India's Aksai Chin since November 1962. Also, Pakistan has illegally ceded 5,800 square km of Indian territory in J&K to China through which the Karakoram Highway has ben constructed.

India's first vital national interest is independence and autonomy in decision-making. There can be no compromises with national level decision-making in important matters, particularly those relating to national security. Whether it is the decision to sign the CTBT or to join the FMCT negotiations, Indian decision-makers must be guided purely by the national interest and not by any extraneous considerations. The next vital interest in order of importance would be to create a secure environment conducive to India's unhindered economic development. India should aim to achieve the status of a fully developed country by 2020-25 and the Indian Government must not tolerate any external interference in this national effort. The early resolution of the territorial and boundary dispute with China is a vital interest for India's security and so is the resolution of the ongoing low intensity limited conflict along the Line of Control (LoC) in J&K and the Actual Ground Position Line (AGPL) at Siachen Glacier. Ensuring that Pakistan's sponsorship of trans-border and trans-LoC terrorism and insurgency in J&K and other parts of India is brought to an early end would also qualify as a vital interest. In fact, finding a long-term solution to the internal and external dimensions of the Kashmir problem is India's foremost vital interest at present.

Another vital interest would be to ensure that a credible nuclear deterrence is firmly in place with China and Pakistan. If nuclear deterrence were to ever fail, this interest would be instantaneously upgraded to the level of a vital or even survival interest and immediate retaliatory action would be warranted. Parallel to this would be work towards total, universal nuclear disarmament and disarmament of other weapons of mass destruction. The protection of Indian citizens against threats to their lives and to care for their well-being at all places and at all times would be vital interests. Other vital interests would include a conflict and tension free internal security environment and the protection of key national infrastructure from physical and cyber attack. Effective control over and the protection of India's airspace is a vital interest that cannot be compromised. As 97 percent of India's trade (by volume) is ship-borne, the guaranteed, unhindered passage of Indian ships and foreign-owned ships carrying goods to and from India through India's sea lanes of communications (SLOCs) would also be a vital interest and the Indian Navy would need to be structured to ensure the protection of these SLOCs both during war and peace. India must spare no effort to defend its vital interests, including the decisive use of military force when necessary and appropriate.

Major interests are important but not crucial to the well-being of a country. Major economic, political and ideological issues that cause serious concern can be negotiated with adversaries even if the negotiations are protracted. Confrontation is rarely desirable to protect major interests. A confrontation free regional security environment is a major national security interest. An early end to the Afghan conflict and the resolution of the ethnic conflict in Sri Lanka would be major interests with diplomatic and military overtones. To enable India to exercise a degree of influence over the nations in India's regional neighbourhood to promote harmonious relationship in tune with India's national interests would be a major national interest. Safeguarding India's interests in its two million square kilometre Exclusive Economic Zone

(EEZ) is an important major interest. The maintenance of the Indian Ocean as a zone of peace is a major interest that also has a bearing on the prevention of armed intervention and the establishment of military bases by inimical external forces in India's regional neighbourhood. India would like to promote the United Nations (UN) as the world's premier peacekeeping, peace enforcement and peace support organisation and continue its support to such operations worldwide. As a corollary, it is in India's interest to oppose the growing tendencies to marginalise the UN since the end of the Cold War.

Another major interest is the resolution of internal ethnic conflicts with fissiparous tendencies and the prevention of terrorism. Linked with this are the proliferation of small arms and narcotics trafficking and organised crime, including the circulation of fake Indian currency to undermine the Indian economy. Since these internal problems have a major external dimension, they need to be approached in a comprehensive inter-ministerial and inter-departmental manner at the national level in conjunction with the concerned state governments. Energy, food, water and environmental security are major interests that require synergised civil and military action plans at the national level. India must at all times maintain access to sources of energy supplies, natural resources and world markets for Indian goods. The prevention of demographic invasions from India's neighbours would also qualify as a major interest. Promoting democracy abroad, particularly in the Southern Asian region, is as important for India as it is for the US. India would need to find ways and means to promote democracy in Afghanistan, Pakistan, Myanmar and even Tibet without direct interference in the internal affairs of these countries.

A peripheral interest is one that does not seriously affect the entire nation's well being even though it may be detrimental to the private interests of Indian citizens and businessmen. Peripheral interests are lower order political, economic and ideological interests.

Concern for the well being of the Indian Diaspora could be called a peripheral interest. However, such interests may at times have to be upgraded to major interests due to the impact of the prevailing situation. The events in Fiji during the summer of months of 2000 when the democratically elected government was overthrown and the Indian minority was subjected to undue harassment provide an example.

While the promotion of democracy abroad is a major interest, the promotion of secular values could be termed as a peripheral interest. Humanitarian interests would also qualify as peripheral interests.

China's human rights violations in Tibet are of immense concern to India because of India's long-standing affinity with the Tibetan people. Pakistan's suppression of the human rights of the people of Pakistan Occupied Kashmir (POK) and the Northern Areas of Gilgit and Baltistan are also a cause for concern. The people in these areas do not enjoy any fundamental rights and those in the Northern Areas have no representation or say in their governance. India needs to bring international pressures to bear on these countries to stop these wanton and unchecked human rights violations.

The two national interests that are most likely to determine whether a country would engage in war are serious military threats to its homeland and major potential dangers to its external environment. The real test of the worth of a nation's political leadership is to correctly assess vital national interests and the likely costs involved in upholding them. Failure to appreciate the intensity of an antagonist's interest, or for that matter an ally's stake, can lead to blunders in foreign policy and disasters in war.

The United Kingdom's invasion of Egypt in 1956, the US intervention in Vietnam in the mid-1960s, Argentina's seizure of the Falklands Islands in 1982 and Saddam Hussein's capture of Kuwait in 1990 are examples of such blunders. The US intervention in Vietnam is a classic example of the political leaders deciding that the issue was a vital interest and merited armed intervention and the US Congress and public thinking otherwise. No issue that is not supported wholeheartedly by the public can be graded as a vital interest without the risk of ultimate failure if the use of force is resorted to. This is, of course, more true of open societies and modern democracies than of totalitarian regimes. India's intervention in Sri Lanka in 1987 was not supported by the public and had finally led to an ignominious abandonment without having achieved any strategic goals.

National interests cannot be easily sub-divided into vital, major and peripheral ones, as they tend to change with changes in the international environment and the prevailing situation at any point in time. The sub-divisions tend to be judgmental and even experienced analysts can and often do wrong. It must be recognised that various political leaders, government functionaries, scholars and academics would have their own concept of what qualifies as a vital, major or peripheral interest. It is necessary to have a parliamentary and wider public debate on these issues to assess whether there is a national consensus. After that it should be left to the National Security Council and its various groups to evaluate India's interests holistically and draw up a list that is both meaningful and achievable.

INDIAN COUNTERMEASURES POST MUMBAI ATTACKS

Immediately after the Mumbai attacks several measures were taken by the Indian administration amidst much public debate- mostly criticism as to how vulnerable Indian cities are to terrorist attacks. These measures were:

- Creation of NSG hubs in the major metropolitan cities
- Diplomatic pressure on Pakistan for the arrest and trial of Lashkar-e-Taiba's top leadership
- Creation of a new National Investigation Agency (NIA)
- Amendment of Unlawful Activities (Prevention) Act
- Increased budget allocation for Homeland Security Agencies
- Coastal Security Scheme
- Creation of a Police Commando Force in Mumbai
- Arrest of key Lashkar-e-Taiba operatives

Within a week of the attacks Indian Prime Minister Manmohan Singh announced the setting up of NSG hubs in different parts of the country. The first phase included setting up of hubs in Mumbai, Kolkata, Chennai and Hyderabad. All four of the hubs have been established and the last one was inaugurated in the winter of 2011. The regional NSG hubs were set up with the intent of reducing response time in case of a terrorist attack. In a country like India, which faces terrorist threat not just from external terrorist groups like Lashkar-e-Taiba but from homegrown terrorist and insurgent groups, even though it is necessary to have these regional hubs for quick deployment and response, security experts also feel that increase in the number of personnel or hubs is not going to solve the problem. Former National Security Advisor M.K. Narayanan said at a conference that the idea of setting up of NSG hubs was 'archaic' and a 'major mistake'. "I am concerned about the current emphasis on increasing the size and numbers of the NSG. I also have reservations about the establishment of four regional hubs. The NSG is an elite special force intended to meet a specific situation and not intended to confront the normal law and order situation… Its strength does not lie in its numbers, its uniqueness lies in the fact that it consists of the bravest of brave personnel, of great virtue and ability, specially trained for undertaking the most difficult tasks... increasing numbers, to my mind, is bound to dilute both quality and capability of the force"

The National Security Guard which was established in 1986 was modelled after the German GSG-9 and raised as an elite anti-hijacking, anti-terror and bomb disposal force. In the years before as well as after the attacks in Mumbai, they have mostly been used for VIP security. In 2012 the NSG for the first time in many years pulled out its 900 commandos from VIP security details and put them to train for and perform counter-terrorism and anti-hijacking operations. The boost that the NSG got after the Mumbai attacks was a step in the right direction but no Mumbai like attack after 2008, the force seems to now be caught up in a fight for budget allocations, equipment acquisition and improving their capability in terms of personnel and training.

As the interrogations of the lone surviving terrorist, Ajmal Amir Kasab, proceeded and reports of Pakistani state support as well as Lashkar-e-Taiba's involvement surfaced, Indian officials blamed Pakistan for providing sanctuary and letting terrorist activities emanate from their soil. Indian administration since then has been trying to pressure Pakistan through diplomatic channels as well as through the international community to crack down on Lashkar-e-Taiba and bring the masterminds of the Mumbai attacks to book. In early January 2009, India sent evidence to Pakistan which linked the Mumbai attacks to Pakistani terrorists including data from the satellite phones which were used by the 10 gunmen to keep in touch with their handlers as well as what was described as 'Kasab's confession.'

The evidence dossier was also sent to countries whose citizens were the victims of the attack such as the United States, as India tried to corner Pakistan diplomatically into bringing the perpetrators to justice.

In a time frame of three years since, 15 such dossiers have been provided to the Pakistani administration by the Indian government and officials of both countries have met on 13 different occasions. And even though Pakistan has acknowledged that the plan to attack Mumbai was hatched on Pakistani soil, India feels Pakistan has done little to cooperate and hasn't taken any real hard steps to crack down on terrorist activity. It has been almost 5 years since the first dossier was provided and on the 5th anniversary of the attacks, Indian officials still press for a speedy and just trial of the masterminds.

Another major initiative taken by the government was the setting up of a federal National Investigative Agency by passing the National Investigative Agency Act and making relevant amendments to the already existing Unlawful Activities (Prevention) Act. Both these measures were taken within a month of the Mumbai attacks and were passed by both Houses of the Parliament almost at the same time.

At present the NIA is functioning as the Central Counter Terrorism Law Enforcement Agency in India and has dealt with 72 cases till date. Even though there was a dire need for a Federal Investigative Agency, the haste in which this Act has been conceived has left unresolved many issues about the NIA's constitutional validity, functioning, and scope.

The constitutional basis for the creation of the NIA remains a matter of debate. The areas of policing and public order lie within the exclusive legislative competence of the States and not with the Centre (Central government). States would be extremely chary of accepting or cooperating with any agency that encroached on that power.

Furthermore, the NIA Act has been drafted in a way that it focuses only on investigation but not on prevention. In order for the NIA to be effective in preventing federal crime, it needs to be able to warehouse, process and coordinate the flow of critical information.

The Amendments to the Unlawful Activities (Prevention) Act which were brought about almost parallel to the NIA Act also felt significant but were vague in character and meaning. The amendments define 'an act of terrorism' but for the Act to have any real prevention or enforcement powers the definition needs to be more specific in sketching out the difference between civilians and combatants as well as between political and personal motives.

Further the Act lacks any kind of provision for a review mechanism. It grants immunity from prosecution or other legal proceedings to the central and state governments, and their employees.

One of the more progressive steps which seems promising and likely to have a real effect on India's counter-terrorism policies is higher budget allocation for the Ministry of Home Affairs which is responsible for internal security, border management, para military forces etc. The allocation for India's homeland security agencies was increased by 25 percent in the budget 2009-2010. The allocation of budget for the Ministry has since increased yearly.

The budget in recent years also included the Coastal Security Schemes which were initiated in 2005, well before the Mumbai attacks in 2008, and completed its first phase in 2011.

The Coastal Security Schemes were initiated with the aim of improving surveillance and patrolling along the Indian coast with the strengthening of the Marine Police Force. Under Phase-1 of the scheme 73 Coastal Police Stations, 58 Out Posts and 30 Barracks were approved with 204 boats and vehicles. Phase-2 was approved in 2010 and is set to be completed by 2015. 131 Coastal Police Stations, 180 boats/vessels, 60 jetties and 373 vehicles have been approved under Phase-2.

The issue of maritime security and the lack of it surfaced and gained much attention after the Mumbai attacks. The fact that 10 men could easily enter Indian waters and gain entry into India's financial capital armed with explosives, made the Indian government a target of the civil society's outrage and frustration.

Candle light vigils and heated public debates forced the administration to review the matter of coastal security and accelerate the implementation of the Coastal Security Scheme. But even though the Home Department and police are regularly claiming to have enhanced the coastal security system, the projects launched for this still remain on paper.

Many coastal states failed to reach the target number of coastal police stations under Phase-1 and yet more have been sanctioned under Phase-2. States are also struggling with the maintenance and repair of equipment and vehicles.

The intelligence community in Mumbai has got around 250 intelligence inputs this year with some referring to the possibility of terrorists using the sea to carry out attacks. Despite this, coastal police stations have not been built and the boats have been under repair for nearly two years.

Yet another example of an ineffective counter-measure is the creation of an elite commando force under the Mumbai Police Department. The commando force called Force One was created for swift action in an event of Mumbai style attack and again it failed to even stand up on its feet. Till 2012, three years after its formation, the force was struggling to get the funds allocated to it by the State government and was struggling to cope with shortage of equipment such as special rifles, bulletproof vests, pistols and even ammunition for training and practice. The most successful of all countermeasures though has been the arrest of key Lashkar-e-Taiba operatives. In 2013, Indian security officials arrested Abdul Karim Tunda- an expert bomb maker for the terrorist outfit. In 2012 approximately 61 operatives were killed in encounters with Indian security forces including Lashkar Division and District Commanders. Around 48 were arrested and 8 sleeper cells were neutralized. The arrests included key recruiter for Lashkar from India and Nepal Mohammad Omar Madni and Chief Coordinator for Jammu and Kashmir Manzoor.

Looking at the numbers, it certainly seems like the intelligence community is successful in gathering critical information as well as preventing further attacks but in my opinion they still have a long way to go. In 2013 itself, there has been a record of 254 infiltration bids made by terrorists along the India-Pakistan border.

In 133 cases, the terrorists were made to 'return' to Pakistan territory, while they successfully crossed over in 84 cases. The operatives that crossed over in these 84 cases could well be planning another Mumbai. As seen in most of the counter measures analyzed above, they were carried out in haste without much deliberation or debate after the attacks in Mumbai.

The poorly formed and impulsive decisions were then tangled in bureaucratic processes, slow paper work and murky politics. A senior journalist, Praveen Swami, commenting on the police reforms after the Mumbai attacks wrote in an article, 'The Indian Fine Art of Faking Security'- "India's post-26/11 police reforms painted stripes on a donkey — and passed it off as a tiger." But the alarming as well as disconcerting fact is that it is not just the police reforms which are being passed off as a tiger but India's counter-terrorism policies as a whole seems to be a striped donkey which when under attack will shed its stripes and show its true colors.

Indian authorities continue to boast and reiterate the fact that they have launched many counter measures post Mumbai and they have been successful because there has not been another Mumbai like attack after 2008. Although that it is true, it is hardly a metric that can be used to measure success for counterterrorism policies. Most of these measures were taken to show to the world as well as to pacify the public sentiment that 'we are doing something.'

Instead, for a review of the success or failure of these measures some basic questions should be addressed: Is the dependence on certain factors that terrorists or anti-terrorists can exploit as vulnerabilities increasing or decreasing? How seamlessly do terrorist organizations and networks interact? How seamlessly do new government anti-terrorist organizational structures and networks interact? Is the international operating environment becoming more or less inviting or restrictive for terrorists or for those combating them? Is it easier or harder today for terrorists to inflict the damage they seek to do?

3

India's Internal Security Policy and Challenges

India was partitioned in the backdrop of large-scale communal riots, but the partition of the country on religious lines, without taking into consideration its multiple identities, instead of bringing the communal tensions down, in fact, worsened the situation. The two-nation theory created Pakistan, and it still survives on this theory. Pakistan finds it difficult to accept the reality that India continues to be a democratic, plural, multireligious society and that India today has more Muslim citizens than Pakistan.

The Government of Pakistan has taken upon itself the responsibility of not only protecting its own citizens, but also the Indian Muslims. The power structure in theocratic Pakistan, dominated by the army, the feudal landlords, the bureaucracy and the religious leaders has been able to retain its hold over the levers of power by playing the anti- India and Islamic cards. Pakistan plays the Islamic card in its foreign policy also. It misses no opportunity to club India as an anti-Islamic country where Muslims are not safe. The continuing tensions between India and Pakistan have a direct bearing on the internal situation in India. They have further complicated the internal security situation.

The management of internal security, therefore, assumes great importance. If the internal security issues are tackled effectively, subversion by the external forces to that extent becomes more difficult. Unfortunately, the rise of contentious politics based on sectarian, ethnic, linguistic or other divisive criteria, is primarily responsible for the many communal and secessionist movements flourishing in India. The presence of hostile neighbours enables the internal conflicts to get external support, which includes money, arms and sanctuaries. The vested interests exploit these conditions to pursue their own agenda.

In a well-established political system and a developed economy, conflicts between the various group identities are kept under check as in due course they get assimilated into the national identity. But that has not happened in India as yet, where the wounds of the partition and the colonial rule have still not fully healed. Moreover, the dependence on the government by a large section of our people for their very survival sharpens these conflicts among them. The democratic institutions and the state structures are still not strong enough to fully harmonise these conflicts in a peaceful manner. Violence erupts when conflicting interests cannot be consensually reconciled. The hostile external forces, taking advantage of this situation through subversive propaganda, further accentuate these conflicts. They give material and ideological support to aggravate this sense of grievance to such an extent that a small minority are willing to become tools in their hands to subvert the stability and security of the country.

In addition, a number of secessionist and the so-called revolutionary movements are operating in India today. Their goal could be to overthrow the government and bring about revolutionary changes in the structure and functioning of the state, or even secession from the Indian Union. Ever since independence, India has been facing all types of violent conflicts based on religion, caste, language, ethnicity and regional loyalties. Political insecurity further compounds the problem. Preoccupied with the problem of survival, the governments in some of the most affected states are not looking at the problem from a long-term perspective. They have bought temporary peace by compromising with the subversive forces. Such shortsighted policies can have disastrous consequences in the long run. Instead of effectively dealing with them in the initial stages when the problem is manageable, they have allowed these anti-national forces to take roots and spread their tentacles far and wide. When a state government is unable to effectively deal with them, instead of strengthening the state police machinery, it rushes to the Centre to hand over its responsibility at the first sign of any serious trouble. It is not surprising that in these states some sections of the police have actually joined hands with the subversive forces against the central forces. "If you cannot fight them, join them". Finding themselves at the mercy of these subversive forces, the people tend to change sides and start supporting them instead of supporting the security forces. It would be wrong to assume that all those supporting, directly or indirectly, these forces are sympathetic to their ideology. Far from it! For most of them, preoccupied with the daily battle of survival, this is the obvious choice, because the police are unable to protect them. Polarisation on caste and religious lines can further reduce the credibility of the police in the minds of the people.

The police-politician-criminal nexus can embolden the criminal elements. Their activities can create an environment of lawlessness, where influential and rich people violate the law with impunity. The police is not the only component of the criminal justice system that has suffered because of this nexus. In fact, the entire criminal justice system is under strain. Not all crimes are being registered and those registered are not being properly investigated; and even out of those charge-sheeted, very few are ending in conviction. The conviction rate in case of heinous crimes is steadily falling. In some North-Eastern states it has reached almost zero level, where the police have stopped even submitting the charge sheets in the insurgency-related cases. When the fear of legal punishment disappears, organised crime finds it convenient to spread its tentacles. The crime syndicates are finding the new communication and information technology very useful. Extortion and payment of the so-called 'protection money' is more widespread than we would like to believe. According to some reports, direct extortion from the government funds runs into hundreds of crores of rupees. Many of the insurgent and militant groups are not driven by ideology, but by sheer greed. Money power is a bigger motivating factor than ideology. Vested interests have developed around these groups with active connivance of corrupt politicians, police officers and civil servants. Some politicians even take their assistance during election times. They have to return their favours when they come to power. This mutually beneficial relationship has seriously damaged the quality of governance in the interior areas. The real losers are the people. The development process gets seriously hampered in a violent environment. When large development funds are siphoned out by this unholy alliance between the criminal and corrupt forces, even the delivery of the most basic services like water, power, healthcare, education and communications becomes a stupendous task.

A vicious circle starts. The deprived and the marginalised sections of the society, unable to survive in the present system, get alienated. The militant and extremist forces thrive in this environment. The rise of Left extremism is more due to these compulsions than on ideological grounds. There are media reports about the carving out of a corridor by the Left extremist forces from Nepal to Tamil Nadu. Even if there is no truth in these reports, the involvement of hostile external forces in support of the Left extremist forces to destabilise the country cannot be ruled out.

The mushrooming of armed 'Senas' on caste and ethnic lines in some parts of the country is a direct consequence of the polarisation of the society. This phenomenon has also affected the police and the administration in general. Loss of public confidence in the capacity of the state to protect their life and property is the primary cause of this dangerous development. Far from controlling them, a politicised and partisan police actually encourages this development.

The tensions in some parts of the country, especially in the tribal areas, due to a perceived threat to their identity is not new, but the rise of so many violent movements is a relatively recent development. In the border states these movements become secessionist because of the support they receive from the hostile neighbouring states.

The rise of fundamentalist forces is posing the most serious threat to India's security. Fired with religious zeal these forces have created an entirely new situation. The intelligence agencies in our neighbourhood and the organisations, like Al Qaida, and Jaish-e-Mohammad, are encouraging the so-called 'Jehadis' to enter India from outside. After first targeting the border states they have now spread deep inside the country. These bands of fanatics are not only indulging in subversive activities, but are spreading the virus of fundamentalism among the Indian Muslims. The break-up of the Indian Union continues to be the main goal of Pakistan's domestic and foreign policy. Easy availability of deadly weapons with the subversive groups operating in India has created new dangers for India's security.

With the 'Golden Crescent', and the 'Golden Triangle' in India's neighbourhood, drug trafficking poses yet another threat to our security. Drug syndicates are generating huge funds, a part of which is being used to give financial support to some of these subversive groups. The intelligence agencies like the ISI are recruiting a number of 'carriers' in drug trafficking as their agents. These agencies provide legal immunity for their criminal activities in their own country in addition to giving them financial and logistical support. Internal security challenges are not confined to any one area, but the North-East, Jammu and Kashmir, and the areas afflicted by Left extremism deserve special mention.

INTERNAL SECURITY THREATS TO INDIA

India's internal security challenges can be categorized under two heads – insurgency and extremism. We will explore the internal security threats to India in these lines.

Insurgency

India faces huge challenges in dousing the insurgency fires in many parts of the country – from the dense forests of Central India covering Chattisgarh, Jharkhand, few districts in Uttar Pradesh, West Bengal, few parts of Andhra Pradesh (so called Red Corridor) to North-East India. We all know the Pakistani sponsored and mooted terrorist activities in the state of J&K since 1989. Besides there are dozens of militant groups in ethnically diverse North Eastern part of the country. Indian strategy so far has been to first let a state handle its law and order situation and intervene only in cases of extreme urgency. This strategy needs a rethink because of signs of consolidation among many of the freedom-seekers e.g. there are indications that Maoists have tried to forge ties with Kashmiri separatists and ULFA to synergize their activities. Furthermore as Left-Wing Extremism (LWE) in India stretches has their proximity to important cities and both north-south and east west lines of communication - termed as "potentially dangerous" by the Indian Army. Therefore for successfully tackling the menace of LWE, two pronged strategy needs to be adopted – focus on socio-economic uplift of the affected areas as it is unfulfilled promise of the Indian state to her citizens (aka Directive Principles of the State) and secondly this is one of the root-causes of the rise of Naxal movement in the Indian hinterland. Sincere efforts must be taken to implement inclusive growth as an objective of public policy. On fighting the insurgency, inter-state cooperation is a must and jurisdictional issues should not be allowed to tackle a nation-wide insurgency. Failing which, it must be emphasized India will face sever governance crisis internally and might even descend into chaos.

Insurgency in NE part of the country goes till 1950s and has its genesis in the way those states were integrated into the Indian Union. Much water has since flown down the river Brahmaputra to reverse the flow of time. Inter-ethnic and inter-religious harmony should be maintained in the highly sensitive region through grass-root level participation of people. Besides illegal migration from Bangladesh rightly fuels resentment among the rightful Indian citizens and there should be no vote-bank politics with this critical development in Assam and other states. Otherwise changed demographics of these states can wreck havoc on the internal security of the country in the coming decades.

For tackling the issue of Jammu and Kashmir, numerous tomes have been written. But in a nutshell, the issue requires firm handling from the Centre. It is widely documented that Pakistani state fuels the seeds of alienation among the Kashmiri youth. Even within the state of J&K, Jammu and Ladakh have not shown secessionist movements and are well-integrated into the mainstream. It is only the Kashmir Valley which has seen such activities and adequate focus should be given towards job creation in this region.

Extremism

Religious extremism is other main internal security threat to the country. Without establishing cause-and-effect for this phenomenon as do most of the Right and Left wing intellectuals, there is urgency to tackle this issue. Fair and transparent law enforcement and quick, efficient judicial apparatus are required to stem the tide of religious extremism in the country – both minority as well as majority. Recent rhetorical statements from the politicians of certain political spectrum to milk this challenge for their advantage are indeed unfortunate.

Other challenges to internal security are astoundingly high level of corruption, political factionalism and caste wars – all of which require seasoned and firm political vision.

EMERGING SECURITY CHALLENGES

Even as India grapples with diverse external and internal threats to its security, many new challenges are emerging on the security horizon. Before the dangers evident in them can be addressed, the emerging threats need to be identified and understood. The major emerging threats are outlined below:

- Increasing demands for electric power to meet the requirements of industry and the growing population will make energy security a primary concern. Energy security will be particularly important in future, as fossil fuels will become more and more inadequate for the nation's increasing energy needs. Domestic oil production has been declining while the demand has been rising steadily. Hence, oil will continue to be a strategic resource and the security of India's oil supplies from abroad as well as that of all oil reserves and installations will need to be ensured.
- India's growing population and the likelihood of mass migrations into India, for example from Bangladesh, will threaten the existing food reserves and endanger food security. The nation will find it extremely difficult to cope with successive failures of the monsoon, if they occur, and the consequent famine-like conditions that are likely to prevail. For almost a decade now, the monsoon has been bountiful in most parts of India. Quite obviously, this cannot continue for long and the law of averages will catch up sooner rather than later.

- The ravages of global warming and changing monsoon patterns are likely to deplete India's water sources and threaten water security even as the increasing population, rapid industrialisation and the enhanced requirements of irrigation raise the demand for water. The Tata Energy Research Institute has estimated that the demand for water will almost double from 564 billion cubic metres (bcum) in 1997 to 1,048 bcum in 2047.14 The situation will be further exacerbated when the Himalayan nation-states begin drawing more water for their own consumption. The amicable sharing of the Ganga River waters between India, Bangladesh and Nepal has already been posing problems. Successive droughts have ravaged some of India's western states during 1999 and 2000 mainly due to groundwater levels having fallen to extremely low levels.
- Information warfare is another emerging threat through which, besides nation-states, non-state actors, individual terrorists and even disgruntled elements within a state can play havoc with a nation's telecom, banking, stock exchanges, power grids, railways and air traffic control infrastructure, besides military communications and networks. The prevention of large-scale damage through a complex cyber-security system requires an inter-departmental approach in concert with industry and private entrepreneurs and can only be undertaken by a duly empowered apex organisation.
- The threats to India's maritime security are increasing exponentially as the world turns more and more towards the exploitation of ocean resources for food, energy and raw materials. This long- neglected aspect needs to be incorporated in the management of national security so that India's ocean resources in its exclusive economic zone (EEZ) are not poached at will by state and non-state actors. Increasing piracy at sea and the possible use of India's island territories by terrorist organisations and for trade in contraband goods are other serious maritime threats.
- Security of the environment is another emerging challenge. The continuing increase in the population will threaten the already depleted forest resources as the area of cultivable land comes under pressure. Also, over exploitation of the oceans may upset the delicate marine balance. Increasing urbanisation is causing its own environmental problems. Soil erosion in some areas, specially in hill states due to the impact of deforestation, and the irreplaceable loss of vital nutrients due to the tendency to harvest three to four crops a year in some other

states, will eventually lay waste vast areas of cultivable lands and severely curtail agricultural production.

- In future, the Indian government will have to increasingly plan for the security concerns of the vast Indian Diaspora, particularly the migrant Indian population employed on temporary work permits in the Gulf countries. The Gulf War in 1990-91 had resulted in the most massive airlift since the Berlin airlift as over 100,000 Indian workforce personnel had to be evacuated from Iraq. The increasing persecution of ethnic minorities of Indian origin in countries like Pakistan will create its own tensions and may force India to intervene in future. The May 2000 coup in Fiji, where the Indian minority was specifically targeted, may be a pointer of the shape of things to come.

Still newer challenges that are emerging include those from organised crime and narco-terrorism. India is flanked by two of the most notorious narcotics producing regions in the world - the Golden Crescent (Afghanistan, Iran and Pakistan; annual production approximately 2,500 tonnes) on the west and the Golden Triangle (Laos, Myanmar and Thailand; 1,500 tonnes) on the east. Money laundering and the issue of fake currency by inimical neighbours are new problems to be contended with. The Asian financial crisis demonstrated that a nation's currency can be undermined through external intervention and its economy can be de-stabilised. The Ministry of Defence (MoD) Annual Report 1995-96 listed several other non-military 'pressures' on the national security environment which could not be ignored. These included "...those relating to trade, intellectual property rights, environment, human rights..." The existing and emerging threats to national security are becoming more and more complex to evaluate and manage in the prevailing era of strategic uncertainty.

Need for a Formal Defence Policy

These threats and challenges to national security require systematic evaluation by an apex body and the formulation of a comprehensive national security strategy to ensure that they are managed well and not allowed to spin out of control. Indian defence analysts have for long lamented the lack of a national security vision and strategy. With his characteristic frankness, K. Subrahmanyam minces no words in bluntly stating that, "It is now well recognised all over the world that India does not have a tradition of strategic thinking... mainly due to the incapacity of our political leaders and top civil servants to take a long-term view of national security. This is compounded by their consequent failure in giving a lead to the armed forces in preparing the country to face its long-term need for defence preparedness." In Brahma Chellaney's view, "The lack of an integrated, long-term national security approach stands out as the biggest failure of nation-building in the half-century that India has been independent. In the absence of such an approach, national security policy-making has been characterised largely by ad hoc decisions to meet new threats and realities." M. D. Nalapat says that national security policy has generally been one of reacting to threats and events and, "A holistic view was avoided as this would have reduced the powers of the separate bureaucracies (in the home and defence ministries especially) dealing with the problem... this uncoordinated response to security threats is a major failing in the system." And, K. N. Daruwalla asks, "Can a country have a military doctrine if it does not posses a strategic one? If your overall objectives and goals are ambiguous and undefined, how can you lay down objectives for your armed forces? How can a military doctrine be embedded in such amorphousness?.... Since the armed forces are required to safeguard national interests, foreign policy objectives should go hand in hand with the development of the military machine." However, Jasjit Singh has expressed the view that, "... the reality also must be recognised that (despite the absence of a formally articulated defence doctrine) the country has managed its defence and military affairs well during the past half century."

Indian policy planners have traditionally fought shy of formally articulating the country's defence and national security policies. Perhaps this reticence owes its origins to an innate sense of refraining from hurting the sensibilities of India's adversaries and neighbours. In its Nineteenth Report, the Estimates Committee had recommended that the country should have a formal National Security Doctrine. When the Standing Committee on Defence (1995-96) in the Tenth Lok Sabha enquired about the action taken on this recommendation, the Defence Secretary replied: "... there is a policy; the only thing is that it is not written down as a separate document and published as such... As a matter of policy we have not published such a document and the Government has not been in favour of publishing a separate document. It is only the United States in my knowledge which annually publishes a document called National Security Doctrine. Non-publication of the document does not mean in any way non-existence of policy." Replying to the debate in the Lok Sabha on the Demands for grants of the MoD, on May 10, 1995, Prime Minister P. V. Narsimha Rao, who was also the Defence Minister, stated: "We do not have a document called India's National Defence Policy. But we have got several guidelines which are followed, strictly followed and observed... This policy is not merely rigid in the sense that it has been written down, but these are the guidelines, these are the objectives, these are the matters which are always kept in view while conducting our defence policy..."

Similarly, the Ministry of External Affairs (MEA) avers in its Annual Report 1998-99 that, "We view foreign policy as an integral part of the larger effort of building the nation's capabilities: through economic development, strengthening social well-being and the quality of life and of protecting India's sovereignty, territorial integrity and security, not only in its defence and economic aspects, but in the widest strategic sense of the term." It says that India's external relations are guided by "well-established principles" which have formed the "basis of our foreign policy for decades" and "enjoy a broad national consensus, thus providing a strong foundation of stability and continuity." However, the report does not spell out what those principles are in specific terms and how they translate into practical execution in furthering national interests and objectives.

It is due to this lack of a long-term national security perspective and the failure to initiate a public debate for the formulation of a national consensus on the vital interests, national security objectives and a synergised national security strategy, that the security pendulum has swung between the interventionist "Indira Doctrine" of the 1970s and 1980s on one end and the conciliatory "Gujral Doctrine" of the mid-1990s on the other. The Indira Doctrine stated that, "India will neither intervene in the domestic affairs of any state in the region, unless requested to do so, nor tolerate such intervention by an external power. If external assistance is needed to meet an external crisis, states should first look within the region (that is, to India) for help." The ill-conceived IPKF intervention in Sri Lanka, as also the stand-off with Nepal on the trade treaty and the successful crushing of the coup in the Maldives could be attributed to the practical application of the Indira Doctrine (dubbed as a "muscular" foreign policy by some non-Indian South Asian commentators). The Gujral Doctrine reflected the recognition that India's policies towards its smaller neighbours within Southern Asia should show greater concern for their security perceptions, instead of sticking to hard-line attitudes that have created tensions in the past. The essence of the doctrine was that India would not insist on reciprocity and would be prepared to go more than half way to improve its relations with its smaller neighbours. Inder Gujral, India's Minister for External Affairs, expected the implementation of his ideas to result in a "fundamental recasting of South Asia's regional relationships... to create a climate of greater confidence and close and mutually beneficial co-operation." The two doctrines would require fundamentally different national security strategies to implement though these would not be mutually exclusive and would even overlap in certain areas. Radically different approaches to national security from decade to decade can only lead to a mismatch between capabilities and intentions and must be resolved through wider national debate.

The closest that government documents in India come to articulating national security and foreign policy objectives are the annual reports of the MoD and the Ministry of External Affairs (MEA). In fact, it was only with the 1997-98 annual report that the MoD for the first time spelt out India's national security objectives. Commenting on this interesting development, Raja Menon wrote recently: "The Annual Defence Report of 1997-98 has many welcome changes and for the first time, the notion of 'sacred territory' has been watered down. In all the previous years the role of the armed forces was depicted purely and solely as the 'defence of our territorial integrity', exhibiting a mindset that was not conducive to understanding coercive diplomacy, the manipulation of risk and the threat of military action."

In its opening chapter entitled "National Security Environment", the Annual Report of 1997-98 stated that India's national security objectives are served by:

- Defending the country's borders as defined by law and enshrined in the Constitution and protecting the lives and property of its citizens against terrorism and insurgencies.
- Promoting further co-operation and understanding with neighbouring countries and implementing mutually agreed confidence-building measures.
- Working with countries of the Non-Aligned Movement to address key challenges before the international community and engaging in co-operative security initiatives such as the ASEAN Regional Forum (ARF).
- Pursuing security and strategic dialogues with major powers and key partners.
- Following a consistent and principled policy on disarmament and international security issues based on universality, non-discrimination and equal security for all.
- Having a secure and effective deterrent against the use or the threat of use of weapons of mass destruction against India.

Post-Pokhran II in May 1998, in the 1998-99 Annual Report, the issue of deterrence against weapons of mass destruction was moved up from the last place to the second place in the national security objectives and was re-worded as follows: "Having a secure, effective and credible minimum deterrent against the use or threat of use of weapons of mass destruction against India. The profile of this deterrent, including accurate and refined delivery systems, will not be circumscribed in range and payload by any outside pressure or influence but will be determined by the country's threat perception at any point of time." Also, a new sub-para on technology control regimes was added: "Insulating the country from the effect of individual or group restrictions on the transfer of material, equipment and technologies that have a bearing on India's security, particularly its defence preparedness. This involves a greater emphasis on in-house research, development and production of the nation's requirements and recourse to feasible alternative sources." In the 1998-99 Annual Report, in the objective on the country's disarmament policy, the phrase "based on the principles of supreme national interest" has been added after the words "and international security issues". Curiously, the report refers to the territorial dispute with China as a "boundary" dispute. A careful reading of the national security objectives enunciated in the annual reports of the MoD reveals a tendency to mix objectives with policy in some cases and shows that the objectives are mere statements of intent in others.

According to the MoD, "... although there has been no specifically written document called India's National Defence Policy, yet it has been articulated clearly and unambiguously through various policy statements over the years. The policy articulated since independence is as follows:

"That our military capability is to be so directed to ensuring the defence of national territory over land, sea and air encompassing among others the inviolability of our land borders, island territories, offshore assets and our maritime trade routes. Government have repeatedly made it clear that it is not our objective to influence/interfere/dominate (the) region on the basis of military strength."

In a submission made by the MoD to the Standing Committee on Defence, it was stated that the following aspects "fully depict the national security interests":

- Defence of national territory over land, sea and air, encompassing among others the inviolability of our land borders, island territories, offshore assets and our maritime trade routes.
- To secure an internal environment whereby our Nation State is insured against any threat to its unity or progress on the basis of religion, language, ethnicity or socio-economic dissonance.
- To enable our country to exercise a degree of influence over the nations in our immediate neighbourhood to promote harmonious relationship in tune with our national interests.

- To be able to effectively contribute towards regional and international stability.
- To possess an effective out-of-the-country contingency capability to prevent destabilisation of the small nations in our immediate neighbourhood that could have adverse security implications for us.

Though national security interests and objectives have been spelt out in bits and pieces by the Government, in annual reports and while answering the queries of the Standing Committee on Defence, as brought out above, these have tended to change from time to time and have not been subject to direct parliamentary oversight. These policy statements are of a transitory nature and could sometimes even be based on the personal predilections of policy makers who may be in power at a given point in time. A case in point is the question of whether or not China poses a threat to India. It is well known that while the Defence Minister was reported to have named China as India's number one threat, the Minister for External Affairs subsequently ruled out such an assessment. Hence, these transitory policy statements do not amount to a comprehensive, nationally debated approach that is sanctified by parliamentary consensus transcending the political divide.

Brahma Chellaney has written: "... it needs to be recognised that national security is much more than defence policy. The defence of India means the defence of its national interests. National security demands integrated planning and co-ordinated use of India's political, military, diplomatic and scientific resources to advance its core interests... Unfortunately, India lacks a long-term national security strategy despite the pressing problems it confronts. There is no integrated policy-making process that seeks to make specific policies compatible with each other... serious efforts have (not been) made to establish institutionalised methods so that policy-making is driven less by personalities and more by long-term integrated planning. A host of functional inefficiencies continue to burden Indian policy-making constricting any government's ability to manage national security in a prudent, cost-effective and result-oriented manner..."

Even the Kargil Review Committee Report has recommended an overhaul of the present system: "The Committee strongly feels that the Kargil experience, the continuing proxy war and the prevailing nuclearised security environment justify a thorough review of the national security system in its entirety."

It clearly emerges that the manifold existing and emerging external and internal threats to national security demand a comprehensive and mature system for their handling and management.

Present Government policies appear to reflect individual ministerial approaches rather than a holistic integrated approach. Coherence in application can only flow from a synergised national security strategy. Only an all-encompassing national security management system can take into account all the prevalent inter-ministerial, inter-departmental and civil-military diversities. The emerging asymmetric threats require systematic evaluation and meticulous planning, so that long-term projections can be made in respect of military force structures and the development of the necessary capabilities.

Only when a comprehensive national security strategy is formulated to deal with the existing and emerging threats on a long- and mid-term basis, can the responsibilities of the armed forces and concerned government departments be clearly visualised. Based on the security objectives and the responsibilities assigned, the Services can review their organisational and force structures and make recommendations to the government to institute the changes necessary to translate policy into action. The virtues of long-term defence planning cannot be over-emphasised. Ad hoc functioning on a year-to-year basis leads to imperfection in decision-making and tends to result in avoidable waste.

MAOISM TERRORISM

Denial was decimated at Dantewada last week. The massacre of 76 lives demands Indians face the harsh truth. Maoism is terrorism. By definition, terrorism is the use of force or violence to intimidate. Maoism is terrorism draped in a fig leaf of virtuous intent, in Marxist-Leninist ideology. It was in November 2004 when Prime Minister Manmohan Singh first declared Maoism as the biggest threat to India. For six years Maoists have been "enemy number one" and grown without fear of retribution.

The Maoists are thriving because India has been hostage to romantic notions of a band of do-gooders chased by evil in uniform. It is time India declares a war on the conditions that foment Maoism and Maoists. Make no mistake, Maoists are extortionists and terrorists masquerading as modern day Robin Hoods aided by a thick fog of sentiments. Yes. Every third person in India, or nearly 400 million people live below the poverty line. It is deplorable and a reflection of failed politics and stalled governance. Maoism has flourished because the vote has become a four-letter word that impales decisions, a disincentive for political parties from doing the right thing. Poor road connectivity, the fading writ of law, abject poverty are all allies of Maoism.

Circumstance of poverty though cannot be an alibi for violence, nor a justification for terror. Not in a democracy which affords citizens many avenues to seek justice. Like fashion victims some commentators find reason to sympathise with the cause of Maoists, to condone criminality and intellectualise the indefensible. Let's not forget the goal of Maoists is to overthrow the Government through an armed struggle. Eloquence is not a substitute for rationale. Those presenting poverty and oppression as justification for stoking terror are ideologically in the company of Osama bin Laden.

Dantewada is just another milestone on the Maoist agenda. Since 2004, India has suffered over 7,000 incidents involving Maoists in which over 5,000 have been killed. In 2009, Maoism claimed a life every eight hours. Apologists for Maoism cite lack of development even as Maoists wrecked over 1,700 schools in just two years-in 2008 and 2009. More lives have been claimed by Naxal violence than jihadi terror in the past decade. Maoist guerrillas have described the state as the "enemy" and the conflict as a "war". A war is being waged against India in 220 of its 600 districts, or one in three districts.

Home to the argumentative billion, India also seems to be the emerging refuge of the banal babel. Every Maoist attack triggers in its wake a tedious tide of rhetoric on the need for a political approach to tackling Naxalism. A day after 76 jawans bled to death, the Government is trapped in a debate on whether it will deploy the army or not, whether it will use air power or not. How can we use force on "our own" ask the pacifists in the system, forgetting that never has India been so bloodied by its "own". This is not the occasion for semantics-military or paramilitary, air power or air force. And the war can't be won with just 7,000 trained men. It calls for a new strike force and drafting of trained ex-servicemen. The operative phrase should be "fitting response".

Every inch of India is ruled by the states and war will essentially have to be waged by states. The Centre can at best be a catalyst, the evangelist. If state governments are not delivering, they should be named and shamed. Yes, the war will not be won by bullets alone.

If India truly aspires to be a superpower then it needs to reclaim both the landscape and the mindspace. It could be a public private partnership. Corporates could be invited to adopt the 100 worst districts under the social responsibility banner to help deliver social infrastructure. On its part, the Government could create a special mechanism to ensure implementation of programmes like NREGA and Bharat Nirman under the supervision of senior bureaucrats and young ministers of state.

As Home Minister P. Chidambaram has said: "We need a strong head, a stronger heart and staying power to win." The massacre has forged a political consensus across the political spectrum. It is a rare moment that must be leveraged. India must respond. India must declare a war, on the conditions which foment Maoism and Maoists.

Maoists Rhetoric on India

India's External Affairs Minister SM Krishna will undertake a three-day official visit to Kathmandu from January 15, 2010. According to the Indian Embassy in Kathmandu, at least five memorandums of understanding will be signed during Krishna's visit. The possible MoUs include construction of a National Police Academy at Panauti in Kavre district, Indian assistance for the Nepal Stock Exchange, construction of roads in the Terai, establishment of a science learning centre and a solar electrification project. Krishna will also take up issues related to Indian security and counterfeit currency issues.

Though the visit is timely and significant, uncertainties over the future of the peace process continue due to differences between the political parties on contentious issues like federalism, rehabilitation of Maoist combatants, and the nature of Constitution. The UCPN-Maoist leader Prachanda has accused the ruling parties of being puppets of the Indian ruling class, accused the Indian establishment of intervening in Nepal's internal affairs and trying to derail the peace process. He also said that the UCPN-Maoist should hold direct talks with New Delhi since the ruling parties are guided by remote control and talks with them to establish civilian supremacy have been failing. The Maoists have made elaborate arrangements to express displeasure during Krishna's visit. Recently, they declared the fourth phase of their nationwide agitation demanding restoration of civilian supremacy and formation of a Maoist-led national government. As part of the fourth round of protest programmes, senior party leaders will visit those locations along the open border with India where India has reportedly occupied Nepal's territories. The Maoists will organise mass rallies at several bordering regions 'encroached' by India and torch the copies of the various treaties with India. They will hold demonstrations outside the Indian Embassy and Singha Durbar on January 19.

Krishna's visit is taking place at a time when the Maoist sponsored anti-India feeling is at an all time high in Nepal. Maoists have been consistently branding the 1950 treaty as unequal, raising issues such as illegal encroachment and the recruitment of Nepalse Gurkhas into the Indian Army. But none of these demands are genuine and valid. The Maoists, in fact, do not want to resolve these issues since these give them huge political dividends to retain public support. Pushpa Kamal Dahal alias Prachanda, during his nine month tenure as prime minister, did not take any steps to withdraw from the 1950 treaty though clause 10 of the agreement cleanly mentions that the "Treaty shall remain in force until it is terminated by either party by giving one year's notice." The issue figured prominently during his visit to New Delhi in September 2008. On this occasion, Prachanda had agreed with India's Prime Minister to "review, adjust and update" the 1950 Treaty of Peace and Friendship and other agreements, while giving due recognition to the special features of the bilateral relationship. Why did Prachanda not use clause 10 of the treaty and agreed to review the same during his visit?

Regarding the Gurkha recruitment issue, Pracahnda preferred to remain tightlipped during his visit to India. On the eve of the visit, Deepak Bahadur Gurung, chairman of the Nepal Ex-Servicemen's Association, warned that his organisation would start a new 'People's War' if the Maoist government stopped the recruitment. Most importantly, Maoists' argument about Gurkaha recruitment being colonial is illogical because Gurkha Nepalese have been joining the Indian Army purely on a voluntary basis. This is not forced recruitment or conscription by the Indian Army.

Given the geographical dynamics in the border region, "encroachment" is more a natural phenomenon than man-made. Rivers flowing from Nepal to India frequently shift their course during the monsoons. As a result, certain portions of the border region either come to Nepal or to India depending on the shifting of the river course. Since farmers from both countries find that part of the land fertile, they encroach upon it for agricultural purposes. In fact, Prachanda during his last visit to India acknowledged the problem of inundation in the border areas and agreed to take up necessary work for its effective prevention on the basis of bilateral consultation. Both countries have already (unofficially) agreed that 98 per cent of the border is demarcated except two disputed areas in Kalapani and Susta. India's former external affairs minister Pranab Mukhrjee during his official visit to Kathmandu in November 2008 talked about it before the media. Interestingly, then the Maoist-led government in Kathmandu did not contradict his view on border demarcation. The issue rose to prominence again only after Prachanda's resignation. The Maoists have accused encroachment of Nepalese territory by Indian security forces in the Dang district.

Maoist Insurrection and the Struggle for Land

India aspires to become an unrivalled regional power by 2015. But, to achieve that, guaranteeing its energy needs (oil and, preferably, gas) is vital and it is in this regard that nuclear energy plays an important role. Since its independence from Great Britain, India has tried to set out from what one might call "an economy of size", taking advantage, in other words, of its geographic and population potential. However, despite enormous social differences revolutionary forces, or the Left, if you like, have had difficulty making progress given that capitalism has developed slowly but constantly. The explanation for this situation is that since independence in 1947 India had relatively developed industry and a wealthy, powerful bourgeoisie very adept both at international politics (one should not forget India's importance in creating the Movement of Non-Aligned Countries) and national politics, integrating social measures-although without abolishing the caste system-with outright capitalist ones.

However, during the last 18 years, India has implemented neoliberal policies, gradually dismantling its centralized economy and privatizing its main sectors under the wing of a battery of laws to protect Direct Foreign Investments, especially those from the United States that have now increased from US$76m to US$4bn. At the moment, India's gross domestic product is about US$786bn, four times that of the rest of countries in South Asia. This policy has led to an increase in the middle classes to around 300 million people, the Bollywood movie watchers and migrants to Europe or the United States and who are more and more isolated from disadvantaged classes not only along traditional caste divisions but in economic matters too. It is reckoned that more than 700 million Indians live in the most absolute poverty. Almost all of them are rural workers who live on small plots of land of less than one hectare and who depend on big private businesses for supplies of seed, fertiliser and other inputs. Furthermore they have to survive amidst impressive industrial projects (especially mining projects) and water projects that flood their land or else expropriate them at absurd prices. To that one has to add the traditional oppression that lower castes have suffered since time immemorial and the ever-increasing presence of paramilitaries in the service of big landowners.

So it is no wonder then that a Maoist insurrection is spreading across India like an oil stain across paper, already affecting 14 of India's 28 States (Chatisgarh, Jharkhand, Uttar Pradesh, Asma, Uttaranchal, Kerala, Tamil Nadu, West Bengal, Gujarat, Andhra Pradesh, Madhya Pradesh, Orissa, Maharashtra and Bihar). In figures, that means the Maoists are in control in 165 districts out of the total of 602 into which the country is divided. In fact in the last five states mentioned one can say that "popular new democratic power" is a reality, given that they are the ones who control the countryside, collect taxes from large businesses within their zones of influence, build dykes and irrigation systems, impart justice, decide land disputes among rural families and have suppressed, for example, child marriage. Prime Minister Singh recognised the Maoist advance on August 23rd 2006 when he declared solemnly to Parliament that the Maoists "have become the biggest internal challenge to security that India has."

To deal with the Maoist surge the New Delhi government put into practice the well known US strategy from Vietnam, later perfected in Central America during the revolutionary processes in El Salvador and, above all, in Guatemala : the creation of strategic hamlets and the formation of paramilitary patrols to defend them (in Guatemala, the Civilian Self-Defence Patrols). In India they are known as Slawa Judum (that translates as "Peace Hunters") and have the status of "special police agents" in rural communities. They are especially active in Chatisgarh and it is against them that the guerrilla offensive is currently aimed. An ambush on March 15th killed 50 out of a joint force of police and paramilitaries. The main activity of the paramilitaries is the forced displacement of rural families to "temporary camps" set up in the areas of Bhairamgarh, Gedam y Bijapur and in which 50,000 people are currently crowded.

Paid by landowners and by the Indian government itself, the paramilitaries earn about 1500 rupees a month (about €26 or US$35). The counter-insurgency war, as in the Central American countries mentioned or in Peru or Colombia, uses terror to try and cut off the guerrilla advance. It is estimated that Salwa Judum has 5000 members and the ideologue, just as with the Colombian paramilitaries protected by current President Alvaro Uribe during his time as governor of the Antioquia province, was the main Congress Party leader in Chatisgarh. This is the party of Prime Minister Singh. To those 5000, one must add about 2000 "anti-terrorist " police who have undergone a similar training programme to that given to the Atlacatl battalion, in El Salvador, which committed countless mass murders, outrages, intimidation and forced displacements. In case this paramilitary force is insufficient to stop the guerrilla, the government also offers bounties of up to a million rupees (about €17,000 or US$23,000) for the betrayal of the main guerrilla leaders.

This strategy is favoured in the "red zone", a category applied by the Indian government to the states of Andhra Pradesh, Madhya Pradesh, Orissa, Maharashtra y Bihar, although in the last few months an impressive guerrilla military campaign has begun in Chatisgarh which has made the new Delhi government focus on this state leaving its plans for the other states in abeyance. The reason the guerrillas are prioritizing Chatisgarh is that this state, along with Jharkand, is turning into the spearhead of the government's neoliberal policies following the signing of juicy, million-dollar contracts with big national and multinational industrial corporations, on steel, iron, coal and electricity, which presuppose a new wave of rural families in exodus to wretched slums in the cities. In fact, the most recent guerrilla attack was on June 3rd against the electricity plant of Narayanpur, a district of Chatisgarh.

The Maoists say little when they carry out their actions. It is a fact that guerrilla control in this state is almost complete, with 10 of its 16 districts in their power and that their military actions are more and more daring, including attacks against officials, police, politicians and strategic economic and industrial targets. The government's aim is to confine the Maoist presence to that "red zone" and avoid it spreading with equal force to the rest of the country. Once that objective is achieved, repression will centre on what can be called "support bases" or liberated zones. Nonetheless, it is the different States that have responsibility for security matters, not central government, which explains why police implement the repression rather than the army, and there are different opinions about the best way to confront the guerrilla. In Andra Pradesh the tendency is to negotiate directly, while in Chatisgarh the paramilitary phenomenon is used, to mention the most extreme examples. These positions are influenced by the role the moderate Left has in different State governments and even in the central government which would collapse without the Left's support, as was pointed out earlier. This is the reason why timid agrarian reform is being advanced throughout India and which has as a pilot experience the one implemented in 2005 in the mother State of the guerrillas, West Bengal.

For the moment the guerrillas are ignoring the cities to focus on total control of the countryside, following the old strategy of surrounding the cities from the countryside. The strategy is to penetrate rural areas, consolidate in them and, once the bases of support are deemed secure, to go on building up effective and efficient links with different cells in other states. It is the classic strategy that has given such good results in Nepal. As with their Nepalese comrades, the Indian Maoists respect local officials-including the police-if the people think they are honest and not compromised by cases of corruption or repression. They also respect businesses established in their zones of influence but they collect from them a "revolutionary tax", which varies between 15% and 20 % of their profits, to fund their operations.

History of the Naxalites

The Indian Maoists are known as Naxalites from the town of Naxalbari in West Bengal, where the first armed actions occurred of an organization called the People's War Group, the armed wing of the Communist Party of India (Marxist-Leninist) which, with the slogan of radical reform of land ownership, forced a stand-off through the 1960s with the Indian government. Although the rebellion they led-land occupations, burning of catastral property registers, forgiveness of rural families' mortgage debts and execution of the most important oppressors and usurers-only lasted three months, it ended with a very severe repression that caused more than 100,000 deaths and the virtual disappearance of the organization's members. But some groups carried on operating, although without mutual contact. This led to the fragmentation of the CPI-ML which lasted until 2003 when the Maoist Communist Centre and the Indian Revolutionary Communist Centre united to form the Maoist Communist Centre of India (CCMI) and, one year later in 2004, the integration of a tendency of the CPI-ML called "Popular War". That is how the Communist Party of India (Maoist) came into being with its main slogan as "the fight against feudalism and imperialism".

If one can believe reports of the Indian intelligence services, the country's Maoists have been tempered in the revolutionary popular war in Nepal where they have won greater political training and military experience. The intelligence services reckon that the People's Guerrilla Army (the Indian Maoists military wing) last year counted on 8000 combatants, 25,000 militia members-protecting support bases, carrying out intelligence work and logistic support for the combatants-and 50,000 political members. Small numbers if one considers that India is a country with 1bn inhabitants. But the rapid development of the Maoist movement has set off alarm bells among India's political elite. The immiseration of two thirds of India's people and their social oppression counteract elite desires to turn India into a regional power via nuclear weapons and an agreement with the United States. Today the Naxalites are a reality that has to be taken into account. Perhaps westerners looking to India have been able to learn that "naxa" in the Indian vocabulary now means "rebel rural worker" and that the current and past struggles of the naxalites are part of modern Indian culture, even of its cinema.

JAMMU & KASHMIR

The problem has been with us since independence even though Pakistan has no legal case. The ruler of this erstwhile princely state decided to accede to India. According to the Independence Act it was for the rulers of the princely states to decide to join India or Pakistan. Pakistan has been disputing the legality of the accession signed by the then J&K ruler, Maharaja Hari Singh. The initial hesitation of the Maharaja to accede to either India or

Pakistan and the unilateral Indian offer to find out the wishes of the people of the state has given Pakistan an excuse to challenge the legality of the accession. It has been doing everything for the last 56 years to grab this state. It has not been able to achieve its objective through wars with India. So, it has started a proxy war since 1989. Waging of a proxy war fits into the Pakistani designs of bleeding India. Unfortunately, the weaknesses of the state and of the administrative systems have provided Pakistan with opportunities to fish in troubled waters. More interested in perpetuating their rule than governing the state, its rulers have been exploiting regional and religious differences. Anti-national forces thrived in this environment and Pakistan has missed no opportunity to support and encourage them. Over the years it has succeeded in building a pro- Pakistan base in the state. Frustrated in their efforts to gain power through democratic means, some politicians joined the anti-India front, more to put pressure on the Indian government than on ideological grounds. In a state, where the overwhelming population was against communal politics at the time of partition, the fundamentalist forces have managed to penetrate into the secular polity. The many serious problems of the people have to be addressed. It is not a coincidence that Pakistan's efforts to destabilise the situation in the state received some success only when our own political mismanagement provided it with an opportunity to intervene, as in 1965 and again in 1989. One of Pakistan's main aims is to divide the polity on communal lines.

The attitude of the Pakistani military government is unlikely to change in the near future. But that does not mean that Pakistan should be allowed to set the Kashmir agenda. Moves will have to be made on all fronts to regain the initiative on both political and diplomatic fronts. The proposals made in the announcements by the Cabinet Committee on Security on October 22 are steps in the right direction, but the ground situation does not justify over-optimism. There are likely to be many ups and downs on this long torturous road to peace in Jammu and Kashmir.

Left Extremism

Making a beginning in Naxalbari in West Bengal and Telengana in Andhra Pradesh in the 1970s, the movement has since spread to many states: Bihar, Jharkhand, Madhya Pradesh, Chhattisgarh and Orissa. The root cause for the rise in Left extremism is the inability of the states to address the many genuine grievances of the people. The gap between the unrealistic expectations, fuelled by populist rhetoric, and their actual fulfilment has increased and not decreased over the years. The younger generation is no longer willing to put up passively with injustice and humiliation without a fight. The bitterness of the angry young man against the prevailing unjust socio-economic system is spilling over. The older generation is not unsympathetic to them. An educational system which produces unemployable young boys and girls has not helped. Pressure on land has made the task of survival on agriculture more difficult. A callous district administration, especially in the rural areas, a clogged judicial system and feudal attitudes have compounded the problem. The land disputes have multiplied, but the land records and the judicial system to settle them is in disarray. There is a sense of frustration and anger.

The most prominent among the groups, that have mushroomed in the recent years, are the People's War Group (PWG) and the Marxist Communist Centre (MCC). But it is not ideology and revolutionary zeal that is driving them. For many, joining these groups is the only way to survive. Their main activity is extortion. Huge funds amounting to hundreds of crores of rupees are being extorted by them. What they cannot get through legitimate means they obtain through arms and explosives. Their tactics are no different from the insurgents and terrorists. Create terror and extort money. They are, however, not secessionists. Their aim is to overthrow what they call an unjust socio-economic system. But they are in no hurry to achieve their ideological aims as long as they can extort enough money. Corrupt politicians, policemen and civil servants have made their own adjustments with these groups. A live-and-let live attitude is mutually beneficial to all of them. Who knows how much money goes to the extremists and how much goes to the others. The real sufferers are the very people for whom the extremists are waging this war against the state.

In public perception a government that is unable to discharge all its responsibilities is more likely to respond when the demand is loud, organised and backed by acts of violence. The many progressive, well intentioned legislations are not being implemented effectively and sometimes have done more harm than good by creating more bitterness and frustration, e.g., the Minimum Wages Act. The marginal and deprived sections of the society are the worst hit.

Social and economic factors are important, but even more important are religion and identity. The secessionist movement in J&K is politically motivated, but its ideological base is built around religious fundamentalism. Fired by religious fervour, the young recruits have no hesitation in attacking ruthlessly what they consider the decayed political and moral order, which they perceive as hedonistic. Once the instruments of governance are discredited, it is not too difficult to justify their destruction as in J&K, the North-East or in the states afflicted by Left extremism. In another sense, however, the aim of all these movements is no different from the aim of legitimate political movements. They too seek to acquire power, measured in terms of exercising influence or control over the people and acquisition of wealth for them is the source of all power. Extortion, therefore, becomes an essential part of their strategy. Their goal and strategy could change during the course of the movement. In the initial stages some of them may only demand economic and political justice or more autonomy in the existing political system, like the Bodos in Assam, but they can take a more extremist stand and demand secession in the later stages.

Effective steps to reduce ethnic and social inequalities, disparities in educational and employment opportunities, and for creating an effective machinery for the redressal of public grievance, are absolutely essential to improve the environment in which extremist violence flourishes. Steps to reduce economic deprivation and improve the delivery of essential services can erode the base of public support on which the extremist movements survive. It is relatively easier to find solutions to seemingly intractable political problems, like in J&K, in an environment where people are by and large satisfied with the functioning of the government agencies and are not deprived of essential services. More than anything else, it is the economic policies that would ultimately determine the future of these movements. A thriving economy, which gives hope and opportunity to the people, is more likely to defeat all types of extremist movements than any other strategy.

The need for a well co-ordinated security apparatus can hardly be overemphasised. It should include the police, the paramilitary forces, the army and the intelligence agencies. A composite force on the lines of the National Security Guards (NSG) should be organised in all the states, even in those states where the internal security situation is not so serious. It is easier to deal with the problems at the initial stages, than later, when the state police is no longer able to cope with them.

But in the states where the situation has gone beyond their control, the Centre, as laid down in the Constitution, is duty-bound to intervene, notwithstanding the fact that law and order is under the State List. The Union government is charged with the responsibility of protecting the states from internal disturbances under Article 353 of the Constitution, even though law and order comes under List-II, the State List. The Union government can issue directions to the state under Articles 257-258. Action for non-compliance of the directions from the Union government can be taken under Article 365. A state government can be dismissed under Article 356, if a situation arises in which the administration of the state cannot be carried on in accordance with the provisions of the Constitution. A national emergency can be declared under Article 352.

But, even if the Centre decides to intervene, the state's role cannot be minimised. The primary responsibility to deal with the security challenges must rest with the state governments. A situation should not be allowed to develop where the state government washes its hands off, or its forces instead of cooperating with the central forces, actually work against them. The many internal security challenges can be met effectively only with full cooperation between the central and the state governments. The police, the paramilitary forces, the army and all the intelligence agencies must act in close co-ordination. The hostile foreign forces can and will take advantage of the internal situation to destabilise the country in pursuit of their own agenda. All serious internal security problems: communal and sectarian violence, organised crime, drug-trafficking, labour and students' unrest, political violence and even economic crimes, if not checked effectively can develop an external dimension. There is an urgent need to make the police and the paramilitary forces more professional. The emphasis has to shift from 'more numbers' to 'more professionally trained forces'.

The internal security problems should not be treated as merely law and order problems. They have to be dealt with comprehensively in all their dimensions and at all levels — political, economic and social. They are all interlinked. At times, the required measures will conflict with each other. Going too far in one direction could be counter-productive. The security requirements have to be met, but that does not mean giving the security agencies a free hand. Striking the right balance is the key to success in meeting these challenges effectively. We need a comprehensive security policy that will be implemented effectively at all levels.

NORTH-EAST

The Naga leadership under Z.A. Phizo had challenged their integration into the Indian Union even before India became independent in 1947. The Naga insurgency started way back in the early 1950s. Since then the insurgencies in this region have multiplied and spread to many new areas. In this extremely diverse and strategically sensitive region, there are different reasons for the ethnic upsurges and insurgencies in different states. Some seek secession from the Indian Union, some others seek separate states and yet others greater autonomy within the existing state. The number of such insurgent groups could reach three-digit figures. In Manipur alone, more than twenty-five groups are operating. Thousands have died in the insurgency-related violence. Insurgencies have seriously affected the economic life of the region. The whole developmental process is seriously hampered because of this unending violence. One can imagine the plight of the people who are already living on the margin. What to talk of getting a share of the fruits of development, they are deprived even of the most basic services. Unfortunately, unlike Jammu & Kashmir, these violent movements do not stir much response in national consciousness. Even serious incidents of violence hardly find any mention in the so-called mainstream media. The geo-strategic importance of the North-East is not sufficiently appreciated even in the security establishment. All the states in the North-East share an international border with other countries and the seven North-Eastern states are linked to the rest of the country only by a narrow strip of land. The lack of physical, cultural and emotional links has encouraged a feeling of alienation, which is being exploited by the nottoo-friendly neighbours to pursue their own agenda. They are giving support and sanctuaries to many of these groups to use them as leverage against a much bigger and more powerful neighbour.

The roots of these many insurgencies in the North-East lie deep in its history and its geography. But, it would be wrong to treat it as one homogeneous region with common problems, or social systems and customs. Even physiographically, the region can be divided into three broad areas — hills, plateaus, and plains. The many ethnic groups, speaking many different languages and dialects, who inhabit this remote part of the country consider themselves as separate people with little in common with the people in the rest of the country. The lack of physical, cultural and emotional links has encouraged this feeling of separation.

The partition of the country seriously dislocated the old system of communications with serious demographic consequences. At the heart of the problem, however, is the new political consciousness and an urge for asserting their identity, especially among the fiercely independent tribal communities. The partition left the entire region land-locked, and even the old road, railway and river-waterway links with the rest of the country were severed, because they all passed through East Pakistan (now Bangladesh). The new rail link via North Bengal is circuitous and too long and expensive for easy access to the region. The air link is not only expensive, but also unreliable due to climatic conditions. The people have to bear enormous additional transport cost for all their supplies. Another intractable problem is created by the influx of migrants from East Pakistan and now continuing from Bangladesh. In the beginning it was confined to the Hindus leaving East Pakistan due to insecure conditions, but later, because of intense population pressure even Muslims started migrating. The fear that immigrant population will one day dominate them is keeping many of the insurgent and secessionist movements alive.

The terrain in this region is eminently suitable for insurgency. The hilly terrain and dense forests provide convenient hiding places to mount ambushes on the moving convoys of the security forces. Large parts of the interior areas have little or no police presence. The insurgent groups virtually control the administration in these areas. After attacking the security force they can easily disappear into the local population. Because of deprivation and alienation, a large section of the people tend to be sympathetic to the members of these groups. It is the alienation of the people that has sustained insurgency all these years, though logistic support and sanctuaries provided by the neighbouring states play a vital role in sustaining them. The dispersion of ethnic groups across the international boundaries has profoundly influenced the nature of political conflicts. However, it needs to be emphasised that internal-external linkages originate with the failure of the domestic political and administrative system in coping with the internal conflicts.

Secessionist leaders often adopt alternative strategies to achieve their goal. They keep on changing their tactics and demands according to the ground situation. The intensity of the conflict depends very much on how strong the public support is. Ethnicity can become an important dimension of internal conflict when it becomes intertwined with other social, political and economic issues. As conflicting groups go from one crisis to the next, they learn by experience to raise their demands to increase their bargaining power. Political changes that offer new opportunities for personal gain and extending their influence can spark violent conflicts. Even though most of them are conscious of the fact that secession is not a viable option, they keep on raising this demand to bring together the various contending conflicts on one platform.

Making common cause against the Indian state is how many of these groups with conflicting ideologies cooperate with each other in their fight against the Indian state. The United Liberation Front of Assam (ULFA) was born out of the demand to throw out the migrants from Bangladesh, and yet its top leaders are today finding sanctuary in that country.

The South Asian countries have more in common with India than with other countries in the region. They do not even have a common boundary with each other. But this reality has not made them friendlier towards India.

History and geography have encouraged negative sentiments rather than positive sentiments about India in these countries. The big powers too have not hesitated to fish in troubled waters. Till the 1970s, China was directly supporting the insurgencies in the North-East. Strategically, politically and economically the North-East is the most sensitive part of the country and should receive the serious attention it deserves.

The ongoing dialogue between the government and the NSCN (IM) is a positive development, but it is going to take a long and torturous route. The NSCN (IM)'s claim on the Naga-inhabited areas in the neighbouring states has created serious complications. The riots in Manipur in 2001 following the extension of the ceasefire to the areas beyond the boundaries of Nagaland are a pointer to the difficult road ahead. The situation in Assam has shown some signs of improvement, but large-scale extortion by the ULFA and other groups is posing serious problems.

The NLFT and the ATTF continue to be active in Tripura. They have sanctuaries in Bangladesh. Mizoram is quiet, but there are problems between the Mizos and the Chakmas, and the Mizos and the Reangs. Thousands of Reang refugees from Mizoram are staying in camps in Tripura. In spite of many rounds of negotiations between the Mizoram government and the representatives of the Reangs, so far no solution appears to be in sight. The unending internecine feud between the NSCN (IM) and the NSCN (K) has spilled over from Nagaland to the neighbouring states and even to Myanmar. A number of Meitie and Kuki groups have sanctuaries in the Chin Hills in Myanmar.

The ULFA and the Bodo groups have sanctuaries in the forests of Bhutan. There are unconfirmed reports of some sort of tie-up between the ULFA and the LTTE. A number of groups have also come up in Meghalaya and Arunachal Pradesh.

Many experts have called the Naga insurgencies as the mother of all insurgencies in the North-East. The level of violence, however, in this explosive region continues to be high in spite of the fact that the ceasefire agreement with the NSCN (IM) has been in place since 1997. This only goes to show how difficult the road to peace is going to be in this trouble-torn region.

It is truism to say that it is not only a law and order problem. It has many other dimensions. No strategy will succeed unless it strikes a right balance between political, economic and security measures.

There is need for closer co-ordination among the policymakers. Ideally, there is need for a consensus among the major political parties. The pursuit of narrow political agenda can be exploited by the subversive groups. Many political leaders in this region indulge in double-speak. They mouth nationalist slogans in Delhi but have no hesitation in making strong anti-national statements and collaborating with the insurgent groups in the state.

Nor do they have any reservation in changing parties. They frequently hop from one political party to another. In Manipur some politicians have changed sides as many as six times in a year. A chief minister changed his party three times in one month, and his coalition partners three times in 48 hours. A party label has very little meaning. Money and muscle power with active support of the insurgent groups play a key role in the elections.

Most of these states are not financially viable. They hardly collect any revenue and depend almost entirely on the Union government for financial support. This has caused lack of responsibility in incurring public expenditure.

For example, Manipur has created a huge bureaucratic structure with a workforce of almost 100,000 on its pay roll. Over 80% of its total revenue (both Plan and non-Plan) is spent on payment of salaries and pensions. Extortion by the insurgent groups, the leakage's of huge funds through corrupt practices leave very little for development. And they conveniently put the blame on the Centre for not giving them adequate funds. Through years of neglect this potentially rich region is today the most backward, almost primitive, part of our country. In these appalling conditions an alienated population becomes an easy target for the secessionist propaganda.

4

Basic Principles of Cyber Security Strategy in India

The Federal Government aims at making a substantial contribution to a secure cyberspace, thus maintaining and promoting economic and social prosperity in Germany. Cyber security in Germany must be ensured at a level commensurate with the importance and protection required by interlinked information infrastructures, without hampering the opportunities and the utilization of the cyberspace.

In this context the level of cyber security reached is the sum of all national and international measures taken to protect the availability of information and communications technology and the integrity, authenticity and confidentiality of data in cyberspace.

Cyber security must be based on a comprehensive approach. This requires even more intensive information sharing and coordination. The Cyber Security Strategy mainly focuses on civilian approaches and measures. They are complemented by measures taken by the Bundeswehr to protect its capabilities and measures based on mandates to make cyber security a part of Germany's preventive security strategy.

Given the global nature of information and communications technology, international coordination and appropriate networks focusing on foreign and security policy aspects are indispensable. This includes cooperation not only in the United Nations, but also in the EU, the Council of Europe, NATO, the G8, the OSCE and other multinational organizations. The aim is to ensure the coherence and capabilities of the international community to protect cyberspace.

CYBER-SECURITY AS SCIENCE

A science of cyber-security has to deal with a combination of peculiar features that are shared by no other area of study. First, the background on which events occur is almost completely created by humans and is digital. That is, people built all the pieces. One might have thought that computers, their software, and networks were therefore completely understandable. The truth is that the cyber-universe is complex well beyond anyone's understanding and exhibits behaviour that no one predicted, and sometimes can't even be explained well.

On the positive side, the cyber-universe can be thought of as reduced to the 0s and 1s of binary data. Actions in this universe consist of sequences of changes to binary data, interleaved in time, and having some sort of locations in space. One can speculate as to why mathematics is so effective in explaining physics, but the cyber-world is inherently mathematical. Mathematics is a natural way for reasoning about it and this point of view is a theme that appears repeatedly in this report. Second, cyber-security has good guys and bad guys. It is a field that has developed because people have discovered how to do things that other people disapprove of, and that break what is thought to be an agreed-upon social contract in the material world. That is, in cyber-security there are adversaries, and the adversaries are purposeful and intelligent.

Thus, the reasoning in cyber-security has to be both about the constructed universe and the actions and reactions of the adversaries. Definitions and concepts will shift over time in cyber-security, as in all sciences. A successfully chosen name is a bridge between scientific knowledge and common sense, between new experience and old habits. The conceptual foundation of any science consists of a complicated network of names of things, names of ideas, and names of names. It evolves itself, and its projections on reality changes. This quote echoes the observations of a presentation to JASON by Peter Gallison of Harvard in which he compared the type of science encountered in cyber security to a "Manichaean science" or science in the presence of adversaries. Particularly important for this type of science (and indeed any branch of science) was the development of a common language so that precise arguments could be formulated that addressed directly the problems of interest. We emphasize this point because the definition of cyber-security itself is imprecise. The subject includes correctness properties like condentiality and integrity, and liveness properties such as are associated with denial-of-service attacks, together with a growing set of unpleasant surprises.

Security Degrades Over Time

We observed earlier that success in cyber-security requires constant attention. Not only do the threats and attacks change, but the old techniques tend to become less effective. Technology advances, and the properties of the security system become better understood.

Unix Passwords

The original UNIX passwords were up to 8 ASCII non-control characters. The passwords aren't stored directly. Rather hashes (some one-way function) are stored. In modern systems these hashes aren't easily read, but if a machine is compromised, then the hashes can be taken away, and one can attempt to break passwords by making up likely candidates, applying the one-way function, and seeing if the result matches any of the hashes.

There are about 2 original UNIX passwords, which seemed like quite a lot at the time. Nowadays, one could imagine trying about 32 million guesses (2) per second on a single CPU core, so testing the entire space would only take about 3 days on 1,000 cores. That's not a particularly large computer, but the calculation is also embarrassingly parallel, so the 1,000 cores could be 1,000 machines in a (small) botnet. Or one could use 9,000 machines, still not a large botnet, and do the whole calculation in one night. For completeness we note that there has been a lot of work on making it harder to guess passwords; for instance, by using much slower one-way functions and much larger spaces. Another approach is to force people to use more complex passwords, but that has other sociological ramications which are unfortunately very difficult to deal with in terms of any science. An extreme version turned up in the recent Russian spy case, where "Ricci said the steganographic programme was activated by pressing controlalt-E and then typing in a 27-character password, which the FBI found written down on a piece of paper during one of its searches."

Lock Bumping

A second example of security decreasing over time comes from the common locks people use on doors. A simple technique called "lock bumping" makes all these locks quite easy to open with just a little practice. The locks were, of course, vulnerable, but it didn't much matter until the technique was popularized starting about 2005. There are plenty of explanatory videos online. The implication for cyber-security is that the nature of the attack can change over time. It will not in general be possible to anticipate all attacks. For this reason it becomes necessary to constantly survey the extant modes of attack to understand the nature of current technology as well as continually attack one's own systems in the hopes of finding heretofore undiscovered attacks.

The Role of Secrecy

All security regimes include some secrets. The TSA doesn't explain everything it is looking for; the credit card processors don't fully explain their criteria, and so on. In the computer science community, security by obscurity is generally considered bad, probably based on examples of awed cryptography. There seems to be little theoretical work on this subject. We mention a few examples of keeping (and not keeping) secrets.

Commercial anti-virus programmes, of the sort that run on your home computer, reveal some of the weaknesses of totally public defences. In principal, a malware author could just buy these, and adjust the malware until none of them detect it. The market has made this easier; there are online services that for a fee will run uploaded malware through a large number of commercial programmes, and report the result.

Game theory and economics teach us that keeping our private valuations secret sometimes adds value. Much effort has gone into auction mechanisms that get bidders to reveal their private valuations.

On the other hand, under various circumstances, this "asymmetric information" can lead to lemon markets, where either no market exists, or only people who are forced to will trade in the market.

Secrecy might also be required by the rules. For instance, the DoD might use logs of network trafc to tune its network defences. These logs might easily contain material that should not be made public. For these reasons, there may be some benefit in exploring the role an enhanced role for secrecy and obfuscation, particularly for DOD systems.

Finally, one might ask if keeping the source code secret adds much to security. First, there may be other reasons for keeping source code secret, such as the trade secrets incorporated in it. Certainly attackers with source code are likely to proceed differently, as they have a better chance of finding attacks based on logical errors, and this would be especially valuable for targeted attacks.

On the other hand, there seems to be no particular shortage of effective attacks when source code is unavailable. But the code owner may have no realistic alternatives to making the source available. As an example consider the following announcement: "The agreement that we signed with the FSB is an extension of Microsoft's Government Security Programme (GSP),"

Microsoft said in a statement on Friday. "The purpose of the GSP is to increase trust with national governments. In the case of the Russian agreement, GSP participation will facilitate the development of the next generation of secured solutions for Russian government agencies based on the latest Microsoft technologies and Russian cryptography."

NATIONAL CYBER SECURITY POLICY

IT as an engine for economic growth and prosperity

The IT sector has become one of the most significant growth catalysts for the Indian economy. In addition to fuelling India's economy, this sector is also positively influencing the lives of its people through direct and indirect contribution to the various socio-economic parameters such as employment, standard of living and diversity among others.

The sector has played a significant role in transforming India's image to that of a global player in providing world-class technology solutions and business services. The government has been a key driver for increased adoption of IT-based products and solutions in the country. It has embarked on various IT-enabled initiatives including in Public services (Government to citizen services, citizen identification, public distribution systems), Healthcare (telemedicine, remote consultation, mobile clinics), Education (e- Learning, virtual classrooms, etc.) and Financial service (mobile banking/payment gateways), etc. In addition, Government sector has enabled increased IT adoption in the country through sectors reforms that encourage IT acceptance and National programmes such as National eGovernance Programmes (NeGP) and the Unique Identification Development Authority of India (UIDAI) programme that create large scale IT infrastructure and promote corporate participation.

Security of cyber space - Need for action

In light of the growth of IT sector in the country, ambitious plans for rapid social transformation & inclusive growth and India's prominent role in the IT global market, providing right kind of focus for secure computing environment and adequate trust & confidence in electronic transactions becomes one of the compelling priorities for the country.

This kind of focus enables creation of suitable cyber security eco system in the country, in tune with globally networked environment and at the same time assures its citizens as well the global community about the seriousness of its intentions and ability to act suitably.

Target audience

The cyber security policy is an evolving task, which need to be regularly updated/refined in line with technological trends and security challenges posed by such technology directions.

This policy caters for the whole spectrum of ICT users and providers including small and home users, medium and large enterprises and Government & non-Government entities.

It proviides an over view of what it takes to effectively protect information, information systems & networks and also to provide an insight into the Government's approach and strategy for protection of cyber space in the country. It also outlines some pointers to enable collaborative working of all key players in public & private to safeguard country's information and information systems. This policy, therefore, aims to create a cyber security framework, which will address all the related issues over a long period. The framework will lead to specific actions and programmes to enhance the security posture of country's cyber space.

Securing cyber space – Key policy considerations

The key considerations for securing the cyber space include:

- The security of cyber space is not an optional issue but an imperative need in view of its impact on national security, public safety and economic well-being.
- The issue of cyber security needs to move beyond traditional technological measures such as anti-virus and firewalls. It needs to be dynamic in nature and have necessary depth to detect, stop and prevent attacks.
- Cyber security intelligence forms an integral component of security of cyber space in order to be able to anticipate attacks, adopt suitable counter measures and attribute the attacks for possible counter action.
- Effective correlation of information from multiple sources and real-time monitoring of assets that need protection and at the same time ensuring that adequate expertise and process are in place to deal with crisis situations.
- There is a need to focus on having a suitable security posture and adopt counter measures on the basis of hierarchy of priority and understanding of the inter dependencies, rather than attempting to defend against all intrusions and attacks.

- Security is all about what people, process and technology and as such there is a clear need for focusing on people and processes while attempting to use the best available technological solutions, which otherwise could prove ineffective.
- Use of adequately trained and qualified manpower along with suitable incentives for effective results in a highly specialized field of cyber security.
- Security needs to be built-in from the conceptual design stage itself when it comes to developing and deploying critical information infrastructure, as opposed to having security as an afterthought.

SECURITY RISKS

As a result of the Internet and e-mail, there has been a sharp increase in security incidents involving the accidental disclosure of classified and other sensitive information. One common problem occurs when individuals download a seemingly unclassified file from a classified system, and then fail to carefully review this file before sending it as an attachment to an e-mail message. Too often, the seemingly unclassified file actually has some classified material or classification markings that are not readily apparent when the file is viewed on line. Sending such material by e-mail is a security violation even if the recipient has an appropriate security clearance, as e-mail can easily be monitored by unauthorized persons.

More important, even if the downloaded file really is unclassified, the electronic version of that file may have recoverable traces of classified information. This happens because data is stored in "blocks." If a file does not take up an entire block, the remainder of that block may have recoverable traces of data from other files. Your system administrator must follow an approved technical procedure for removing these traces before the file is treated as unclassified.

Some organizations have found it necessary to lock their computer drives to prevent any downloading of files from the classified system. If an individual wishes to download and retransmit an unclassified file from a classified system, the file must be downloaded and processed by the system administrator to remove electronic traces of other files before it is retransmitted.

Inappropriate Materials

Sending e-mail is like sending a postcard through the mail. Just as the mailman and others have an opportunity to read a postcard, network eavesdroppers can read your e-mail as it passes through the Internet from computer to computer. E-mail is not like a telephone call, where your privacy rights are protected by law.

The courts have repeatedly sided with employers who monitor their employees' e-mail or Internet use. In an American Management Association poll, 47% of major companies reported that they store and review their employees' e-mail. Organizations do this to protect themselves against lawsuits, because the organization can be held liable for abusive, harassing, or otherwise inappropriate messages sent over its computer network. In the same poll, 25% of companies reported that they have fired employees for misuse of the Internet or office e-mail.

In the past couple years, *The New York Times* fired 23 employees for exchanging off-colour e-mail. Xerox fired 40 people for inappropriate Internet use. Dow Chemical fired 24 employees and disciplined another 230 for sending or storing pornographic or violent material by e-mail. Several years ago, Chevron Corp. had to pay $2.2 million to plaintiffs who successfully brought a suit of sexual harassment, in part because an employee sent an e-mail to coworkers listing the reasons why beer is better than women.

Security of Tools

Secrets in the computer require the same protection as secrets on paper. This is because information can be recovered from a computer hard drive even after the file has been deleted or erased by the computer user. It is estimated that about a third of the average hard drive contains information that has been "deleted" but is still recoverable. Computers on which classified information is prepared must be kept in facilities that meet specified physical security requirements for processing classified information. If necessary to prepare classified information on a computer in a non-secure environment, use a removable hard drive or laptop that is secured in an approved safe when not in use. Alternatively, use a typewriter. Check with your security office concerning rules for traveling with a laptop on which classified or other sensitive information has been prepared. Laptop computers are a particular concern owing to their vulnerability to theft.

Computer Passwords

Passwords are used to authenticate an individual's right to have access to certain information. Your password is for your use only. Lending it to someone else is a security violation and may result in disciplinary action against both parties. Never disclose your password to anyone. Memorize it – do not put it in writing. If you leave your terminal unattended for any reason, log off or use a screen lock. Otherwise, someone else could use your computer to access information they are not authorized to have. You will be held responsible if someone else uses your password in connection with a system transaction.

Do change your password regularly. Use a password with at least six and preferably eight characters and consisting of a mix of upper and lower case letters, numbers, and special characters such as punctuation marks This mix of various types of characters makes it more difficult for a hacker to use an automated tool called a "password cracker" to discover your password. Cracking passwords is a common means by which hackers gain unauthorized access to protected systems.

Social Engineering

"Social engineering" is hacker-speak for conning legitimate computer users into providing useful information that helps the hacker gain unauthorized access to their computer system. The hacker using social engineering usually poses as a legitimate person in the organization (maintenance technician, security officer, inexperienced computer user, VIP, etc.) and employs a plausible cover story to trick computer users into giving useful information. This is usually done by telephone, but it may also be done by forged e-mail messages or even in-person visits.

Most people have an incorrect impression of computer break-ins. They think they are purely technical, the result of technical flaws in computer systems which the intruders are able to exploit. The truth is, however, that social engineering often plays a big part in helping an attacker slip through security barriers. Lack of security awareness or gullibility of computer users often provides an easy stepping stone into the protected system if the attacker has no authorized access to the system at all.

Computer Applications in Business

Computer Applications in Business provides an overview of the integrated software packages most often used in the workplace. By the end of this course, you will have a sound understanding of the basic features and business applications for the word processor, spreadsheet, database, and presentation software in your choice of either Microsoft Works Suite or Microsoft Office Professional packages.

This process of completing this course, you will also learn how to problem solve and use the Help function and online tutorial assistance for your software. Finally, as this is an online course, you will learn about using the Internet and e-mail.

Delivery Method

There is continuous enrolment for this course. Delivery is self-paced, allowing you the flexibility to proceed through the course according to your own schedule.

Prerequisites

None. Students will need access to a PC with full internet access and MS Office Professional (XP preferred) including Access database software or MS Works (the 2002 or newer Works 'Suite' with Word included is preferred). This course is not ideal for those using the MS Office 2007 version.

Exclusions

Students with credit for CMPT 109, 150 or a similar course may not take CMPT 119 for further credit.

Objectives

- Answer questions regarding your computer's hardware, software, and basic operations.
- Set up your computer for World Wide Web connection.
- Use e-mail to send messages and file attachments.
- Participate in on-line discussion groups.
- Describe the types of documents created with a word processing programme.
- List the principal features of a word processing programme.
- Create and format a business letter.
- Create and format a schedule containing a table.
- Design either a textual or a visual message for a public audience.
- Select and use style features to create new documents.
- Use the Help system to answer questions and troubleshoot problems.
- Describe the purposes of a spreadsheet and define its vocabulary.
- Set up and analyse itemized lists of numbers, such as the various types of budgets or financial statements.
- Perform and manipulate the calculations to achieve meaningful information.
- Present the numerical data in the spreadsheet in a graphical format.
- Conduct "what if" simulations of the numerical statements.
- Import spreadsheet reports and charts into word processing and/or database documents.

- Define the purpose of a database programme.
- Describe the components of a database.
- Plan a simple two-table database.
- Use wizards to enter and to search data, and to create a report.
- Enter data in a form.
- Merge data with a document.
- Create mailing labels.
- Analyse data in a database.
- Privacy issues related to databases.
- Plan a presentation.
- Apply good design principles to a presentation.
- Examine examples of a presentation.
- Describe the purpose of presentation software.
- Describe the components of a presentation.
- Create a presentation outline.
- Apply and modify a design template.
- Add clip art and charts to a presentation.
- Run a slide show.

Small, rural high schools are constantly trying to determine what type of computer training should be provided to students to meet the needs of business in the surrounding area. Many students in high schools today are not college bound and attempt to find local employment after graduation. Leaders in the community are also interested in retaining as many young people as possible in the area by helping them find local jobs through adequate high school training.

Changing Face of Business

Reports of shipments of personal computers to small businesses and home offices are growing at a 16% annual rate. The power of the computer, the fax machine and voice mail allow a small company to do almost anything a larger corporation does. New technology has streamlined every part of our business lives.

The challenge for small firms is to apply these technologies appropriately. After investing in a computer, for example, most discover other peripherals they want to incorporate into their office systems. The bottom line is that even small businesses can, and do, utilize computers and related technologies in their day-to-day operations. This means that even a high school graduate who does not plan to further his or her formal education should have some knowledge of computers. In addition, it is important to bridge the gap between basic theory and computer applications. There is a strong correlation between high anxiety and reduced computer competence. Experience with computers in school tends to reduce anxiety on the job and leads to more productive workers. A good computer course also shows students how the computer can be utilized in many diverse fields.

Identifying Skills

Businesses must be periodically surveyed for information on the type of skills needed by their workers. In today's evolving world of work, required skills change as fast as the available technologies.

In Nebraska, for example, the Manpower company surveyed offices from Lincoln west to the Colorado border by sending a questionnaire on office automation topics to over 2,500 businesses.

The results indicated that word processing was the number one activity, using a spreadsheet was number two, and manipulating a database was number three. Lotus 1-23 was the most widely installed software. WordPerfect was the most popular word processing package, capturing 40% of those responding to their survey. Service companies were the largest number of respondents, with government second and retail/wholesale businesses third.

Previous to its decisions on what type of computers to purchase and which software packages to teach, Auburn High School needed to know similar information. They wanted to provide their students specific experience with the computers and applications being utilized by business and industry in the local geographic area. This would reassure their students that they would be employable after graduation. It would also assist the local communities by keeping young people in the area and not have them travel to find jobs elsewhere. Upon the suggestion of Auburn's computer programming teacher, Claudette Stevens, a comprehensive survey of local area businesses was conducted in southeast Nebraska in two rural counties, Richardson and Nemaha. All of both counties' businesses were identified from the telephone book and local Chamber of Commerces, totalling 627. A random sample of 150 (approximately 25%) of these firms were contacted by telephone. All companies that were contacted agreed to answer the questions on the survey.

Examining the Survey Results

Almost half of the small, rural businesses contacted (46%) are still not using computers. Of those using computers, over 68% said they purchased them mainly for accounting. However, most companies indicated they use computers for a variety of functions. Surveyed companies reported using a total of 38 different software packages. The most common type of programme used was for accounting, the second most common was word processing, and the third most common software produced customer receipts.

The questionnaire also dealt with the amount of knowledge new employees were expected to possess. Only one employer expected to hire a person with a bachelor's degree in computer science, and that job also required a four month period of intense training. A majority of companies expected to hire employees with basic knowledge on how to use the type of computer the firm owned. Some companies wanted potential employees to have an amount of keyboarding skills; other firms wanted general computer ability.

CHALLENGES TO INDIA'S NATIONAL SECURITY

As brought out earlier India has carried a niche for itself in the IT Sector. India's reliance on technology also reflects from the fact that India is shifting gears by entering into facets of e-governance. India has already brought sectors like income tax, passports.. visa under the realm of e -governance. Sectors like police and judiciary are to follow. The travel sector is also heavily reliant on this. Most of the Indian banks have gone on full-scale computerization. This has also brought in concepts of e-commerce and e-banking. The stock markets have also not remained immune. To create havoc in the country these are lucrative targets to paralyse the economic and financial institutions. The damage done can be catastrophic and irreversible.

Existing Counter Cyber Security Initiatives

National Informatics Centre (NIC). A premier organisation providing network backbone and e-governance support to the Central Government, State Governments, Union Territories, Districts and other Governments bodies. It provides wide range of information and communication technology services including nation wide communication Network for decentralized planning improvement in Government services and wider transparency of national and local governments.

Indian Computer Emergency Response Team (Cert-In). Cert-In is the most important constituent of India's cyber community. Its mandate states, 'ensure security of cyber space in the country by enhancing the security communications and information infrastructure, through proactive action and effective collaboration aimed at security incident prevention and response and security assurance'.

National Information Security Assurance Programme (NISAP). Government and critical infrastructures, Highlights are :-

This is for

(a) Government and critical infrastructures should have a security policy and create a point of contact.

(b) Mandatory for organizations to implement security control and report any security incident to Cert-In.

(c) Cert-In to create a panel of auditor for IT security.

(d) All organizations to be subject to a third party audit from this panel once a year.

(e) Cert-In to be reported about security compliance on periodic basis by the organizations.

Indo-US Cyber Security Forum (IUSCSF). Under this forum (set up in 2001) high power delegations from both side met and several initiatives were announced. Highlights are:-

(a) Setting up an India Information Sharing and Analysis Centre (ISAC) for better cooperation in anti hacking measures.

(b) Setting up India Anti Bot Alliance to raise awareness about the emerging threats in cyberspace by the Confederation of Indian Industry (CII).

(c) Ongoing cooperation between India's Standardization Testing and Quality Certification (STQC) and the US National Institute of Standards and Technology (NIST) would be expanded to new areas.

(d) The R&D group will work on the hard problems of cyber security. Cyber forensics and anti spasm research.

(e) Chalked the way for intensifying bilateral cooperation to control cyber crime- between the two countries.

Challenges and Concerns

Some challenges and concerns are highlighted below :-

(a) Lack of awareness and the culture of cyber security at individual as well as institutional level.

(b) Lack of trained and qualified manpower to implement the counter measures.

(c) Too many information security organisations which have become weak due to 'turf wars' or financial compulsions.

(d) A weak IT Act which has became redundant due to non exploitation and age old cyber laws.

(e) No e-mail account policy especially for the defence forces, police and the agency personnel.

(f) Cyber attacks have come not only from terrorists but also from neighboring countries inimical to our National interests.

Recommendations

Certain recommendations are given below:-

(a) Need to sensitize the common citizens about the dangers of cyber terrorism. Cert-in should engage academic institutions and follow an aggressive strategy.

(b) Joint efforts by all Government agencies including defence forces to attract qualified skilled personnel for implementation of counter measures.

(c) Cyber security not to be given more lip service and the organisations dealing with the same should be given all support. No bureaucratic dominance should be permitted.

(d) Agreements relating to cyber security should be given the same importance as other conventional agreements.

(e) More investment in this field in terms of finance and manpower.

(f) Indian agencies working after cyber security should also keep a close vigil on the developments in the IT sector of our potential adversaries.

Conclusions

There is a growing nexus between the hacker and the terrorist. The day is not far when terrorists themselves will be excellent hackers. That will change the entire landscape of terrorism. A common vision is required to ensure cyber security and prevent cyber crimes. The time has come to prioritize cyber security in India's counter terrorism strategy.

NEED FOR A COMPREHENSIVE CYBER SECURITY POLICY

As in most countries around the world, the cyber security scenario in India is one of relative chaos and a sense of insecurity arising out of the periodic reports of cyber espionage, cyberterrorism, cyber warfare and cyber crime. The complexity of the issue has resulted in a virtual paralysis. Legal and law enforcement mechanisms have not shifted gears fast enough to grapple with growing cyber crime.

Periodic newspaper reports indicate that a wide variety of offensive measures are being contemplated by various agencies, but that is all. The lack of a coherent cyber security policy will seriously interfere with India's national security and economic development.

It is essential that more attention at the highest levels is paid to ensuring that cyber-related vulnerabilities that can impact on critical sectors are identified and removed.

A coherent and comprehensive cyber security policy will have several major elements, including accurate conceptualisation of cyberspace threats; building of robust cyberspace through a variety of measures, including technical, legal, diplomatic, international cooperation; creation of adequate organisational structures; strengthening of PPPs; HR development; and implementation of best practices and guidelines. The list is only illustrative.

India's approach to cyber security has so far been ad hoc and piecemeal. A number of organisations have been created but their precise roles have not been defined nor synergy has been created among them. As it transcends a vast domain, this falls within the charter of the NSCS. However , there appears to be no institutional structure for implementation of policies. Neither the private sector nor government has been able to build information systems that can be described as reasonably robust. There has not been enough thinking on the implications of cyber warfare.

Meanwhile, many countries are seriously engaged in attending to their cyber security doctrines and strategies. The US, Russia, UK, France, Australia, Germany, New Zealand, South Korea, China, Brazil, South Africa, Denmark, Sweden, EU, Singapore, Malaysia – the list is long and growing – are actively engaged in ensuring a safe and secure cyber environment for their citizens. The international community is also engaged in a variety of discussions. NATO has taken the task of creating cyber security institutions in member countries.

A group of governmental experts (GGE), set up by the UN Secretary General, gave a report in 2010 on "developments in the field of ICT in the context of international security". The report noted that there was increasing evidence that states were developing ICTs as "instruments of warfare and intelligence, and for political purposes". To confront challenges in cyberspace, the GGE recommended cooperation among likeminded partners, among states, between states, and between states and civil society and the private sectors.

The draft cyber security policy document put out by the DIT for public discussion is an important step but it is essentially a departmental effort, not taking a whole- of-government approach. DIT does not have jurisdiction over departments.

The document lists a number of major stakeholders, including: (1) National Information Board (NIB); (2) National Crisis Management Committee (NCMC); (3) NSCS; (4) Ministry of Home Affairs (MHA); (5) Ministry of Defence; (6) DIT; (7) DoT; (8) National Cyber Response Centre (N CRC); (9) CERT -In; (10) National Information Infrastructure Protection Centre (NIIPC); (11) National Disaster Management Authority (NDMA); (12) Standardisation, Testing and Quality Certification (STQC) Directorate; and (13) sectoral CERTs. However, only CERT-In is mandated under the IT Amendment Act, 2008 to serve as the national agency in charge of cyber security.

The Act also provided for a national nodal agency for protection of CII but it is not clear whether such an organisation exists other than on paper; NDMA and some others play only a peripheral role; and many of the sectoral CERTs are yet to come up. In the meantime, real oversight over cyber security may be said to be distributed amongst the Ministries of Communication and Technology, Home Affairs and Defence, and the office of the NSA.

Need For A Nodal Authority

The NIB is tasked with national-level policy formulation and creation of suitable institutions and structures on Cyber and Information War (CIW). It is considered that the Secretariat of the NSC needs to be suitably structured and strengthened with the appointment of a Director General (DG) as head of CIW. To ensure the desired level of coordination, the DG must be suitably empowered and should be a person who combines a technical, operational and innovative mind with a proactive and decision-oriented approach.

The NIB as structured finds it difficult to meet frequently. It is therefore recommended that a smaller effective and flexible apex body be created to oversee and deliberate on policy and other issues in respect of CIW, with coordination and monitoring left to the DG. This apex body could constantly review the situation and institute remedial measures, where required. With experience, and confidence in delegation it could possibly take on the role of the NIB.

Asuggested structure with charter of the apex and executive bodies. As these include public and private agencies, the Planning Commission's experience, which incorporates expertise from all fields, could serve as a guide. The success of the Indian BPO industry is based on ensuring demanding security requirements of clients. This experience can usefully be adapted and harnessed. Tasked as it is, the NIB could under its powers establish this apex body and DG CS&IW office as proposed. Permanence in functioning could be ensured by the allocation of business rules.

CYBER SECURITY AND CRITICAL INFRASTRUCTURE PROTECTION IN INDIA

Cyber Security of India is an essential part of National ICT Policy and Strategy of India. Despite some very good suggestions and critical evaluations, the Government of India (GOI) has not considered it necessary to take some action in this regard. There has been repetitive wake up calls given to the GOI but it seems the GOI is in indefinite sleep.

On the other hand, the International Community is stressing really hard to make cyber security an essential part of their day to day lives. Dartmouth's Institute for Information Infrastructure Protection (I3P) has recently provided its cyber security research recommendations.

They are in the form of a set of recommendations for advancing research in cyber security that can be implemented in the next five to 10 years. The report recognises four areas of need that emerged during the forum:

(1) A coordinated and collaborative approach is needed.

(2) Metrics and assessment tools must be developed.

(3) An effective legal and policy framework for security must be created.

(4) The human dimension of security must be addressed.

It may be a coincidence that similar suggestions were provided by Mr. Praveen Dalal, Managing Partner of Perry4Law to the Government of India. He has also provided the Indian Policies and Strategies for Critical ICT Infrastructure Protection and Management in India. The stress upon Legal Enablement of ICT Systems in India is very important to make Cyber Law of India strong and effective.

There are lot of Problems through which the present Cyber Law of India is passing through. A good account of the same can be found at this nice piece of work.

The problem still remains the same. In India we don't have a dedicated resource that is taking care of Techno-Legal Laws of India in a holistic manner. Of course, we have a Cyber Law Database of India.

We also have a Techno-Legal ICT Regulations Database in India. These two resources are tracing back the history of cyber law in India. However, we need a resource that can trace both history of cyber law in India as well as its current position and the prospective future of the same. The task is very difficult but it has been successfully achieved by Mr. Praveen Dalal, Managing Partner of Perry4Law. He has successfully come out with a "Dedicated Resource" on cyber law in India. The same is titled "Legal Enablement Of

ICT Systems in India" and is the exclusive, most comprehensive and holistic web resource in India dealing with Techno-Legal ICT Laws and Regulations in India.

All the cyber law observers can now access information about cyber law in India and the changes that are proposed or actually made from time to time. The resource is very futuristic and promising in nature and it would be good idea if the Government of India (GOI) consults the same while making, amending or reformulating techno-legal laws in India.

One of the important aspects of this resource is that it is the exclusive resource that is providing a "Constitutional Analysis" of the present as well as proposed techno-legal laws in India. Therefore all of the "Civil Liberty Crusaders" keep a close eye upon this resource for issues like Privacy Rights, Life and Liberty, Right to Speech and Expressions, etc.

For instance, surveillance has become a controversial issue since the Information Technology (Amendment) Bill, 2008 (Bill, 2008) has been proposed. Surprisingly some people are justifying these wide and unregulated powers as justified under the garb of security that does not exists at all in India. There is only one answer to the pro surveillance argument and it is a Benjamin Franklin quote: Those who would give up essential liberty to purchase a little temporary safety deserve neither liberty nor safety.

E-Surveillance should not be a substitute for cyber security and cyber forensics capabilities.

Privacy Rights must be respected and followed in both letter and spirit in India. He Bill, 2008 has seriously compromised these Fundamental Rights. So friends, wake up and be a vigilant and legally aware citizens. We will keep on spreading the "Cyber Law Awareness" in India so that we may have an informed citizenry.

INDIA'S CYBER SECURITY CHALLENGE

The evolution of technology impacts the nature of conflict and war. Amongst the recent aspects of involving in conflict is "no contact war" (NCW) wherein there is no "physical" or "kinetic" action across borders. Operations are conducted in a covert manner using resources such as agents in the information domain to weaken or strike at an adversary to achieve political objectives. These are clouded in ambiguity and deniability. The enemy is unseen and the victim unsure of how and where to react.

Several states are on the way to achieving this capability. Historically speaking, China studied Gulf War I in detail and analysed that it could not defeat the USA with numbers or in technology. It therefore adopted the concept of asymmetric war based on vulnerabilities of the USA in the cyber domain. This was structured around the concept of " Wangluohua" – networkisation as a part of unrestricted and asymmetric warfare. Amongst others, a Task Force was created for Information War (IW), four universities set up, hacker groups supported, regular exercises held and IW units raised in 2003. Through a process of cyber espionage, reverse engineering, source-code sharing, manufacture of hardware, supported by a huge human resource (HR) base, China has greatly developed its capacity in this regard to formidable proportions. Unlike any other forms of warfare, there is no convention or ban on sharing of information with respect to the cyber domain. Thus countries which are inimical could put together resources. Additionally, this capability could be shared with terrorist and fundamentalist groups to wreak mayhem on an intended adversary.

As India progresses, its reliance on the Internet will increase at a rapid pace. Globalisation and governance require a wired society. Along with this India's vulnerability to the threat of IW will become greater. This danger must be foreseen and planned for. Failure to do so can result in a catastrophe and severely affect the country's status and international partnerships, especially in the financial sector. To understand the impact of IW a hypothetical situation at the end of this decade is presented here.

REGIONAL SECURITY SCENARIO, 2020

The regional situation is uncertain. Relations with China and Pakistan have not seen any major change. The J&K dispute and the boundary issue with China have not been resolved and tension prevails. Pakistan continues to flounder, with an unsettled situation in Afghanistan. India's continued growth in the region of 7 to 9% has generated an increased demand for water, energy resources and raw materials. Competition for resources and global business has grown. Global warming has had adverse environmental and demographic effects.

Back To The Future: 1997 To 2012

How bad will it be? An indicative answer emerges if we look back 15 years ago, i.e. 1996-97. Vast changes have taken place in this period. The rate and pace has been exponential in every field, whether it is the economy, the telephone revolution, industrial growth, standard of living, left- wing extremism, threat of terrorism, regional instability or the very way in which the government functions. In retrospect, despite the political instability of that period, India in a manner was much safer and insulated. Applying the same escalatory model, the security situation in 2020 is bound to be far more complex and dangerous. The standard of living will go up, however, it will be a more wired society with the e-governance, communication, power and transportation NWs, financial transactions, health and medicine, all dependent on the cyber domain. Alongside will be the aspect of increased transparency and instant dissemination or democratisation of information. All this will also create vulnerabilities and impact on security with disastrous consequences.

Events Of 30 June 2020

It has been a long hot day in a summer of internal and regional tension. At 1900 hours, when everyone is likely to call it a day, Internet traffic has broken down all over. CERT-In sends a message to the National Security Council Secretariat (NSCS) and the National Command Post that "Large-scale movement of several different zero day malware programs on Internet affecting critical infrastructure." Copies are sent globally. Soon thereafter come in reports from different ministries, state governments, establishments and institutions all over the country. Ascenario of what could happen in isolation, or in combination, in the next few hours, follows.

- Telephone NWs Collapse: BSNL exchanges hang and switching centres of mobile NWs (hardware mostly of Chinese origin) shut down or behave erratically. Defence NW routers are failing and rebooting. Close to 1000 million telephones are functioning erratically, Setting the Scene affecting every aspect of life. Worrisome messages abound. There is panic and uncertainty.
- Satellites out of Control: Communication, remote sensing and surveillance satellites are thrown out of gear. TV and other transmissions are disrupted, spreading alarm. The Indian GPS system, operationalised in 2016, malfunctions, affecting traffic and security systems.
- SCADA Systems Controlling Power Grids Collapse: The whole of North and Western India and some other regions suffer a power blackout. This affects all services, including rail and road traffic. There is chaos on the roads as traffic lights and systems are not working and the police are unable to cope with the rush-hour flow. Reports of accidents and traffic jams come in from all over the country. It also results in looting and police are unable to control the mobs.
- ATC Management Collapses: The international air traffic control (ATC) system, based on communication NWs and the Internet, is malfunctioning. Manual backup systems cannot meet the requirements.

There is chaos at airports like Delhi and Mumbai which handle 2000 to 3000 flights a day. There are reports of at least three mid-air collisions from different parts of India. Rumours abound and there is widespread alarm and hysteria.

- Railway Traffic Control Collapses: The complex Indian Railway management and traffic system is clogged. Rail traffic on a number of routes is suspended due to power failure. There are reports of derailments and accidents. The metro and local train systems in major cities are also suffering from chaos.
- Oil Refineries: There are messages of explosions and devastating fires in major refineries with extensive damage and loss of life. Pipelines are ruptured and oil flow is disrupted.
- Collapse of Financial Services: Dedicated denial of service (DDOS) attacks paralyse the financial systems. There is data theft, destruction and clogging. Millions of transactions are distorted. Banks cut off the systems from the Internet. ATM machines across the country hang. There is talk that money has run out with resultant panic.
- Collapse of Health and Civic Services: Health and civic services, dependent heavily on the Internet, collapse. Data in respect of emergency facilities are not available. Coupled with power and communication failures, the situation in hospitals is close to breaking point.
- Chemical Plants: The safety systems of chemical plants, governed by computer systems, fail. Lethal clouds of noxious gases billow, creating panic and deaths.
- Defence Forces: A large tri-service exercise, that has been underway, is in a crucial phase. There is complete dislocation due to failure of communication and GPS systems as also large-scale DDOS attacks. Amongst others:
  - Avionics on the latest MMCR aircraft blank out.
  - Computer-controlled systems in the C-17 not responding.
  - The ANTPQ-37 WLRs go into seizure.
  - The newly developed tri-service logistic management system is affected by virus and fails.

Damage and Loss

Millions of Indians have been affected. The loss of lives has been in thousands. Given the reach of the media as also the visibility that any such event would invite, it could, in a few hours constitute a disaster for the country far greater than all the wars and natural catastrophes put together. It would expose India as weak and unprepared, unsafe to live in, an unreliable business partner and vulnerable in every sense of the word. India's credibility as a country would be affected without a shot having been fired in anger. It is difficult to imagine a greater national humiliation.

The other aspect is that there would be no attributability. When investigated, these attacks will appear to have come from all over the globe as also servers within the country. Much as India would like to retaliate, there would be nobody who could be definitely identified. Even if identified, it could be denied.

The foregoing scenario, which is only partial of what could happen, must serve as a wake-up call for urgent measures in this regard.

SECURING CYBER SPACE - SCOPE OF ACTION

Cyber security and cyber defence

Cyber security is the activity of protecting information and information systems (networks, computers, data bases, data centers and applications) with appropriate procedural and technological security measures. In that sense, the notion of cyber security is quite generic and encompasses all protection activities.

Cyber defence relates to a much more specialized activity linked to particular aspects and organizations. The distinguishing factors between cyber security and cyber defence in a network environment are the nature of the threat, the assets that need to be protected and the mechanisms applied to ensure that protection. Cyber defence relates to defensive actions against activities primarily originating from hostile actors that have political, quasi-political or economic motivation that have an impact on national security, public safety or economic well being of the society.

The cyber defence environment requires deployment of technologies and capabilities for real-time protection and incident response. Generally, cyber defence is driven by intelligence on the threat to achieve the kind of defence that directs, collects, analysis and disseminates the relevant actionable intelligence information to the stakeholders concerned for necessary proactive, preventive and protective measures. The effectiveness of cyber defence lies in the proactive nature of security counter measures as well as in ensuring resilience and continuity of operations, despite the possibilities of successful attacks.

Cyber intelligence and cyber defence

The value of collecting intelligence information about threat sources and possible cyber attacks cannot be underestimated. A well-deployed cyber attack can yield vital information that compromises communication and encryption ciphers. It tends to project the power of the attacker and demoralize the victim. However, the changing phase of cyber attacks as well as ever- increasing sophistication of attack methods have complicated the efforts of collecting valuable intelligence information for effective proactive, preventive and protective measures. Generally, attacks directed against Govt. and critical information infrastructure can be categorized as either

massive attacks, aimed at disabling the infrastructure rendering it unusable or inaccessible to users; or targeted attacks, aimed at collecting sensitive/ strategic information. Massive attacks generally take the form of denial of service attacks against the infrastructure. The targeted attacks involve a good deal of customization and personalization of attack methods and levels of technological and operational sophistication. Skillful execution of attack and the methodology used to conceal any traces of attack complicates the task of advance intelligence information collection and/or attack detection.

Priorities for action

Assuring security of cyber space requires careful and due attention to creation of well defined systems and processes, use of appropriate technology and more importantly, engaging right kind of people with suitable awareness, ethics and behavior. Considering the transnational character of information technology & the cyber space, the technical & legal challenges in ensuring security of information, information systems & networks as well as related impact on socio-economic life in the country, the priorities for action for creating a secure cyber eco-system include series of enabling processes, direct actions and cooperative & collaborative efforts within the country and beyond, covering:

- Creation of necessary situational awareness regarding threats to ICT infrastructure for determination and implementation of suitable response
- Creation of a conducive legal environment in support of safe and secure cyber space, adequate trust & confidence in electronic transactions, enhancement of law enforcement capabilities that can enable responsible action by stakeholders and effective prosecution
- Protection of IT networks & gateways and critical communication & information infrastructure

- Putting in place 24 x 7 mechanism for cyber security emergency response & resolution and crisis management through effective predictive, preventive, protective, response and recovery actions
- Policy, promotion and enabling actions for compliance to international security best practices and conformity assessment (product, process, technology & people) and incentives for compliance.
- Indigenous development of suitable security techniques & technology through frontier technology research, solution oriented research, proof of concept, pilot development etc. and deployment of secure IT products/processes
- Creation of a culture of cyber security for responsible user behavior & actions
- Effective cyber crime prevention & prosecution actions
- Proactive preventive & reactive mitigation actions to reach out & neutralize the sources of trouble and support for creation of global security eco system, including public-private partnership arrangements, information sharing, bilateral & multi-lateral agreements with overseas CERTs, security agencies and security vendors etc.
- Protection of data while in process, handling, storage & transit and protection of sensitive personal information to create a necessary environment of trust.

Partnership and collaborative efforts

Government leadership catalyzes activities of strategic importance to the Nation. In cyber security, such leadership can energize a broad collaboration with private-sector partners and stakeholders to generate fundamental technological advances in the security of the Nation's IT infrastructure. First, in support of national and economic security, the Government should identify the most dangerous classes of cyber security threats to the Nation, the most critical IT infrastructure vulnerabilities, and the most difficult cyber security problems. Second, the Government can use these findings to develop and implement a coordinated R&D effort focused on the key research needs that can only be addressed with such leadership. While these needs will evolve over time, this cyber security policy provides a starting point for such an effort. Public- private partnership is a key component of this cyber security policy. These partnerships can usefully confront coordination problems. They can significantly enhance information exchange and cooperation. Public-private engagement will take a variety of forms and will address awareness, training, technological improvements, vulnerability remediation, and recovery operations. These actions will help in leveraging rapid technological developments and capabilities of private sector.

Security threat and vulnerability management

All infrastructure facilities face a certain level of risk associated with various threats. These threats may be result of natural events, accidents or intentional acts to cause harm. Regardless of the nature of the threat, facility owners have a responsibility to limit or manage risks from these threats to the extent possible.

This is more so, if the facility is a part of nation's critical information infrastructure. As such focus of these efforts would be:

1) To prevent cyber attacks on critical ICT infrastructure
2) Reduce vulnerability of critical ICT infrastructure to cyber attacks.
3) Enhancing the capability of critical ICT infrastructure to resist cyber attacks
4) Minimize damage and recovery in a reasonable time frame time

The key actions to reduce security threats and related vulnerabilities are:

1) Identification and classification of critical information infrastructure facilities and assets.
2) Roadmaps for organization-wise security policy implementation in line with international security best practices standards and other related guidelines.
3) Process for national level security threat & vulnerability assessments to understand the potential consequences.
4) Use of secure products/services, protocols & communications, trusted networks and digital control systems. Internet Service Providers (ISPs) would be closely associated in providing for secure information flow through their networks and gateways. Appropriate legally binding agreements need to be in place to support law enforcement, information security incident handling and crisis management processes on a 24x7 basis.
5) Identification of national level security organization (CERT-In, DIT) to act as a nodal agency and co-ordinate all matters related to information security in the country, with clearly defined roles & responsibilities.
6) Emergency preparedness and crisis management (Mirror Centers, Hot/warm/cold sites, communication, redundancy, and disaster recovery plans, test & evaluation of plans etc.

7) Periodic as well as random verification of the level of emergency preparedness of critical information infrastructure facilities in resisting cyber attacks and minimize damage & recovery time in case cyber attacks do occur.
8) Development of comprehensive repair and maintenance policy so as to minimize false alarms and increase cyber resource availability to all users efficiently.

Security threat early warning and response a) National cyber alert system:

(i) Rapid identification, information exchange, and remediation can often mitigate the damage caused by malicious cyberspace activity. For these activities to take place effectively at a national level, it requires a central nodal agency (CERT-In, DIT) to perform analysis, issue warnings, and coordinate response efforts. Because no information security plan can be impervious to concerted and intelligent attacks, information systems must be able to operate while under attack and also have the resilience to restore full operations in reasonable time frame. The National Cyber Alert System will involve critical infrastructure organizations, public and private institutions to perform analysis, conduct watch and warning activities, enable information exchange, and facilitate restoration efforts.

(ii) The essential actions under National Cyber Alert System include:

- Identification of focal points in the critical infrastructure
- Establishment of a public-private architecture for responding to national-level cyber incidents
- Tactical and strategic analysis of cyber attacks and vulnerability assessments
- Expanding the Cyber Warning and Information Network to support the role of Government in coordinating crisis management for cyberspace security;
- Cyber security drills and exercises in IT dependent business continuity plans of critical sectors to assess the level of emergency preparedness of critical information infrastructure facilities in resisting cyber attacks and minimize damage & recovery time in case cyber attacks do occur.

Sectoral CERTS

In order to effectively deal with targeted cyber attacks on sensitive and strategic sectors, it is essential to operationalise sectoral CERTs in all identified critical sectors such as finance, defence, energy, transportation, telecommunication etc. These CERTs would be responsible for all coordination and communication actions within their respective sectors and should be in regular touch with CERT-In for any incidence resolution support as well as dealing with cyber crisis requiring broader action.

Local incident response teams

Each critical sector organisation should have an identified team of personnel who will be part of the respective local Incident Response Team. This team would:

- Identify the correctness of the severity level of any incident
- Contain, Eradicate and Recover
- Seek necessary resources and support from the corresponding Level II Incident Resolution Team
- Provide regular updates to higher management regarding progress of the incident handling process
- Escalate to an expert team/sectoral CERT or CERT-In, if unable to resolve within the prescribed time frame/reasonable time frame.

Security best practices - compliance and assurance

Critical Information Infrastructure Protection

The primary focus of these efforts is to secure the information resources belonging to Government as well as those in the critical sectors. The critical sectors include Defence, Finance, Energy, Transportation and Telecommunications. Consequently, many in the industry and critical infrastructure organizations have come to recognize that their continued ability to gain consumer confidence will depend on improved software development, systems engineering practices and the adoption of strengthened security models and best practices. The designated agency of the Government would coordinate the efforts towards protection of critical information infrastructure in the country and enable development of expertise in communication, interception, monitoring and early warning, and surprise vulnerability checks with due authorization.

(a) Implementation of security best practices in Govt. and Critical sectors: In order to reduce the risk of cyber attacks and improve upon the security posture of critical information infrastructure, Government and critical sector organizations are required to do the following on priority:

1) Identify a member of senior management, as Chief Information Security Officer (CISO), knowledgeable in the nature of information security & related issues and designate him/her as a 'Point of contact', responsible for coordinating security policy compliance efforts and to regularly interact with the Indian Computer Emergency Response Team (CERT-In), Department of Information Technology (DIT), which is the nodal agency for coordinating all actions pertaining to cyber security
2) Prepare information security plan and implement the security control measures as per international security best practices standards and other guidelines, as appropriate
3) Carry out periodic IT security risk assessments and determine acceptable level of risks, consistent with criticality of business/functional requirements, likely impact on business/functions and achievement of organisational goals/objectives.
4) Periodically test and evaluate the adequacy and effectiveness of technical security control measures implemented for IT systems and networks. Especially, Test and evaluation may become necessary after each significant change to the IT applications/systems/networks and can include, as appropriate the following:
   - Penetration Testing (both announced as well as unannounced)
   - Vulnerability Assessment
   - Application Security Testing
   - Web Security Testing
5) Carry out Audit of Information infrastructure on an annual basis and when there is major up gradation/change in the Information Technology Infrastructure, by an independent IT Security Auditing organization
6) Report to CERT-In cyber security incidents, as and when they occur and the status of cyber security, periodically.

Government Networks

The government agencies need to set an example in the development and use of secure computer and communication networks. For this purpose, a part of departmental budget should be earmarked for IT and information security needs. Besides this, all ministries/departments and other agencies of the government should ensure that they take necessary precautions and steps to promote the culture of information security amongst their employees and attached agencies. Necessary change in office procedure should be undertaken to bring in vogue, reliable and robust paperless offices where required. Top-level management of government departments should pay attention to the development of suitable information security policy and guidelines and encourage the use of appropriate technology and applications in the organization.

Government secure intranet

There is a need for priority action to create a countrywide secure intranet for connecting strategic installations with CERT-In as the nodal centre for emergency response and coordination. This intranet will facilitate faster and efficient information sharing between strategic installations and CERT-In as well as supporting crisis management and disaster recovery during national IT security emergencies.

Information security Assurance Framework

In order to ensure implementation security best practices in critical sector organizations and periodic verification of compliance, there is a need to create, establish and operate a 'Information security Assurance Framework', including creation of national conformity assessment infrastructure. Information security Assurance Framework is aimed at assisting National level efforts in protecting critical information infrastructure. It supports Government, Critical Infrastructure Organizations and other key IT users of nation's economy through series of "Enabling and Endorsing" actions.

Enabling actions are essentially Promotional/Advisory/Regulatory in nature and involve publication of "National Security Policy Compliance requirements" and cyber security guidelines and supporting documents to facilitate cyber security implementation and compliance.

Endorsing actions are part of national conformity assessment infrastructure. These are essentially commercial in nature and may involve more than one service provider offering commercial services after having fulfilled requisite qualification criteria and demonstrated ability prior to empanelment. These include:

Assessment and certification of compliance to international IT security best practices, standards and guidelines (Ex. ISMS certification, Trusted company certification *for Data security and privacy protection*, IS system audits, Penetration testing/Vulnerability assessment etc.)

Government and critical infrastructure organizations can make use of CERT-In evaluated and empanelled third party agencies for their organisation/site specific IT security assessment services (including ISMS assessment, risk assessment, network security profiling, penetration testing, vulnerability assessment, application security testing etc.) under specific contract and pre-determined rules of engagement. Contact details of the agencies empanelled by CERT-In are available at 'http://www.cert-in.org.in')

IT Security product evaluation and certification as per accepted international standards.

These actions provide an assurance that the process of specification, implementation and evaluation of a IT security product has been conducted in a rigorous and acceptable manner.

IT security manpower training, qualification and other related services to assist user in IT security implementation and compliance.

Data security and privacy protection for 'Trust and Confidence': In order to stay competitive in the global market place, business entities have to continually generate adequate levels of trust & confidence in their services in terms of privacy and data protection through the use of internationally accepted best practices and ability to demonstrate where necessary.

Quality and protection of electronic records: Organizations need to ensure that important data/records are protected from loss, destruction and falsification, in accordance with statutory, regulatory, contractual, and business requirements.

Where a follow-up action against a person or organization involves legal action (either civil or criminal), electronic evidence needs to be properly collected, retained, and presented to conform to the rules for evidence laid down in the relevant jurisdiction(s). It is a good practice to have audit logs recording user activities, exceptions, and information security events and retained for an agreed period to assist in future investigations.

E-governance

All e-governance initiatives in the country should be based on best information security practices. Government should encourage wider usage of Public Key Infrastructure (PKI) in its own departments. There is a need to empanel Information Security professionals/ organizations to assist E-Governance initiatives and monitor quality of their performance/service through appropriate quality standards.

Secure software development and application

Software development process, whether in-house or outsourced, needs to be supervised and monitored using a system development life cycle methodology that includes information security considerations and selection of appropriate security controls and countermeasures.

Open standards: To minimize the risk of dependency on proprietary IT products, open standards need to be encouraged.

A consortium of government and private sector needs to be created for enhancing the use of validated and certified IT products based on open standards.

Security crisis management plan for countering cyber attacks and cyber terrorism

The Crisis Management Plan for Countering Cyber Attacks and Cyber Terrorism outlines a framework for dealing with cyber related incidents for a coordinated, multi disciplinary and broad based approach for rapid identification, information exchange, swift response and remedial actions to mitigate and recover from malicious cyber related incidents impacting critical national processes.

The Crisis Management Plan for Countering Cyber Attacks and Cyber Terrorism describes the following aspects:

- The Critical Sectors, Nature of cyber crisis and possible targets and impact of particular type of crisis on these targets.
- Focused cyber attacks affecting the organisations in critical sector such as Defence, Energy, Finance, Space, Telecommunications, Transport, Public Essential Services and Utilities, Law Enforcement and Security would lead to national crisis.
- Different types of cyber crisis described include Large-scale defacement and semantic attacks on websites, Malicious code attacks, Large scale SPAM attacks, Spoofing, Phishing attacks, Social Engineering, Denial of Service (DoS) and Distributed DoS attacks, attacks on DNS, Applications, infrastructure and Routers, Compound attacks and High Energy RF attacks.
- Incident prevention and precautionary measures to be taken at organisational level which include implementation of Information Security Best Practices based on ISO 27001 standard, Business Continuity Plan, Disaster Recovery, Security of Information and Network, Security Training and Awareness, Incident Management, Sharing of information pertaining to incidents and conducting mock drills to test the preparedness of Critical Infrastructure organisations to withstand cyber attacks.

Security legal framework and law enforcement

A sound legal framework and effective law enforcement procedures are essential in deterring cyber-crime. In this direction, recent amendments to the Indian IT ACT 2000 provide for an excellent means to enable adequate trust and confidence in the online environment and enhance law enforcement capability to deal effectively with cyber crime. Besides this, for greater international cooperation, there is a need to harmonize national laws and enforcement procedures. Priorities for action include:

- Dynamic legal framework that is in tune with the technological changes and international developments in the area of information security (Ex. Electronic signatures, national encryption policy etc.)
- Dedicated cyber-crime units with skilled and competent manpower
- Dedicated state-of-the-art facilities for law enforcement for cyber crime prevention and prosecution
- Dedicated state-of-the-art training facilities for law enforcement and judiciary to assist them in keeping track with developments
- International cooperation agreements facilitating sharing of information and crime prosecution

Combating Hi-Tech Crime/Cyber Crime

The Hi-Tech Crime/Cyber Crime covers any crime committed against or using IT systems including hacking, web site defacements, identity theft, stealing personal information, Internet fraud or online child abuse.

Criminals have sought to exploit the Internet as it offers a rapid and productive means of communicating as well as a good chance of anonymity. Although the threats in cyber space are similar to those in the physical space (be it theft, fraud or terrorism), IT has changed the way in which these activities are perpetrated.

The Hi-Tech/Cyber Crime strategy aims to focus on issues such as e-crime reporting, crime reduction and prevention, legislation, response, role of business-industry-public and international cooperation.

Security information sharing and cooperation

The cyber threat sources and attacks span across countries. As such, as there is a need for enhanced global cooperation among security agencies, CERTs and Law Enforcement agencies of various countries to effectively mitigate cyber threats and be able to respond to information security incidents in a timely manner.

The priorities for international cooperation are:

- Information security and Information Assurance Technology to prevent, protect against, detecting, responding, and recovering from cyber attacks in critical information infrastructure that may have large-scale consequences.
- Collaboration in training personnel for implementing and monitoring secure government intranets and cyber space
- Joint R&D projects in frontline and futuristic technologies
- Coordination in early warning, threat & vulnerability analysis and incident tracking
- Information security drills/exercises to test the vulnerability & preparedness of critical ectors.

5

India's Maritime Security Challenge

Indian maritime history begins during the 3rd millennium BCE when inhabitants of the Indus Valley initiated maritime trading contact with Mesopotamia. The Roman historian Strabo mentions an increase in Roman trade with India following the Roman annexation of Egypt. By the time of Augustus up to 120 ships were setting sail every year from Myos Hormos to India. As trade between India and the Greco-Roman worldincreased spices became the main import from India to the Western world, bypassing silk and other commodities.

Indians were present in Alexandria while Christian and Jew settlers from Rome continued to live in India long after the fall of the Roman empire, which resulted in Rome's loss of the Red Sea ports, previously used to secure trade with India by the Greco-Roman world since the Ptolemaic dynasty. The Indian commercial connection with South East Asia proved vital to the merchants of Arabia and Persia during the 7th–8th century. On orders of Manuel I of Portugal, four vessels under the command of navigator Vasco da Gama rounded the Cape of Good Hope, continuing to the eastern coast of Africa to Malindi to sail across the Indian Ocean to Calicut. The wealth of the Indies was now open for the Europeans to explore. The Portuguese Empire was one of the early European empires to grow from spice trade.

MARITIME CHALLENGES

India's main strategic challenge comes from its prosperous northern neighbour; China. Without entering into a detailed discussion about respective capabilities and intentions, it can be said that China and India, are going to make uneasy neighbours. For the two nuclear-armed nations to rise, almost simultaneously, without conflict will require either adroit diplomacy or a miracle; possibly both. The all weather Sino-Pakistan alliance, with its strong anti-Indian slant, further complicates our security problems. The Kashmir and Sino-Indian border disputes, although far from the sea, could have maritime repercussions if India attempts to employ countervailing strategies in the Indian Ocean. Our cautious and hesitant reaction to border intrusions by both China and Pakistan, earlier this year, raised questions about India's political resolve and military preparedness in the face of repeated provocations. The incidents also conveyed the warning that we need to be prepared for collusive action by both armies. To exacerbate India's security predicament, the Pak Army-ISI combine awaits the withdrawal of US forces from Afghanistan to unleash its strategic reserve of Taliban on Kashmir.

Within the Sino-Indian strategic equation, the maritime dimension is a relatively new factor. The rapid growth of both economies has led to increasing reliance on energy and raw materials, and transported by sea. This has focused sharp attention on the criticality, for both economies, of uninterrupted use of the sea-lanes for trade and energy transportation. Thus, while the PLA Navy makes forays into the Indian Ocean, the IN has newfound commitments in the South China Sea. The seas around us are rife with hazards and uncertainties; whether it is rampant piracy, maritime terrorism, and proliferation or inter-state tensions. Natural disasters and the impact of climate change, too, present a severe threat to coastal nations and low-lying islands in our region. After its sterling performance during the 2004 tsunami, it will be the unstated expectation of our neighbours that the IN will promptly come to their assistance in times of natural calamity. Against this backdrop, and given the trans-national reach and versatility of maritime power, not only is the IN going to find greater salience in India's national security matrix, but will also play a vital role in sustaining India's economic prosperity. India's long-term maritime roadmap, therefore, requires special focus on three vital factors.

The navy's biggest challenge is going to be the timely replacement of ageing platforms and obsolescent equipment. The envisaged order of battle of about 150-170 ships and submarines, and possibly 250-300 aircraft assumes certain delivery rates from shipyards and aircraft factories; which they seem incapable of meeting.

At the same time, our other major source, of hardware, the Russians, have brazenly reneged on costs as well as delivery schedules, in violation of solemn agreements. One of the more serious challenges before the navy's leadership will be to persuade the Russians as well as Indian DPSUs to deliver on time and within cost.

The failure to acquire even a reasonable level of self-reliance in major weapon systems in the past 66 years has made India the biggest importer of arms world-wide; and this must count as a failure of the DRDO and DPSUs. Crafting a viable and time-bound strategy which will persuade the DRDO to develop, reverse-engineer or import the technology for weapons and sensors for our indigenously built warships will constitute another major challenge for the IN.

China's pursuit of a, so called, 'string of pearls' strategy tends to draw considerable attention in strategic circles due to its high-profile economic connotations. While India may not be able to match China's financial munificence, the navy's 'foreign cooperation' initiatives have ensured creation of a favourable maritime environment in the region. Apart from activities such as exercises, joint-patrolling, port calls and flag-showing deployments, the navy's out-reach also includes provision of maritime security on request by neighbours. Agreements exist with almost all IOR countries that permit IN ships, submarines and aircraft to avail of refueling and turn-around facilities at very short notice.

Maritime Game-changers

Against this background, there is expectation that the IN could tilt the balance in the South Asian power-game. While a Maritime Strategy is in place, given India's current national security outlook, the crafting of a cohesive national strategy appears an unlikely prospect. Nevertheless some aspects of the Navy's force-accretion plans, which will endow the nation with a number of powerful maritime capabilities, bear mention here.

- Intense maritime activity in the Indian Ocean and the huge area that has to be kept under surveillance requires substantial reconnaissance and anti-submarine capabilities. The expected advent of the PLA Navy, especially its nuclear submarines, into the Indian Ocean will lend urgency to the maritime domain awareness (MDA) task. The IN has evolved a multi layered surveillance capability with deployment of task-optimised aircraft, as well as unmanned aerial vehicles for each layer. The 'icing on the cake' is the recently launched GSAT-7 communication satellite, meant exclusively for IN use, which will facilitate the networking of sensor and weapon data across its vast footprint.

- The arrival INS Vikramaditya, with its complement of MiG-29K fighters and Kamov-28/31 helicopters, will boost the navy's capability to exercise sea-control and to project power over the shore. Current plans envisage a second (and perhaps third) indigenously-built carrier joining the fleet in the 10-15 years. Given the wealth of carrier operating experience available in the IN, these ships are capable of tilting the balance of power in our region.
- Operationalization of the SSBN Ariihant will ensure that India has an invulnerable 2nd strike capability; thus enhancing the effectiveness and credibility of its nuclear deterrent vis-a-vis adversaries; China and Pakistan. As the Service responsible for safe and efficient conduct of SSBN operations, the IN will also be custodian of their nuclear-tipped ballistic missiles, thus enhancing its status and importance in the national security totem-pole.
- The induction of the nuclear-powered attack-submarine (SSN) INS Chakra has placed a powerful weapon of offence and sea-denial in the hands of the IN. Unlike warships which remain vulnerable to detection and attack from all three dimensions, a SSN on patrol vanishes from sight; to reappear as the deadly nemesis of ships and submarines. Apart from the anti-shipping role it can also undertake, with virtual impunity, tasks as varied as surveillance, special-operations, intelligence-gathering and land-attack.

MARITIME SECURITY AND INDIA'S CONCERNS

"Now that we are free, we have once again reiterated the importance of the sea. We cannot afford to be weak at sea... history has shown that whatever power controls the Indian Ocean has, in the first instance, India's sea-borne trade at her mercy, and in the second, India's very independence itself."

Pt Jawaharlal Nehru

Maritime Security. The term 'maritime security' represents the broadest approach to issues and aspects, which pertain to the sea and have an important bearing on the country's security. This goes far beyond the military aspect although military power and security remains the final arbiter of national security. The concept as it relates to the maritime environment, therefore, includes activities such as seaborne trade and commerce and the facilities/infrastructure required for sustaining their efficient pursuit, the management of living and non-living resources of the sea, maritime environmental issues and the delimitation of international seaward boundaries, along with the deployment and employment of Indian and foreign military forces in the Indian Ocean.

Of the three major oceans of the world, the Atlantic and much of the Pacific are serene. The Indian Ocean and its contiguous waters present a plethora of security issues. Given its centrality, the emerging multi-polar influences will continue to converge and will be further catalysed by the strategic sea-lanes and the significance of West Asia, a sub-region that remains volatile and unstable. Besides, the Indian Ocean is located at the crossroads of terrorism originating from 'two banks' to its west and east that are hotbeds of Islamic fundamentalism, thus making it a de-facto 'lake of jihadi terrorism'. The Indian Ocean is also an area of conflict. Some conflicts are internal and remain localised, but other local and regional conflicts are of global significance and are prone to foreign political and military interference. According to a recent analysis of global conflicts by the Heidelberg Institute for International Conflict Research, altogether 42 per cent of world conflicts can be associated with Indian Ocean countries. The list is extensive, but notable conflict areas are Israel and Palestine, Iraq, Sudan, Afghanistan, Somalia and Pakistan. Though the causes of these conflicts vary, many can be associated with weak or failed states, significant levels of poverty, poorly developed institutions, the absence of democracy, corruption, competition for scarce resources, interference by foreign powers, the global war on terror and last but not the least, what can be termed 'turbulence' in the Islamic world.

INDIA'S MARITIME STAKES IN THE SOUTH ASIAN LITTORAL

Lately, two advancements including India have assimilated dialogs inside oceanic circles. In the first place, the Indian Navy situated a guided rocket frigate, the INSKarmuk, off the Andaman and Nicobar Islands, prompting theory that New Delhi is executing arrangements to secure the eastern Indian Ocean. The Straits Times even proposed that India is bracing the Bay of Bengal to keep Chinese submarines from going by the Indian Ocean locale (IOR). A couple days after the fact, amid U.S. guard secretary Ashton Carter's visit to New Delhi, India and the United States consented to sign a logistics trade agreement in the coming months. The assention—a key foundational agreement went for operationalizing India-U.S. sea collaboration in the more extensive Asian hall—drove some political reporters to presume that New Delhi has assented to banding together with Washington in an oceanic coalition went for countering China.

Speculation surrounding India's real intentions in the Indian Ocean—though overblown—is not entirely off the mark. India's efforts to reclaim its maritime space have been evident since January, when New Delhi positioned two P-8I maritime reconnaissance aircraft in the Andaman Islands following reports that a Chinese submarine tender had ventured close to the strategic archipelago.

Last month, the Indian Navy deployed another P-8I maritime surveillance aircraft, this time to the Seychelles, for surveillance missions and antipiracy patrols. The trigger for the move, analysts claim, was again growing concern in New Delhi that a Chinese submarine support ship had come too close to the Andaman and Nicobar Islands, suggesting the presence of a People's Liberation Army Navy (PLAN) submarine in the region.

While there have been clear signs of India's consolidation of its naval power in the Andaman and Nicobar Islands, some analysts see the recent developments as part of a larger strategic design in the wider eastern littoral. It is not happenstance, for instance, that India's new aircraft carrier, the INS *Vikramaditya,* visited ports in Colombo, Sri Lanka, and Malè, Maldives, in January; it is rare for an Indian aircraft carrier to visit two South Asian littoral states in the same deployment.

Nor is New Delhi's expansion of maritime aid to smaller Indian Ocean states in the past twelve months purely coincidental. Recent gestures of naval assistance, including sending a high-end patrol vessel to Mauritius in February 2014 and two advanced light helicopters to Maldives last week, underscore India's security stakes in its maritime neighborhood. Unsurprisingly, the Indian Navy's operations in the western Indian Ocean now involve top-end capabilities and high-value strategic platforms assigned diplomatic messaging missions. Some see this pattern of deployments as a clear illustration of New Delhi's ambition for a larger maritime profile in the IOR.

More importantly, India appears to be fine-tuning its combat machinery in the South Asian littoral. Impelled perhaps by China's growing naval forays into the Indian Ocean, New Delhi has been strengthening its Andaman and Nicobar Command for a more robust defense of the near littoral.

In an amphibious exercise conducted in April, the three arms of the Indian military combined seamlessly to practice defensive missions in the strategically located islands.

The Indian Navy, which commissioned an air base on the southern tip of the island chain in 2012, has now proposed the Maritime Infrastructure Perspective Plan to transform smaller naval detachments at the Lakshadweep and the Andaman and Nicobar Islands into larger maritime hubs. Meanwhile, New Delhi has also signed agreements to develop an island in both Mauritius

(Agalega) and Seychelles (Assumption). To this end, India is undertaking infrastructure projects that would, among other things, enhance the capabilities of the regional defense forces—hinting at greater strategic synergy in regional maritime endeavors.

Despite actively seeking maritime influence in the regional commons, however, India has desisted from projecting combat power in its near seas. The Indian Navy's operational approach has been, to the contrary, remarkably collaborative, with increasing attempts to improve tactical coordination with regional maritime agencies in the protection of vital sea lanes and crucial trade chokepoints.

The navy's flagship endeavor in South Asia is still the Milan exercise—a cooperative meeting of regional navies in Port Blair every two years with a singular focus on humanitarian operations. Furthermore, India's naval leadership continues to promote the Indian Ocean Naval Symposium, a collaborative endeavor that addresses the complex operational challenges faced by regional navies, such as floating armories and illegal acts of violence by on-board security personnel at sea.

India's effort to expand security cooperation with the United States underscores the country's realistic appreciation of Asia's evolving maritime architecture.

Despite being the most capable maritime force in South Asia, the Indian Navy does not have the capacity to underwrite security in the South Asian littoral—especially with rising transnational crime and environmental degradation. Since 2011, India, Sri Lanka, and Maldives have combined forces in a trilateral security effort led by their respective national security advisers, creating a regional mechanism for tackling nontraditional threats in South Asia.

Despite limited success, the initiative has helped showcase India's security efforts in the regional commons, especially the Indian Navy's continuing efforts to assist the maritime agencies of Mauritius, Maldives, and Seychelles in building capacity as well as the provision of local surveillance and hydrographical services.

A key component of the Indian Navy's operational doctrine is the diplomatic dimension of regional maritime missions. Intent on improving the tenor of nautical outreach in the neighborhood, the navy's latest maritime strategy document supports nautical multilateralism. The document describes India's outreach in the IOR as a series of bridge-building initiatives that seek to combine security with development.

India is also refining the content of its bilateral maritime relationships. The Indian Navy recognizes that it must share responsibility for the region's littoral spaces with friendly maritime agencies to create the operational capacities needed to shoulder the regional security burden. The importance of sharing operational responsibility goes beyond considerations of preserving the balance of power to also include nontraditional security and developmental initiatives. To this end, Indian policymaking is ever more cognizant of the imperatives of maritime economics in South Asia: "blue economy" projects, sustainable growth, maritime infrastructure, and renewable energy feature prominently in the contemporary discourse on maritime security.

India's principal predicament in the Indian Ocean, however, is still finding the right balance in its maritime relationship with China. While the PLAN's growing presence and influence in the IOR is a source of abiding concern for the Indian Navy, New Delhi feels compelled to desist from publicly voicing its anxiety. This is in spite of deepening misgivings about the composition of PLAN antipiracy patrols in the region (now comprising submarines, amphibious ships, and guided missile frigates), as well as Beijing's maritime Silk Road proposal, which Indian observers allege is a pretext for a robust naval presence in the Indian Ocean.

There is also suspicion in New Delhi that China's IOR blueprint includes plans for the construction of multiple logistical facilities. Since February, when the Chinese government signed a ten-year agreement with Djibouti to set up a rest and replenishment facility in the northern Obock region, Indian strategic circles have been abuzz with speculation about an operational Chinese naval base in the IOR. Beijing officially described the new facility as "Djibouti's participation in developing the 21st-century Maritime Silk Road," but many in New Delhi are convinced that it is meant to provide cover for PLAN operations in the region.

These fears and suspicions explain why New Delhi recently chose to emphasize its stakes in the Indian Ocean. India realizes that it must stress its geopolitical interests in South Asia, while creating the capacity to play a security role in the wider Asian littoral. To achieve these strategic objectives, India must act in concert with friendly states—both in the Indian Ocean and beyond.

India's widening spectrum of maritime operations and partnerships should be viewed in the context of South Asia's evolving maritime politics. More frequent deployments in the regional commons and the improving maritime relations with the United States are all signs that New Delhi is willing to act creatively to protect its regional equities. In the near future, the Indian Navy can be expected to combine political outreach and economic engagement with a hard-power presence and traditional maritime operations in a bid to emphasize its strategic leverage in India's near neighborhood.

MARITIME SECURITY STRATEGIES

We know that it is possible to mobilize sufficient resources to deal with difficult and asymmetric security threats, as shown by the successful suppression of Somali piracy since 2012. However, the upsurge in 'irregular arrivals' from Somalia to Yemen and a number of recent heroin seizures in the Indian Ocean illustrate that we are dealing with a 'moving target'—criminals are opportunists and move between different areas of illicit and licit business depending on enforcement and profitability. For many poor people, the pay-offs from illicit activities are so high, and the licit alternatives so unrewarding, that interdiction and prison will not deter them from trying their luck again.

A maritime security strategy should therefore move on from only targeting the foot soldiers of maritime crime to putting more pressure on its organizers, as the profits are ultimately consumed and invested on land. We can also do more to offer viable economic alternatives to coastal communities who are in a better position to end maritime crime simply by refusing to protect criminal interests, and police illegal goods that are often ultimately destined for developed country markets. Finally, we need to build more inclusive maritime security communities. Repeated interaction, cooperation and common protocols and practices in one arena of maritime security will facilitate communities to take effective action across issues in the long run, as shown by the European Coal and Steel community which became the basis for the European Union.

Community Building in Action

Several presentations showcased such community building in action. Interpol, partly inspired by the Global Directions International Maritime Security Conferences, has launched a range of initiatives on fisheries crime and identified clear links between illegal fishing and other organised crime at sea. However, Interpol can only give detailed information on criminal activity; it ultimately relies on its members to enforce the rules.

Traditionally, it has been the role of the flag state to enforce its laws and to check on its ships. Unfortunately, this area of the international system at sea has been undermined by the inability of manyflag states to effectively administer their vessels, and in some cases by the sale of the flag state registries of poor nations to opaque businesspeople who compete on anonymity, ask few questions and impose no rules. It has become impossible to trace ship owners through these registries. These trends can only be reversed if port states take action against ships with problematic flags of convenience, in particular those suspected of fisheries crime.

ECOWAS is another important emerging maritime security community, with countries surrounding the Gulf of Guinea realizing the costs of maritime crime across different sectors of the economy, and the extent of lost government revenue when port incomes are jeopardized through rising insurance costs.

The Need for cooperation between actors

Cross-border cooperation, information sharing and joint manoeuvres create trust between countries and new protocols are making it harder for criminals seek shelter in a neighbouring jurisdiction, making interdiction hugely more effective. As we build security communities we also need to ensure that they include all the relevant stakeholders and all those who can contribute to a positive outcome.

All too often we find that there are few bridges between the private sector, the humanitarian sector and the security forces when tackling problems of maritime security and in the aftermath of natural disasters. Sometimes the private sector will have important information and a direct interest in maritime security and could be more involved in its provision, both financially and operationally. A good example of this is theMaritime Trade Information Sharing Centre for the Gulf of Guinea set up at the Regional Maritime University in Accra, Ghana. The capacity of the humanitarian and development sector can be greatly augmented by working with the military. A presentation on Operation Patwin showed the phenomenal capacity of the Royal Navy to provide timely aid to typhoon-stricken communities in the Philippines.

The strategic lesson is for us to understand how capacity building which promotes communication, information sharing and co-operative action in coastal regions increases capacity not only to deal with crime, but also resilience against natural disasters.

Building greater resilience

However, we also need to recognize that naval capacities to deal with the arrested criminals or those trafficked or exploited by them often exceed those of the littoral states. The success of the Somalicounter-piracy strategy has driven significant security sector reform throughout the Horn of Africa which has enabled over 1000 pirates to be prosecuted. This shows the equal importance of work ashore if efforts at sea are not to be an expensive and time-consuming piece of theatre.

Climate change will put ever greater pressure on food resources and create more migration as communities find their traditional livelihoods compromised. Equally, increasing economic globalization means that natural hazards mix with technology to create domino effects across the globe, making developed countries vulnerable to disruptions and disasters in developing nations. It is best to prepare for such events long before they happen. The maritime security communities we are building now are a very good basis for creating greater resilience.

INDIA'S MARITIME SECURITY POLICY

The question posed by the title of my talk today is what are the maritime dimensions of India's foreign policy? The answer is not far to seek. With any policy that has an outward orientation, as does foreign policy, the overlap with security, land, and maritime frontier dimensions is difficult to ignore. For Peninsular India, the lure of the sea around it, has moulded and set the course of the history of the people who inhabit it. The ocean also brought traders and colonizers. Our vantage location with the Indian Ocean literally at our feet, became in those early times, also a source of vulnerability, laying bare our unpreparedness to face external threat.

Learning lessons from the broad sweep of history, Pandit Nehru concluded: "We cannot afford to be weak at sea. History has shown that whoever controls the Indian Ocean has, in the first instance, India's sea-borne trade at her mercy and, in the second, India's very independence itself." We forget this lesson of history at our own risk. All the more reason, therefore, that our engagement and interaction with the world, should internalize awareness of these risks and vulnerabilities and prevent their return, in new forms, to haunt us again and threaten our development and wellbeing. India is naturally a maritime nation-a coast line of over 7500 kms; the Lakshwadweep and the Andaman and Nicobar chains stretch over 600 islands, with southernmost tip just 90 nautical miles from Indonesia and the northern most tip less than 10 nautical miles from Myanmar. Our EEZ is more than 2.5 million square Kms. The mining areas of over 150,000 sq Kms allotted to India under UNCLOS are about 2000 kms from our southernmost tip. We have significant interests in Antarctica as well. Our inseparable bonds with the Indian Ocean region are not merely geographical but of deeper civilizational significance. Historical, cultural economic and political linkages have been forged between India and the Indian Ocean over millennia.

India is almost an island as far as trade is concerned. In the absence of good regional land connectivity, the bulk of our trade is seaborne. India's global mercantile trade has grown phenomenally and now constitutes 41% of our GDP. 77% of our trade by value, and over 90% by volume is carried by sea. India is now projected to become the fourth largest economy in the world by 2020, after China, Japan and the US. Our dependence on sea borne trade is expected to expand exponentially.

The maritime dimension is also vital for our energy security. India's oil consumption is expected to rise to 245 million tons annually by 2020, with the country likely to be the world's single largest importer of oil by 2050. Our economic growth would continue to be critically depended upon unhindered flow of oil. The sea borne terrorist attacks on Mumbai-26/11, focused the need for strengthening maritime and coastal security against threats from sea. Clandestine proliferation networks also use seaways for proliferation activities. It follows that our foreign policy has to focus on these critical aspects for our national development and security.

India has a vision of the Indian Ocean region unshackled from historical divisions and bound together in collective pursuit of peace, and prosperity. As a mature and responsible nation, one of our foreign policy interests is to evolve a regional architecture based on the twin principles of shared security and shared prosperity. India is well poised to play a substantive and formative role in this regard. We have friendly and productive bilateral relations with almost all the states in the Indian Ocean region.

Our bilateral relations with Sri Lanka, Bangladesh, Indonesia, Mauritius, Maldives, Myanmar, Seychelles, Oman, Mozambique South Africa and others facilitate access to a wide swathe of the Indian Ocean. Maritime Security is an important dimension of our relations with ASEAN countries, in particular Singapore and Vietnam.

Many of these are territorial neighbours but all are our maritime neighbours. We have historical and civilizational ties with many of these countries. Some of these countries have large Indian communities. The broad spectrum of our ties with these countries has a strong economic and socio-cultural dimension.

The Indian Navy has contributed towards expanding our diplomatic engagement in the region and beyond. An active Indian naval presence is welcomed in many waters, near and far from our shores. In cooperation with the Indian Navy, we are looking at ways of long term engagement with many of these countries in capacity building including training assistance, refit of ships joint exercises, coordinated patrols, supply of hardware and product support. We are also prepared to assist countries to conduct EEZ surveillance.

Maritime Security is emerging as an important element of our dialogue architecture with various countries, including with the United States. This includes periodic bilateral exercises, information exchanges through maritime domain awareness, sharing of best practices in areas such as search and rescue, maritime safety, pollution control, maritime law enforcement that could cover counter narcotics and counter piracy, training, exercises and humanitarian assistance and disaster relief and exchange of views on promoting a regional security architecture that enhances maritime security.

In addition to bilateral interactions, we are actively engaged with almost all regional bodies that are either based in or border the Indian Ocean region-ranging from SAARC, BIMSTEC, EAS, ARF, ASEAN, GCC, SADC to the AU. Prime Minister's participation in the second India-Africa Forum Summit held in Addis Ababa on May 25 2011 was indeed a milestone. Our aim is to build a web of cooperative relations that brings together all the stakeholders based on mutual interest and benefit. India's 'soft power' attributes give us an advantage that few countries have.

The scourge of piracy off the Somali coast poses a serious problem for safety of maritime traffic as well as the well-being of crew members. The Gulf of Aden is a major trading route for India. Approximately US $ 110 billion of our trade passes through it. India contributes around 7% of the world's merchant mariners and thus has an abiding interest in their safety and security. In the UN and other multilateral fora,

India has urged greater international cooperation in anti-piracy efforts, including welfare of the hostages. It was at India's specific instance that the UN Security Council, vide resolution 1976 of April 11, 2011, for the first time strongly condemned the growing practice of hostage-taking by pirates operating off the coast of Somalia, expressed serious concern at the inhuman conditions hostages face in captivity, recognized the adverse impact on their families, called for the immediate release of all hostages, and called upon States to cooperate, as appropriate, on the issue of hostage-taking.

On India's intervention, the Contact Group in its Communiqué, issued at the latest (9th) Plenary Meeting on 14 July 2011, expressed outrage at the suffering of innocent seafarers held hostage by pirates, including reports of increased violence and even torture, and called for continued international focus on comprehensive counter-piracy efforts and sustained contribution to them. In addition, India is engaged with other countries on capacity-building and consultations in the area of anti-piracy to devise measures for keeping open access points to avoid choking international trade.

The Indian Navy commenced anti-piracy patrols in the Gulf of Aden from October 2008. Since then, 25 Indian Navy ships have been deployed in the Gulf of Aden to provide point to point escort to merchant vessels passing through the 490 nautical miles(nm) long and 20 nm wide Internationally Recommended Transit Corridor (IRTC) in the Gulf of Aden. In addition to escorting Indian flagged vessels, ships of other countries have also been provided protection. Since October 2008, Indian Navy ships have escorted more than 1500 ships, including more than 1350 foreign flagged vessels from different countries. Indian ships thwarted more than 26 piracy attempts; no ship under Indian escort has been hijacked by pirates. Indian Navy and Coast Guard through their effective vigilance have successfully thwarted attempted piracy attempts in our EEZ.

With increased presence of naval forces off the coast of Somalia and in the Gulf of Aden, pirates have moved to other areas and increased pirate activity has been witnessed in the larger Indian Ocean area outside the Internationally Recommended Transit Corridor (IRTC), including close to the West Coast of India. As the piracy prone area has expanded eastwards, the Indian Navy has made additional deployments off the Eastern and North Eastern Arabian Sea.

India, as a founder-member of the 'Contact Group on Piracy off the Coast of Somalia' (CGPCS), established in January 2009, has been fully engaged in the efforts of the group to share information, coordinate actions of navies in combating piracy in the Gulf of Aden, raising public and merchant marine awareness and, examining legal and criminal justice issues with respect to apprehended pirates. Further, the Indian Navy has proactively cooperated with other navies through the SHADE (Shared Awareness and De-confliction) mechanism and otherwise. Our Navy deserves high commendation for the professional manner in which it has conducted anti-piracy operations.

Questions have been asked as to the judicial process for handling captured pirates. In principle India does not support establishment of any international judicial tribunal under Chapter VII as such action would interfere with the national legal sovereignty of States.

On basis of legal opinion, India is inclined to support the establishment of a special chamber within the national jurisdiction of a State or States in the region, with UN participation. This option is considered suitable besides being cost effective, as it would strengthen the existing jurisdiction with the established procedures. It also provides opportunity in capacity building for countries in the region.

Further, this arrangement provides proximity for the purpose of transfer of suspects by patrolling naval states and also the transfer of those convicted to third States for imprisonment. We in MEA are also at an advanced stage of drafting a new bill on piracy that would help in the prosecution of captured pirates. Let me turn to some of the multilateral initiatives which are of significance for maritime security.

The Indian Ocean Naval Symposium (IONS) was launched in February 2008 as a cooperative maritime security initiative following a meeting of Chiefs of Navy of nearly all littoral States of Indian Ocean in New Delhi. The Charter of Business of IONS is to provide a framework to promote shared understanding of maritime issues facing the littoral States of the Indian Ocean region; enhance regional maritime security and stability; establish and promote variety of cooperative mechanisms and develop inter-operability in terms of doctrines, procedures etc. IONS, an inclusive and consultative regional forum provides a platform for all IOR littoral navies to periodically and regularly discuss issues that bear upon regional maritime security.

As per the charter the membership of IONS will be open to any country whose territory abuts or lies within the Indian Ocean. Other countries can become Observers if they meet the agreed criterion. The Chairmanship of the IONS initiative will be rotated every two years. The text of Charter of Business has incorporated suggestions by various countries including India, Australia, France etc. Member States are expected to approve the Charter during next meeting of IONS scheduled in 2012 to be hosted by South Africa. It would then come into force and guide the future activities of IONS initiative. The Navy and MEA have worked closely on the IONS initiative.

In out diplomatic engagement with the ASEAN, the ARF has recognized that maritime security is an indispensible and fundamental condition for the welfare and economic security of the region. India is supportive of international and regional cooperative efforts in this regard. We are already working with ASEAN and other ASEAN Regional Forum members to ensure security of sea lanes against threats posed by piracy and other transnational crimes, and also to build capacity in the field of maritime security. Maritime security issues are one of the core focus areas of our navy in bilateral and multilateral interactions with other navies.

The Indian Navy has been hosting the Milan series of biennial exercises since 1995 for building friendship and mutual understanding among participating navies of ARF countries. Cooperation and exchange of best practices on the maritime security issues were the core theme of Milan 2010 held at Port Blair in February last year. India and ASEAN trade relations have expanded in recent years to over 46 billion dollars. Nearly 50% of India's sea borne trade is east bound-heading towards markets in ASEAN (with which we have an FTA in Goods that came into force in July 2010), East Asia, the United States and Canada. India has also invested in off shore energy development projects in partnership with Petro Vietnam.

The South China Sea is an important shipping route. India supports the freedom of navigation in the South China Sea. At the recent ARF meeting in Bali, India noted that the parties concerned were engaged in discussions to address the South China Sea issue and welcomed the recently agreed guidelines on the implementation of the 2002 Declaration of the Conduct of Parties between China and ASEAN.

The Regional Cooperation Agreement on Combating Piracy and Armed Robbery against Ships in Asia (ReCAAP) is the first regional Government to Government agreement to promote and enhance cooperation against piracy and armed robbery at sea in Asia.

To date, 15 states have become Contracting Parties to ReCAAP. The ReCAAP initiatives have contributed significantly towards maritime security in the region. The ReCAAP has been recognized as a model organization by IMO for cooperation of regional governments to combat piracy and armed robbery. India is a founding member of ReCAAP and contributed financially towards the running of the Information Sharing Centre (ISC) of the ReCAAP ISC. Our contributions in ReCAAP have contributed towards enhancing our stature as responsible maritime state in the region. In addition, it has also helped our ongoing regional engagement initiatives.

The ASEAN+8 Defence Ministers Meeting (ADMM Plus) Plus is a significant milestone in the evolving security architecture in the Asia Pacific region. The ADMM Plus has identified five areas of cooperation – maritime security, humanitarian assistance and disaster relief (HADR), military medicine, counter-terrorism and peacekeeping operations. India is seen as an important stakeholder in the ADMM Plus activities.

We expect maritime security to be an important issue that would be discussed in the context of the East Asia Summit which will be held later this year. During my visit to Japan, it was agreed to establish an India-Japan-United States trilateral dialogue on regional and global issues of shared interest. Maritime security would be one important issue that will be discussed in this Initiative. In fact, the evolution of the Asia-Pacific Security architecture will depend to a large measure how states are able to pull together interests and capabilities to address common threats and preserve and protect the Global Commons, including maritime security.

A word about neighbourhood policy particularly with maritime neighbours. Issues like coastal security consolidation and fisheries cooperation are also very much within the domain of our foreign policy concerns, as any analysis of neighbourhood policy would indicate. The salience of creating a fisheries management policy in the Palk Straits and the Gulf of Mannar through cooperation between India and Sri Lanka is receiving considerable focus of late. This involves close coordination with the Navy, the Coast Guard, and the State Governments concerned.

The issue of maritime boundary delimitation with our neighbours is also dealt with in the Ministry of External Affairs. Competing demands for natural resources, including energy sources, can come into play. The challenge is to find solutions that are mutually acceptable. Conserving and protecting precious marine biology and the oceanic environment through cooperation between littoral states is another important aspect of this maritime dimension. The effects of global warming and climate change on sea levels can have critical human security related repercussions on low lying countries, and the small island developing states. All this falls within the ambit of foreign policy concern.

The development of port and harbour infrastructure both on our coastline in order to improve our global trade turnover, cannot be divorced from the steps being taken in our neighbourhood to develop ports or modernize them with foreign assistance. The economic and security repercussions of such moves have been the subject of intense scrutiny and analysis by our strategic and security experts. The naval outreach and capability of a number of countries has been growing in the Indian Ocean region. Our own capability to be infrastructure builders in our immediate neighbourhood and region needs to be enhanced significantly. Our naval cooperation in the neighbourhood needs further stepping up. Capacity building, training, equipment and vessel supply are all areas that need further attention. With the region, we need to build a common vision of maritime security, conflict prevention, the unhindered passage of trade, counter terrorism and piracy, disaster prevention and humanitarian relief, and the peaceful settlement of disputes, in a balanced and inclusive manner that safeguards these regional and global commons.

It goes without saying that our ability to shape our maritime security environment will require the development of a credible naval presence with adequate assets commensurate with our defence and security interests as well as those required to discharge the role and responsibility expected of India by the international community.

As a diplomatic instrument, the Navy has key attributes-access, mobility, reach and versatility. We need to embed these attributes within the larger vision of India's role in the global arena. A flexible but proactive maritime doctrine is essential to safeguard and project our national interests overseas. The Navy and our foreign policy establishment need to establish closer coordination in this regard.

THE ROOTS OF INDIA'S MARITIME GROWTH

Although India's ancient maritime tradition pre-dates Greek, Roman and Carthaginian exploits in the Mediterranean, not enough is known about it, because we had neither a Herodotus nor Thucydides to record history; and our past suffers from a lack of documentation. For this reason, we have had to accept accounts, authored by Western historians, which rarely make mention of the seafaring skills of the ancient Arabs, the Chinese, or Indians. And yet, tangible evidence of India's widespread cultural, religious and linguistic imprint – dating back 2-3 millennia-is available. It is found, not just around the Indian Ocean rim, but extending, from the Mediterranean to the Pacific.

A lone Indian voice in this historiographic void is that of Sardar KM Panikkar; statesman, diplomat and visionary. According to Panikkar, due to its earlier civilization and its predictable system of monsoon winds, it was the Indian Ocean region, and not the Mediterranean or Aegean Seas, which saw the world's first oceanic sailing activity. Arguing that ancient Hindus possessed the skills to construct sturdy ocean-going ships and knew the use of a magnetic compass for accurate navigation, he clinches his extensive arguments by stating that: *"Millenniums before Columbus sailed the Atlantic and Magellan crossed the Pacific, the Indian Ocean had become a thoroughfare of commercial and cultural traffic."*

Panikkar paints a fascinating picture of India's maritime past as he describes the activities that took place in the 4th century BCE Mauryan Empire. He provides evidence that the waters of the Bay of Bengal witnessed a continuum of commercial colonization as well as cultural and religious osmosis by sea from India's east coast ports to south-east Asia. The existence of ancient Hindu kingdoms right across SE Asia, then known as *Suvarnabhumi*, is still vividly evident in the architecture, culture and religious beliefs of this region.

Panikkar also reminds us that this cultural empire could not have been sustained without the endeavours of skillful and courageous Indian seafarers who braved the turbulent Bay of Bengal for generations. Significantly, Panikkar debunks the thesis that overseas travel for Hindus had been banned by a Brahmanical fiat; saying that the 'ban' perhaps applied only to people in north India.

The Decline of India's Maritime Power

From the 5th century AD command of the eastern waters and Malacca Straits passed into the hands of a great Indian maritime power, known as the Sri Vijaya Empire, based in Sumatra. The Sri Vijaya kings retained mastery over the surrounding waters through a powerful navy, and controlled all shipping traffic. In the year 1007 AD, the Indian Emperor Rajendra of the south Indian Chola dynasty fitted out a powerful fleet and challenged the Sri Vijayas. The ensuing 100-year war weakened both empires and heralded the serious decline of Hindu sea power.

During the 12th and 13th centuries, as Central Asian hordes poured down our mountain passes to conquer the rich Gangetic plain, India's maritime power gradually withered, and oceanic trade passed into the hands of the Arabs. In May 1498, when the Portuguese adventurer Vasco da Gama arrived off Calicut, the Sultanate of Delhi was ruled by the Afghan Lodhi Dynasty, while Southern India was divided between the Bahamini and Vijayanagaram kingdoms. None of them were blessed with a maritime vision, much less a navy; and India's maritime prowess went into rapid decline. Panikkar, however, reminds us that there were brave and resolute sea captains who led indigenous naval forces, and put up determined resistance against seaborne interlopers. While nautical heroes like Kunjali Marakkar and Kanhoji Angre constitute bright spots in an otherwise bleak maritime scenario, they commanded coastal forces which could never match the oceanic supremacy of the Europeans.

Fifteenth century Europe had seen many advances in the areas of shipbuilding and ocean navigation as well as metallurgy and cannon founding. We must note that it was this technological edge, which enabled European merchant-adventurers, to undertake long-distance voyages into uncharted oceans, and to overwhelm natives of eastern lands. The toe-holds they gained, in the form of trading posts, eventually metamorphosed into full blown empires. Panikkar consistently emphasizes that India's fate has been determined not on land frontiers, but on the oceanic expanse that washes its three sides. He declares that India will be in peril if the Indian Ocean ever ceases to be a 'protected sea.' Lamenting our inherited sea-blindness, Panikkar sounded a clear warning in 1945: "*While to other countries, the Indian Ocean is only one of the oceanic areas, to India it is the vital sea. Her future is dependent on the freedom of its waters.*"

Having established India's historical maritime credentials and the criticality of our maritime security to national survival, let me change tack from Panikkar to Mahan and seek the latter's wisdom regarding the purpose of sea power.

THE ESSENCE OF THE MARITIME DOCTRINE

India's Maritime Doctrine frequently resembles a catalogue of core military concepts for readers to absorb and integrate, retracing, for example, the etymology of the word doctrine to the Latin *doctrina*, a 'code of beliefs' or a 'body of teachings'. Military doctrine is defined as providing 'the conceptual framework for understanding the role, scope, and application of military power, and underpins the formulation of military strategy'. The document's pedagogic vocation is clearly laid out by the then acting Chief of Naval Staff, Admiral Sureesh Mehta, who states in the foreword that the doctrine 'provided a common language and a uniform understanding of maritime concepts', as well as serving as the 'foundation for the Navy's operating, planning, organizational and training philosophies'.

Although Admiral Mehta claims that 'in view of the ongoing transformation of both the nation and our navy, a review was overdue', the changes made in the latest version of the maritime doctrine seem more subtle than substantial. Many of the more important modifications in the doctrine appear to flow from the lessons and reforms put in motion after the devastating 2008 terrorist attacks in Mumbai, in the wake of which the Congress-led government decided to entrust the Indian Navy with the overall responsibility for coastal security, bringing both the State Coastal Police and Coast Guard under its wing.

As a result, the 2009 version attaches greater importance to 'synergy' and 'intelligence-sharing', both viewed as being sorely lacking when Pakistan-trained militants slipped in from the Arabian Sea to leave a trail of bloody mayhem. Some of the former chapters, such as those outlining the 'concepts of maritime power', or 'India's maritime environment and interests' have been revamped somewhat, and an entirely new chapter on 'Naval Combat Power' has been added. This chapter, however, remains in the same abstract and didactic mould as most of those preceding it, merely outlining in half a dozen pages the fact that naval combat power comprises three elements: conceptual, physical and human, and listing different categories of vessels. This educational aspect of the Indian Navy's doctrine stands in interesting contrast to those promoted by its sister services, the Indian Army and Air Force, who both define their warfighting roles in detail. This difference in approach is clearly recognized in the opening of the doctrine, which states the following: 'The doctrine primarily addressed the military-strategic level, whilst it also covers the operational level. Tactical issues have been deliberately kept outside the purview of this doctrine, as several other naval publications comprehensively address these aspects'. This self-carved doctrine, moulded from a professedly higher strategic level, and which merely skims tactical issues rather than directly addressing them, is key to understanding what distinguishes the Navy from the other branches of the Indian Armed Forces. Indeed, the Navy views itself as being a multidimensional service, capable of taking on many roles, of which warfighting is but one aspect.

This is reflected in the most absorbing section of the maritime doctrine, which lays out four roles for the Indian Navy: military, diplomatic, constabulary and benign. These four roles echo to a certain degree those already identified more than 10 years prior in the Indian Navy's first Strategic Defence Review, which were then defined as the following: sea-based deterrence, economic and energy security, forward presence and naval diplomacy.

Two important elements are worth noting, however. First, what was defined as naval diplomacy in 1998 has been split into two different roles – benign and diplomatic – in 2009. The Indian Navy has long recognized the potential offered by vessels in terms of diplomacy and soft power projection. This has been reflected both in words, via the earlier version of the maritime doctrine, which defined the Navy as an 'effective instrument of India's foreign policy by generating goodwill through maritime diplomacy'; and in actions, as over the past decade the Indian Navy has frequently displayed with a certain panache its desire and capacity to be viewed as a provider of public goods as well as a reliable partner. Indian ships have thus taken part in a wide range of humanitarian and disaster relief operations over the years, whether it be in the wake of the devastating 2004 tsunami, or in 2008 after the Nargis cyclone. India has also engaged in NEOs or Non-Combatant Evacuation Operations, such as in 2006, when four Indian warships successfully evacuated more than 2,000 Indian, Sri Lankan and Nepalese citizens from a war-torn Lebanon. Interestingly, NEOs are classified as being a form of 'maritime mission and support', thus falling under the Navy's diplomatic, rather than its benign role, in the 2009 doctrine.

This provides an indication of the growing elasticity of the Navy's perceived soft power role, where set distinctions are blurred and seem to overlap. Through its multiple and increasingly institutionalized naval exercises with both regional and extra-regional navies, and its hosting of multilateral initiatives such as the Indian Ocean Naval Symposium, the Indian Navy, as some US Naval War College analysts have noted, 'clearly sees a comparative advantage for their service as a diplomatic instrument for New Delhi'. The 2009 version of the maritime doctrine goes so far as to wax in lyrical terms that the mere presence of an Indian warship with its multi-ethnic and multi-religious crew in a foreign harbour will contribute to India's image as a vibrant democracy abroad.

Another interesting evolution is the sheer width of the gamut of potential military roles laid out for the Indian Navy, which, crammed into a small box, appear to encompass every possible wartime function.

The question is whether the Indian Navy currently has the requisite ability to accomplish all these tasks, whether simultaneously or even sequentially. But before engaging in such a discussion, it is necessary to pinpoint the more advocatory elements to what remains first and foremost the doctrine of an individual service in a country where no official National Security Strategy yet exists, and where both civil-military and inter-service relations remain exceedingly complex. In his seminal study of civil-military relations, Samuel Huntington identified four potential roles for the military in politico-military affairs: advisory, representative, executive and advocatory. Doctrines, especially when they are released by individual service headquarters, can serve as vital advocatory platforms. This is even more the case in countries such as India, where, as it shall be shown, military leaders have, for various reasons, almost systematically been marginalized from the decision-making process in matters of national security.

A Complex Institutional Backdrop

Studies of inter-war doctrinal development in Europe have pointed to the centrality of domestic politics. Indeed, while military doctrine is ultimately preoccupied with state survival, it also provides a reflection of the allocation of power within a state. Therefore, in order to understand the interests that civilian and military officials bring to bear in the formulation of doctrine, one must also take 'into account the cultural dimension of domestic politics and organizational life'. In India's case, civil-military relations, long marked by Nehruvian fears of creeping praetorianism, have led to a highly unwieldy and cumbersome system which has had an acutely deleterious effect on doctrinal and organizational development. Fearful of a drift towards a militaristic state in the vein of Pakistan, India's post-Independence leaders rigorously implemented a tight bureaucratic control of the young nation's armed forces. The Raj-era post of commander-in-chief of the Indian military was abolished, and the service headquarters were downgraded to become 'attached offices', organizationally external to the MOD and therefore removed from major decision-making. Political scientists have noted that 'over time, concerns about the distribution of military power within a state become institutionalized and shape decision makers' opinions about military policy'. In India this has led to a dysfunctional state of affairs in which although 'Indian power is growing each year, no single agency in the country combines military, diplomatic, economic and intelligence capabilities into a coherent national strategy'. The prolonged absence of a Chief of Defence Staff despite a widespread recognition of its urgent necessity means that the prime forum for inter-service discussion continues to be the COSC, or Chief of Staff Committee, which has no decision-making powers, but which is chronically 'plagued by the ills inherent to a committee'.

In private, Indian officers, while not questioning civilian control over the military, deplore the 'unholy alliance between corrupt bureaucrats and unscrupulous politicians', with more than 80 per cent of those polled for a 1997 Rand monograph stating that their vision of the nation's interest frequently differed from that of the government.

In public, officers affiliated to academia or think tanks call more tactfully for a greater 'cross-pollination of national security structures with military expertise', 'which could pave the way for institutional equity'. In their recent study of India's military modernization, Professors Sunil Dasgupta and Steve Cohen observe that many of the IAS officers seconded to the Ministry of Defence are bereft of solid expertise, despite their overwhelming influence.

The problem seems to be not so much the civil-military relationship in itself (that is, between the military and elected officials) but rather the extent of technocratic ossification which has occurred over the years and which, in the view of the military, presents a formidable 'bureaucratic barrier preventing them from making a direct appeal to political leaders'.

This has led to some incidents where the Navy has locked horns with the Ministry of Defence and Ministry of External Affairs, most notably over the 2008 decision to conduct anti-piracy operations off the coast of Somalia. Some have ventured that the tension may have revolved around the MEA's initial refusal to allow the Indian Navy to conduct naval interceptions.

Caught in such a difficult institutional setting, it is natural for the Indian Navy to seek to relay its interests and perceptions through indirect means, most notably via the widespread diffusion of a doctrine. The desire to influence and impact decision-makers, as well as the public writ large, is made clear from the very beginning: 'The Indian Maritime Doctrine is the capstone doctrinal publication of the Indian Navy, which is aimed at not just the professional sea warrior, but also the thinker, planner, supporter and stake-holder amongst the Navy, other armed forces, government, think tanks, media and the larger public of India'.

The reticence of India's politico-bureaucratic nexus to expedite the institutionalization of an overarching military command structure has also had a negative impact on inter-service relations and interoperability.

Although the strategic conceptualization of a blue-water navy has been present in India since Independence, the Indian Navy has traditionally been the least favoured branch of the Indian armed forces in terms of resources. This is due in part, as we shall see, to India's long-standing continentalist tradition, but also to more prosaic immediate post-Independence concerns.

Indeed, after a series of brutal frontier conflicts in which navies played at best a secondary role, India's main priorities were to strengthen its land borders and build up its Army and Air Force, which were the primary actors in the event of a conflict with China or Pakistan.

The Indian Navy, no longer considered as relevant, was relegated to the backseat, its share in the defence budget even plummeting at one stage to a dismal 3 per cent. Under the tenures of Indira and Rajiv Gandhi, the Navy spasmodically regained impetus, but it has only really been over the past 15 years that India's political leadership has actively endorsed an ambitious blue-water role.

Nevertheless, to this day the Navy's share of the defence budget remains considerably lower than that of the Army or the Air Force, and even the most optimistic predictions for its future allocation doubt it will climb much above 20 per cent in years to come. Former Naval Officers' frustration with their service's continued 'Cinderella status' and over what they perceive to be a ponderous, strategically myopic Army is occasionally made manifest, as is the long-standing tension between the Navy and Air Force over the sensitive issue of naval aviation. Both in its doctrine and Maritime Military Strategy document, the Indian Navy appears intent on overcoming these inter-service squabbles and 'trying to carve out a role for itself in support of joint operations-particularly support for armed forces in wartime'. Former Chief of Naval Staff Arun Prakash, while railing against the 'intellectual and doctrinal cul-de-sac' that the Indian Army 'has been driven into', also suggests that the Navy can provide the Army with valuable tactical options by applying 'intense seaward pressure on the enemy'. The idea that the Indian Navy can be highly effective as a game-changing flanking force is one which has gained some credence since the Navy's 'silent Kargil victory'.

It is maybe not a coincidence if the service with the smallest portion of the defence budget is also that with the most active official publication record, with the release of two only marginally different versions of the same doctrine in an interval of five years, interspersed with the release of a Maritime Military Strategy in 2007. In the Navy's view, everything must be done to awaken India's sluggish maritime consciousness.

The Underlying Motivations of an Aspirational Doctrine

Theorists have identified three core motivations driving military organizations' quest for more influence: the wish for enhanced autonomy, the desire for greater prestige and the more functional hunt for additional resources, all of which are frequently interconnected. These three core motivations can all be discerned in some way or another in India's Maritime Doctrine.

Indeed, the 2009 maritime doctrine indicates that the Indian Navy is clearly demonstrating its desire for:

- *Greater Prestige* by having a greater say in the definition of the country's core security interests. This is accomplished through a sustained defence of how the sea can bolster overall national strategy, as well as by the advancement of the unwavering 'logic of geography'. India's centrality in the Indian Ocean and peninsular formation, it is argued, are sure indicators of the nation's maritime destiny, and therefore, as a corollary, of the Navy's great importance. Mention is also made of the pivotal role the sea plays in India's economic development, as close to 90 per cent of India's external trade is maritime. The Navy, therefore, is to some extent the ultimate guarantor of India's sustained economic development, by virtue of its role in upholding freedom of navigation and ensuring the safety of SLOCs.
- *Greater Autonomy* by becoming the core element in India's second-strike nuclear deterrent. This is maybe one of the more important aspects of the document, and one which has the greatest transformational potential for the Indian Navy. Both the 2004 maritime doctrine and the 2007 Maritime Military Strategy placed emphasis on the need for India to invest in a triad of aircraft, sea-based assets and mobile land-based missiles in order to vaunt a credible second-strike capability. The 2004 doctrine professes that 'It has become an unstated axiom of the post cold war era that an independent foreign policy

> posture is inexorably linked with this ... deterrent capability', and the 2007 Maritime Military Strategy adds that 'the most credible of all arsenals in a second strike is the nuclear-armed missile submarine'. Since then, India's first indigenously launched nuclear submarine, the ATV (Advanced Technological Vessel) has been launched, and it was recently announced that the construction of its second submarine at a classified facility in Visakhapatnam had been initiated. The second submarine should be ready for sea trials by 2015, by which time India will also have been operating an Akula II class nuclear submarine on lease from Russia. In the 2009 maritime doctrine, sea-based nuclear strike is given pride of place as a key element in the Indian Navy's overall ability to deter, which is designated as 'the primary military objective for the IN'. The maritime doctrine then adds, 'The ways and means of deterrence by the IN would include developing a sea-based nuclear second-strike capability, in keeping with the Indian Nuclear Doctrine that lays down a "No First Use" Policy'. Reprising the arguments put forward in the 2007 Maritime Military Strategy, the document states that, in order to be 'credible and survivable', India's nuclear second-strike capability needs to also be sea-based.

Despite this intense focus on paper, it remains unclear whether in the short-to-medium term the Navy is both willing and able to make the high degree of economic and technological investment required for deploying and sustaining a nuclear submarine fleet.

Experts have pointed out that if the Indian Navy were to maintain a flotilla of four to five missile-armed submarines on constant patrol, this would engulf much, if not all of its present budget. It remains unclear, as of now, whether the financial burden of India's nascent underwater deterrent will be shouldered by the Navy or by specific government-funded allocations. If this financial millstone is tied around the Indian Navy's neck, it will require a far larger slice of the defence cake.

If not, it appears impossible for it to be able to both remain a carrier-centric force and simultaneously pursue its nuclear ambitions.

Some difficult trade-offs and cornelian choices will need to be made, and it is revealing that when the official announcement of the construction of a second ATV was made, there was reportedly some grumbling amongst the more carrier-focused officers of the IN, who expressed their desire to see 'the focus ... also shift to the surface vessels that need to be part of the flotilla that normally accompanies the Air Defence Ship (India's first indigenous aircraft carrier, currently under construction)'.

It is also unclear when the submarines will be truly operational. The INS *Arihant,* which was launched with great fanfare in 2009, had been described at first as a 'technology demonstrator' rather than as a combat vessel. Recently however, statements from the Naval Chief of Staff have indicated that the INS *Arihant* will be deployed on deterrent patrols as soon as it is commissioned in 2012.

Furthermore, information surrounding the precise armament system of the ATVs is shrouded in opacity. The vessels, which were constructed with extensive Russian assistance, seem to be lighter versions of the Soviet Charlie class submarine, a model of which the Indian Navy operated on lease for three years from 1988 to 1991.

It remains unclear whether India's Defence Research and Development Organization (DRDO) intends to equip the submarines with short-range ballistic missiles under the Sagarika Programme, or with nuclear-tipped cruise missiles. In both cases, the relatively short range of the planned strike systems will compel the submarines to be on constant vigil uncomfortably close to the prospective target.

For the short-to-medium term, it may be in the Indian Navy's functional interest to work towards a latent sea-based nuclear capability rather than to expend its valuable resources in deploying a task force of operational submarines, thereby applying subtle pressure on the Indian government to increase its share of the defence budget.

Beyond the simple desire for additional resources, however, the integration of the Indian Navy as the central pillar of the nation's nuclear triad would grant it considerable institutional prestige, as well as a degree of operational autonomy.

In order to fulfil their role as a survivable deterrent, nuclear submarines on patrol must dissolve into the lower levels of the ocean, where their acoustic signature is the most reduced. While cruising at such depths, maintaining communications with shore-based national command centres is a great degree more challenging than for land-based nuclear forces. The survivability of the nuclear submarine as the ultimate vector for LAA (launch after attack) hinges upon its furtiveness and absolute discretion as to its precise patrol route. The induction of a submarine-centred nuclear deterrent will therefore need to be accompanied by a revamped system of command and control which, while leaving critical second-strike decisions in the hands of elected officials, would also entrust a far greater degree of operational responsibility to the Indian Navy than ever before.

Greater Resources by stressing the need for a large blue-water fleet capable of accomplishing the exceptionally wide range of war and peacetime roles laid out. The tasks set out for the Navy in the Maritime Doctrine are multiple and wide-ranging, whether it be in peacetime or in war.

While it is clearly stipulated that the Indian Navy is to remain a carrier-centric fleet focused on sea control, the service is also expected to be capable of enforcing blockades, enacting sea denial, mine warfare, harbour defence and anti-submarine warfare. A Carrier task force is presented as being a versatile force-multiplier: 'a self contained and composite balanced force, capable of undertaking the entire range of operational tasks'.

Yet India currently only floats one ageing carrier, which is rasping its last after several refits, in the hope that its successor, the *Vikramaditya,* will not fall prey to further delays.

Walter Ladwig's detailed assessment in a previous chapter of the force structure and procurement patterns of the Indian Navy reveals that the Indian Navy is modernizing, but not growing. Indeed, while India's fleet now boasts more advanced platforms than at the end of the 1990s, it has in fact stagnated in purely numerical terms, contracting from 51 capital ships in 1991 to 50 today.

The gradual withering of its submarine fleet, in particular, is cause for concern, as is the Navy's relative paucity in terms of anti-submarine warfare capability. This puts into question the Indian Navy's ability to enact a credible strategy of sea denial geared towards an extra-regional power such as China and suggests that the fleet may be becoming increasingly unbalanced in favour of surface ships.

It appears clear that to be able to accomplish all the different tasks, missions and objectives outlined in the doctrine, the Indian Navy would need to undergo an exponential increase in size and resources.

And yet, as retired naval officer Ashok Sawhney recently highlighted, the Navy's capital budget, that is, the portion of the budget devoted to funding new acquisitions, amounted in 2009 to 2.5 billion dollars out of a total of 4 billion. This amount, notes Sawhney, remains very modest when compared with some of the other naval budgets in Asia such as China, Japan or South Korea, pegged respectively at 32,55 11.6 and 4.2 billion dollars.

Although the Navy's overall budget will continue to expand in nominal terms due to the overall increase in the defence budget enabled by India's sustained GDP growth, it will be hard pressed to fulfil the terms set out in its own doctrine if it does not receive a more generous allocation. The issue of budgetary shortfalls becomes even more stark if one considers, as mentioned previously, the prohibitive costs associated with developing and sustaining a viable sea-based nuclear deterrent.

A reprioritization of the Navy over other services will only occur, however, once the fossilized continentalist tradition which still holds sway over the higher echelons of India's leadership has given way to the more strategically minded outlook evident in the maritime doctrine. The latter must therefore be viewed above all as a well-crafted statement of aspiration, and as a savvy demonstration of what the Indian Navy could be ... rather than what it currently is.

6

Modernization of Indian Defence Industry

The Indian defence industrial base and production capacity is now one of the largest in the world. This has painstakingly been built both pre-independence (1947) and also made rapid strides during the decades after independence. India now has 40 Defence Ordnance Factories and 8 Defence Public Sector Undertakings. These produce a large range of armaments, ammunition, vehicles, helicopters, fighter aircrafts, sophisticated electronics equipment, missiles and naval crafts. The defence sector is fully government controlled with the ultimate aim to reduce dependence on imports and become self reliant in this critical sector at the earliest.

Notwithstanding the large industrial base and advancement in various technologies, research and development in defence has not kept pace with the requirement of modern and high technology weapon systems. This has resulted in import of major armaments and other systems involving critical technologies. Till the 80's India was largely dependent on Soviet Russia and other East Bloc countries for its defence requirements.

As a matter of fact the entire tank fleet, mechanized infantry BMP/ICV fleet, Air Defence systems, bridges, and a large portion of field Artillery presently in front line service in the army is of Soviet/Eastern bloc origin. Despite the economic upheaval in India in 1991 coinciding with the end of the cold war, the two countries continued their defence relationship. The Indo-Russian defence programme is currently set to continue until 2010, but the future is not certain. India in the last 6-7 years has bought the SU30 aircrafts, 310 T-90 battle tanks (347 more are on order), the air craft carrier, Smerch rocket launchers etc. The view on further major purchases is divided due to a number of problems being faced on maintenance support of current and past equipment.

The era of liberalization which commenced in 1991, coincided with the enhanced role of the private sector in defence. Up to the late 90's the private sectors' role was mainly limited to providing large quantities of raw material, sub assemblies and limited quantities of high technology items to the Ordnance Factories, Defence PSU's and the Army's repair agencies.

In May 2001, the government decided to open up defence to private participation up to 100%, with FDI permissible up to 26%. With this change in policy a larger role for the private sector has emerged. Initially, the private sector was slow to absorb this change primarily due to the large requirement of funds, uncertainties of sustained defence requirements and long lead times for trials and eventual introduction of equipment. However, over the last 4-5 years with the active participation of various chambers of commerce a number of large private sector companies have successfully entered the defence sector with tie ups both with large foreign defence conglomerates and defence PSU's/Ordnance Factories.

As per SIPRI Book of 2008, US military spent $547 billion in 2007 which corresponds to 4%of its GDP. UK ranked second with a spend of $60 billion, India ranked 10th in global spending with an expenditure of $ 24 billion of which approximately $10 billion was on capital expenditure, 80% of this was towards buying new equipment. ABOUT $11 BILLION ARE FOR CAPITAL PURCHASES during 2008-2009.

With the entry of the private sector, large resources in terms of latest technologies, management and scientific skills, and its ability to raise large sums of money have brought defence production to center stage. This will not only enhance best practices but will assist in increasing indigenous production, employment and move faster towards the aim of self reliance. It is in this stage of transition that India needs large scale infusion of the latest technologies which is critical to self reliance. This can be best provided by collaboration with foreign companies excelling in a range of diverse equipments. Both the private sector and defence establishments are moving in this direction, albeit a little slow.

India is likely to reach an annual budget of $40 billion by the end of the 11th defence plan (2011-2012). Of this, about $16-17 billion would be available for capital expenditure. An analysis of major purchases during the last 5-6 years shows that major contracts have been signed for the Air Force and Navy. Defence observers feel that this trend is likely to continue. Big ticket contracts like 126 jets to replace the ageing MIG-21 worth about $10 billion, 6-C-130 aircraft, six refuellers, long range maritime patrol air craft for the Navy, utility helicopters for the Army and Air Force are on the anvil.

Indigenous defence industry and foreign manufacturers need to closely observe the Armys requirement. Large induction of four types of 155mm guns, the TCS, BMS, dry and wet bridges, fuzes, bi modular charge systems, specialist vehicles, Air Defence gun and missile system, night vision devices are among a host of requirements the Army wants urgently. Conceptually the Army works on an equipment profile of 30: 40: 30, this implies that 30% of the equipment of a type is approaching obsolescence, 40% is current and 30% is state of the art. The best example to illustrate this is the tank profile, while the T-55 is approaching obsolescence, the T-72 is current and the T-90 is state of art. If this concept is interpolated to others, the requirement of hardware over the next 5 to 10 years can be assessed broadly. Collaboration and transfer of technology will be the mantra in all these requirements.

Defence Procurement Procedure-2008 is in place wef 01 September 08. Very clearly India has entered free market economy in defence requirements.

The Indian defence industry is in transition with increased participation from the private sector. In all fairness Indian industry is nascent and catering for the huge demand of defence equipment by themselves is extremely difficult, thus the window of opportunity for foreign manufactures to partner with Indian industry and provide Indian Defence Forces the state of art equipment is for real.

INDIA'S DEFENCE INDUSTRY: A HISTORICAL OVERVIEW

Looking into the Post-Independence Era

The pre-independence (pre-1947) defence-industrial infrastructure in India was limited. It generally catered to the lowest spectrum of defence production—repair and overhaul of imported weapons systems. The then ruling British followed a policy of retaining strategic capabilities for themselves while allowing the native Indians to assist in the tactical dimensions, confined to minor works in most endeavours.

An example of this policy is evident from the fact that while the Royal Air Force retained the strategic elements like the bomber force and used their own formations, the Indian Air Force (IAF) was left with only tactical elements—supporting them with secondary and tertiary roles that mainly included repair and similar minor works. The Walchand Aircraft Factory (WAF) in

Bangalore was wholly engaged in repair and maintenance of aircraft at that time. From March 1942 till the end of World War II, it was employed for the servicing of American aircraft and was managed, for part of this period, by the US Air Force.

Mazagaon Docks (Mumbai) and Garden Reach Shipyards (Calcutta) similarly existed prior to India's independence to repair warships. However, apart from such single air or ship industrial units, India's defence-industrial capacity during times of pre-independence mainly consisted of what is known as Ordnance Factories (OFs). These factories had been set up primarily to supplement land-based weapons and equipment produced in Britain. Before 1947, there were 16 OFs, all located on Indian territory.

The gun and shell factory at Cossipore (near Kolkata), established in 1801, an ammunition factory at Kirkee of 1889, a rifle factory at Ishapore of 1901, a gun carriage factory at Jabalpur of 1904, and others were built mainly to produce for the British forces. During World War II, possible threats to the sea lanes of communication in the Indian Ocean and requirements of the allied forces in the region, made it necessary to double the number of factories during this time. The filling factory at Khamara and the light machine gun factory at Hyderabad were amongst such new factories. In brief, pre-partition Indian defence-industrial capacities were confined only to a supplementary role and were placed at the lowest end of the production spectrum.

Post-independence, the Indian leadership wanted self-sufficiency in every sphere of activity. This objective was obvious because India was never allowed to develop industrial competencies. The same objective was no different in the field of defence production. Right from the first Prime Minister Jawaharlal Nehru, every successive Indian leader sought self-sufficiency in defence production.

The need to establish a comprehensive defence-industrial infrastructure thus constituted a primary objective of the political leadership. Right from the beginning, India's industrial policies emphasised 'core' industries to be taken care of by the central government and others by the states. Defence industries, considered as critical national assets, obviously came under the exclusive control of the central government. The first Industrial Policy Resolution of 1948, consequently revised under the Second Five-Year Plan in 1956, made it clear that core industries, including munitions, aircraft, shipbuilding, iron and steel, heavy machine tools, heavy electrical plants, atomic energy and similar others were to be placed under exclusive central government control. During this period, many industrial units related to these fields were established under the strict supervision of the central government, known as 'basic' (Schedule A) industries. The Defence Science Organisation was also established during this period to take up the challenge of undertaking R&D activities. As demands for defence R&D grew, this organisation paved the way for the creation of the Defence Research and Development Organisation (DRDO) in 1958, which to-date remains the most important contributor to India's defence R&D activities. It has got nearly 50 laboratories, spread all across the country, and other scientific establishments and institutions like the Council of Scientific and Industrial Research (CSIR).

At independence, India's defence-industrial production was mainly coming from the existing 16 OFs. These factories were engaged in the production of low technology items like small arms and ammunition, mines and other explosives.

Their cumulative value of production was estimated at roughly US $7-8 million during the time of India's independence. Despite the first India-Pakistan War (1947/48) and the need to boost defence-industrial production, no new factory was built during the first decade (1950s). It was during the late 1950s that the need to construct more factories was contemplated. It is also during this time that peace time civilian production in defence industries was emphasised, especially by the then Defence Minister, V. K. Krishna Menon. The policy of production for civilian markets was primarily aimed at maintaining operational capacities during slack periods of demand as well as keeping the level of productivity high by the manufacturing units. By the end of the 1950s, the number of defence-industrial units almost remained the same. The production from these ordnance factories was still geared to low-technology items.

Apart from OFs, and various defence science and technology establishments, the Indian government also created a number of production establishments to take care of various productions in the field of defence. These, like others, were under the exclusive control of the government although they were created as corporations, commonly known as 'Defence Public Sector Units' (DPSUs).

There are eight DPSUs in the country, devoted to the production of different military systems and components. They are: Hindustan Aeronautics Limited (HAL), Bharat Electronics Limited (BEL), Bharat Earth Movers Limited (BEML), Mazagaon Dockyard Limited (MDL), Garden Reach Shipbuilders and Engineers Limited, Goa Shipyard, Bharat Dynamics Limited (BDL) and Mishra Dhatu Nigam Limited (MDNL). Both, DPSUs and OFs, are administered by the Department of Defence Production under the Ministry of Defence. Both sets of industries have their own research and development units although the overall R&D activities are met by the DRDO. Bharat Electronics Limited (BEL) was the first DPSU, established in 1954, to manufacture electronic equipment primarily for the defence sector. Over the years, more than half of BEL's overall production has turned into products for the civilian market. And it is not the only production entity that has changed that way.

In the post-independence period, till the war with China in 1962, India's defence-industrial base was too weak to take the responsibility of all defence needs. The self-sufficiency model had been adopted since the beginning but as years passed and demands for security grew, India found it difficult to create an industrial base as it was hit primarily by two important factors – lack of sufficient funding and access to modern defence technologies. The Indian leadership was aware of these two problems but they also had a number of other issues to handle. The country was just independent, had already fought a war with Pakistan, did not even have a rudimentary industrial base, and faced numerous nation-building and socioeconomic problems, independence, found it pragmatic to follow a policy of controlling critical industries, including defence, though this is widely debated now. Although both defence and non-defence critical industries were under exclusive state control, the former—due to their strategic importance—became a 'closed' sector.

The leadership also desired and pursued what is commonly known as comprehensive industrialisation. This meant that more and more big industries emerged to cater to needs that were vast, like steel, coal, mining, etc. Thus, big state-owned companies like the Steel Authority of India Limited (SAIL) was established.

This was also evident in the defence sector where large industrial units were created to cater to the demands of the vast armed forces. As mentioned, the two problems of lack of investment and access to technologies became acute as the defence industries expanded, making many units perform below par. Also, investment pattern in this sector was not uniform. Critical establishments like the Hindustan Aeronautics Limited (HAL) and DRDO received more funds than others, such as OFs. The ever-growing demands of the armed forces and the problems in the defence sector in meeting those led many to criticise existing policies followed by the then ruling party. The government, in turn, was hard pressed for funds that were essential and was aware of long-term returns for investment in the defence sector. In brief, policies to maximise production in order to attain self-sufficiency in the defence sector although they were considered far-sighted, did not match expectations, thus leading to further constraints.

From Self-Sufficiency to Self-Reliance

The self-sufficiency in defence production was in fact realised from the beginning, and was complemented by the concept of self-reliance after a few years of persistence and failure. Self-reliance, as far as India was concerned, meant—apart from its own production base for support—a degree of dependence on reliable foreign sources for access to technologies, supply of components and complete systems. This, in turn, was debatable as foreign partners to achieve such long-term self-reliance were not forthcoming during the first few years as the West was considered to be unreliable both for military and political reasons. India tested self-reliance by meeting urgent and immediate demands through imports from abroad while simultaneously striving for indigenous capabilities in defence production. The west European weapons systems, primarily British, French and Swedish, were considered first choice in the Indian arsenal during the first few years; however, after the 1962 war with China, many western countries along with the United States were reluctant to co-operate with India which made a major adverse impact on India's defence production activities. The post-War scenario witnessed a slow entry of the Soviet Union as a major supplier, the position is still retained by its successor Russia. The post-1962 scenario was marked by utter confusion in the decision-making circles, which in turn impinged the defence industry.

India was humiliated in the war with China and thus started looking into its existent defence-industrial capabilities and found to its horror that all was not well. For example, the Indian Air Force (IAF) needed a high-altitude supersonic interceptor against the threat of the B-57 bomber of Pakistan (supplied by the United States) and the Tu-16 bomber of the Chinese Air Force (supplied by the USSR).

The requirement especially assumed a serious dimension after the war with China, when India looked outward and found out that only three fighter aircraft worth-considering were available in the market. India neither wanted to buy the British Lightning nor the Soviet MiG-21, and preferred the American F-104.

This system was already supplied by the United States to Pakistan and despite repeated efforts India could not obtain it. India's effort to upgrade the existing HF-24 to supersonic capability was not considered by the Americans, either. It was at this time that the USSR came to India's rescue when they not only decided to supply the MiG-21 and other weapons but also gave a go-ahead for license production. India's quest for self-reliance got a major boost through this license production arrangement. This was indeed a turning point in India's self-reliance activities. The Soviets proved to be a trusted friend whose military supplies constitute more than 70 percent of India's total weapons acquisitions now. This friendship immensely benefited India's defence industry as it improved many notable weapons systems and components from this experience. In brief, India's self-reliance model in defence production was given a life lease by the Soviets.

After 1962, India sought to make up for the lacuna as well as boost defence production to match requirements. New ordnance factories were planned and established during the next three decades. The number of OFs thus grew to thirty-five by the mid-1980s. And, by the mid-1990s, it had reached thirty-nine. The fortieth ordnance factory (at Nalanda, in the state of Bihar), started in 1999/2000. These OFs were established in different parts of the country: Ten of them cater to materials and components, ten for weapons, vehicles and equipment, ten for ammunition and explosives and five for other ordnance items. By the early 1990s, they were producing more than 1500 items of arms, ammunition, equipment and components. By the early 1990s, the OFs collectively reached place 45 on the list of the largest arms producing companies in the world, and were placed at 29 in 2000.

The OFs, with a cumulative work force of 1,75,000, have been engaged in various types of land-based weapons. During the period under examination, the bulk of the production, nonetheless, still constituted of large quantities of relatively low-to medium-technology items. These, among others, included small arms, anti-tank and anti-aircraft guns, mortars, associated ammunition, rocket projectiles, bombs, grenades, mines, transport vehicles, leather items, parachutes and ordnance clothing for the armed forces. The establishment of the Heavy Vehicle Factory at Avadi (in the state of Tamil Nadu) in the early 1960s was crucial for the production of tanks and combat vehicles. This is where the first series of tanks, called 'Vijayanta' were manufactured under license from the British firm Vickers. This was followed by the manufacture of the ex-Soviet T-72 'Ajeya' MBTs. Although this project was taken up during the 1970s, it finally rolled out in 1988. In some projects, however, the level of indigenization has been pretty high, for example, up to about 80 percent in the case of 'Sarath' infantry combat vehicles. The overall performance of the OFs during that period was modest, although a lot could have been done to improve the performance of many factories. Hindustan Aeronautics Limited performed modestly during this period. Created in 1964 through an amalgamation of two aircraft companies, Hindustan Aircraft Limited and Aeronautics India Limited, HAL has become the only major aerospace company. With a total work force of nearly 45,000, it stands as the 57th largest defence company in the world.

During the beginning, it was primarily catering to maintenance and overhaul but over a period of time has slowly developed itself to undertake assembly, license manufacture and indigenous design and development. During the 1960s and well beyond, it was engaged in various license manufacture projects, amongst others the MiG-21 series aircraft, HF-24 Marut transonic fighters, 'Kiran' HJT – 16 jet trainer.. Apart from this, it also undertook to license manufacture 'Cheetah' (Aerospatiale SA 315 B) and 'Chetak' (Aerospatiale SA 316 B) helicopters. Bharat Electronics, set up in 1954 to manufacture electronic equipment, was perhaps the only DPSU which showed positive production results during the same period. Other DPSUs such as BEML, BDL, MDL were engaged in production, which may again be termed as modest. Bharat Dynamics Limited, established in 1970, is the other DPSU, which was engaged in the production of missiles and associated products. Except during the 1990s, it had engaged in the past in license manufacture of some of the low range missile series. To sum up: While the Indian defence industry was expected to raise its production level during the half a century (1960s to mid-1980s), both its objectives of self-reliance through indigenous activity and more active collaborative activity, have brought very limited results. Some analysts even term this phase as an 'era of license-manufacture', nothing more. While plant utilisation capacities remained at the lower end, with around 40 to 50 percent, the quality, range and mode of production was modest and generally confined to low and medium technologies.

Gaps Galore

From the early 1960s till the early and mid-1980s, license production and direct purchase and acquisitions remained the predominant form of supply for the Indian defence forces. Analysts like Ajay Singh argue that there was a gap of nearly three decades in India's effort toward indigenous production. This gap was especially evident in the fields of design and development, which constitutes the upper spectrum of self-reliance. A fighter aircraft between Marut and the Light Combat Aircraft (LCA), a basic trainer aircraft between HT-2 and HPT-32, an intermediate trainer between Kiran and an yet-to-be fully developed Advanced Jet Trainer (AJT) are some of the examples that typify both the technology and production gaps.

Weapons for the army had been manufactured under license with no significant design activities undertaken till the 1980s when a tank and a small arms project commenced. The first was a Main Battle Tank (MBT, named Arjun) while the last is known as the Indian Small Arms Systems (INSAS). The Situation was a little better for the Indian Navy, where at least some ship platforms were designed indigenously. The period thus witnessed a time gap in the design and development while emphases were more on license production and acquisitions that led to two problems – below par quality performance of the defence industry, although the quantum of production was on expected lines and lack of or little funding for critical and strategic sectors of the defence industry including R&D. Analysts also argue that given the situation even half the allocation for acquisitions would have been sufficient to ensure delivery on time, if not at the required level of technology.

PROBLEMS AND PROSPECTS: AN ASSESSMENT

India's quest for self-reliance has produced mixed results. Some of the lessons that India has learnt in the past fifty years are worth noting here. First, a combination of factors have led to the indigenous design and development component of self-reliance slowing down to almost zero for over a quarter of a century after 1962. This has led not only to a huge technology gap but also contributed to severe difficulties in technology assimilation in the industrial sector. However, since the mid-1980s, activities toward achieving a greater degree of self-reliance have taken up momentum. The technology gap also widened the scope for acquisition of production technology rather than design technology from foreign sources. This in turn has created a license production regime at the cost of indigenous production. During the 1990s, the activities to encourage joint ventures and co-production in the defence-industrial sector is largely seen as a step to reduce license regime and boost indigenous industrial capabilities. How far this will achieve desired results are yet to be seen as such activities are only of recent origin and they need lead time to prove themselves.

For example, the market for Brahmos missiles is estimated to be large, but it depends on how much is it likely to penetrate the cruise missile market at a global level. Success of this kind will not only validate India's defence-industrial capabilities to meet domestic demands but also increase its confidence in many ways.

Second, private participation in the defence-industrial sector has started after a long delay. This is attributable to several factors, ranging from the socialist and protective nature of the defence sector to fears of what is called 'security diffusion'.

The latter especially relates to a fear of below-expectation performance by the private sector as it is hardly specialised to meet strict high military standards, hence compromising security standards. This kind of fear has been criticised by many who argue that private participation is essential in the defence sector which is primarily technology driven and capital intensive. The recent opening up of the defence sector for private participation has generated a lot of interest in the country.

Institutions like CII caution that while such initiatives are always welcome, the government should come out with a clear 'road-map' for the private sector participants in defence so as to enable them to prepare themselves for the new reality. Fears regarding the ability of the private sector to match expectations of the country in the highly demanding and technology-dominated industrial sector are countered by industrialists like Atul Kirloskar (Chairman of Committee on National Defence, CII), who claim to have absolute faith in their abilities.

Many also claim that given a chance, the secondary role of the private sector can be turned into a primary one in a short period of time. Some of the leading industrialists even claim that they have or intend to possess capabilities to produce complete weapons systems.

Several companies like Mahindras and Mahindras (M&M), the Tata Group, Kirloskar Brothers, Larsen and Toubro (L&T), and many others have already jumped into the fray to obtain orders from the defence industry. Since 2002, the Government has received more than ten applications from the private sector to manufacture weapons systems. It has recently awarded five licenses to L&T and M&M to produce military vehicles and some weapons systems.

Third, the government has emphasised measures to enhance the defence industry to cope with future challenges. Such measures are carried out by both OFs and DPSUs, apart from respective branches of the Government and the armed forces. Digitalisation, strict quality control, performance-related benefits, professional management systems, allowing the private sector to carry out R&D activities in the government-owned laboratories, are some of the measures which have come up in recent years and are likely to impinge the defence-industrial landscape.

A simplification of production and procurement rules promise better buyer-seller relations. There were some protests coming from employees' unions of OFs and DPSUs against privatisation. The Government has assured these unions that employees' interests will be borne in mind but that it will give priority to performance.

In one instance, the Defence Minister is reported to have appealed to the workers in one DPSU to not to worry about possible relocations due to privatisation and assured them to take effective steps to safeguard their interests. It seems that rationalisation of the defence industry is on the cards which might bring some unrest in the form of reduction of employment in the defence-industrial sector.

There are even rumours that some of the units, especially from the ordnance sector might be closed down. The private sector participants are, however, optimistic.

They argue that their factories can effectively be converted into profit making civilian units. In several rounds of interviews with senior officers and industry analysts by the author, it seems that some of the industrial units may come under close scrutiny. Conversion to civilian production in their cases is not ruled out. In brief, significant rationalisation, diversification and closer private participation are coming and are likely to influence India's defence industry in many ways.

India's defence-industrial strategy is directed primarily toward achieving self-reliance. Presently, there is a clear imbalance in requirements by the armed forces. While roughly 70 percent of requirements are met through arms imports, the domestic sources supply the rest.

The current strategy is geared to reverse this trend with the primary aim of supplying three-fourth of the requirements through domestic sources.

India's decision to allow private participation in the defence-industrial sector is seen as a dual aim, namely to achieve much-needed capital and production enhancement and, secondly, to open up to the external market through their presence. There is also an effort to adopt suitable strategies to make select sectors like aerospace and electronics globally competitive.

DPSUs like HAL and BEL are now much in demand and are trying to become viable global giants, not to be included in SIPRI's List of Top 100 Defence Companies for their sheer size only but for their performance.

And, the overall strategy is to make the defence-industrial sector act as a locomotive for economic development. In this regard, an emphasis on dual-use technologies and production is contemplated which could benefit both the defence and civilian sector.

The current strategy also looks into various options toward minimising the state investments in the defence sector while encouraging private and foreign portfolio investment in existing Indian defence companies. Such a tall order for the defence-industrial sector is often regarded as unrealistic by many in India but that is another matter. If recent changes in various policies related to the defence industry are supposed to have any meaning, then, despite all problems, there is something to be optimistic about in the Indian defence industry.

TRENDS IN THE 1980S AND 1990S

Defence Production during the 1980s and 1990s

The of model of self-reliance, adopted by the defence industry during the 1960s and continued since then, became more prominent during the mid-1980s. After a critical gap in access to defence technology for more than two decades, the defence industry started looking for enhancement of its performance level. This period was also witnessing profound changes in the international security environment. Global defence expenditures rose to an all time high in 1987 and then fell sharply during the late 1980s and early 1990s.

Major production initiatives were curtailed and funding slashed. The Cold War came to an end but South Asia faced a security threat of a different kind. The superpower involvement in Afghanistan left a huge quantum of surplus small arms, which were redirected toward armed violence in Kashmir and Northern Sri Lanka and the volume of general lawlessness and crimes grew manifold. This was also the time when Pakistan was developing its clandestine nuclear programme which reached a critical threshold in 1987. The decision to accelerate India's nuclear programme gained momentum as of the early 1980s when leadership received positive information on the fact that Pakistan was working on a nuclear programme. Although the option had been kept open since the late 1960s, Indian leadership had gone slow after the 1974 Pokhran nuclear test, classified by India as a PNE (Peaceful Nuclear Explosion).

As is mentioned before, defence production was quite modest during the previous decades and it was desired that it should pick up momentum. Hence, one may notice a kind of upswing in India's defence production activities during the early 1980s, which continued thereafter. This was due both to internal and external factors, as cited above, but was more driven by a sense of urgency that was long lacking. It is also interesting to note that while during the 1960s and 1970s the overall expenditure toward defence lay well below the 3 percent mark of the GDP, it started expanding beyond this mark for some years in the 1980s, only again to fall well below this mark in subsequent years. Major acquisitions from abroad coupled with major initiatives in indigenous defence production, including R&D, activities mark this period. The OFs during this period were engaged primarily in manufacturing a series of licensed production items and were also striving for indigenous design and development.

MBTs, ICVs, and small arms were some of the products which were produced with interest. In the MBT series, 'Ajeys', a licensed manufactured version of the T-72, was considered as a major step forward which emboldened the OFs further to produce 'Arjun', an MBT conceived during the 1970s and designed and developed in the 1980s and 1990s, which came out for serial production during the mid-1990s. Arjun is dubbed as a fine indigenous product by India although a minor portion of its components were imported which have subsequently been modified. Similarly, Sarath ICV was developed with full indigenous activities and is doing well for the armed forces. The latest generation INSAS, the 105mm light field gun, mortars, carbines, light machine guns, and related ammunition were produced in several of OFs. Of note is the latest generation of 5.56mm INSAS assault rifle, which is said to be an equivalent of an AK-assault rifle. Production of all these systems were going on with average to expected turnover during the 1990s. In the field of aerospace, a series of new projects were begun and licensed production continued during this period.

After the MiG 21 aircraft, Marut transonic fighter, HAL started looking for new products. Since the early 1980s, among others, it has taken up the license manufacture of Jaguar deep penetration strike aircraft (from France). The first aircraft of this type was delivered to the Air Force in 1987/88. HAL had already handed over the contemporary version of the Mig (named MiG-27M), which was license manufactured for the Indian Air Force. During the mid-1980s, HAL produced the first Dornier Do-228 transport aircraft and, had indigenously designed the modified version of the Kiran trainer by 1989/90,. In fact, production of Kiran MKII (license manufacture) and Dipak basic trainer aircraft had commenced in 1983/84. During the 1990s, it engaged in manufacturing the R-25 and R-29 B aero-engine for fighter helicopters. It is modernising the Air Force fleet of Jaguar and is also engaged in the overhaul of airframe and accessories of the Mirage-2000 series of fighter aircraft. Among its most recent pride, is the indigenously designed prototype of the Advanced Light Helicopter and the involvement in the initial stages for the Indian AWACS project and, along with the Aeronautical Development Agency (ADA, based in Bangalore), its responsibility for the design and development of the Light Combat Aircraft (LCA).

The LCA has been in the news for quite some time because of long delays in flight testing. Tests of the engine for the prototype (GE-404, supplied by the General Electric Corporation of the United States), however, were successful. Apart from undertaking these programmes, which are primarily for military uses, it has contributed significantly to the civilian sector as well, as is explained later. It is worth noting that HAL has contributed at various stages to India's space programme. Light alloy structures, specially designed tanks, and many other components of India's PSLV programme were manufactured by HAL. It is during the early 1980s that India undertook a major initiative in the production of missiles.

In 1983, an Integrated Guided Missile Development Programme (IGMDP) was initiated under the Defence Research Development Organisation (DRDO). This programme was crucial to India's national security as for the first time it made a decision to produce its own brand of missiles.

Although missile technology was and its applications were long in existence in many parts of the world, it took India some time because during the 1970s it was going for indigenous development only. For this purpose, a new DPSU, named Bharat Dynamics Limited (BDL), was created. Since its establishment in 1970, it has been engaged in production activities, both through license manufacture and, since the 1980s and 1990s, through indigenous development. In the latter, it is closely linked with the DRDO, which is responsible for R&D activities in missile technology. BDL entered into an agreement with the French company, Aerospatiale for license manufacture of the SSI anti-tank guided missile. Production of this series was continued during the whole of the 1970s and early 1980s. It is to be noted that the content of indigenously produced parts in this missile was more than 70 percent while only the warhead contained more than 80 percent. This was hailed as a major success. The next series of anti-tank guided missile replaced SSII in 1985 when serial production of 'Milan' started. The first indigenously developed 'Nag' ATGM to replace Milan has been well underway for quite some time and has already been introduced with the armed forces. Two more versions of short range surface-to-air missiles, Trishul and Akash, after necessary tests and extensive user trials, have been inducted.

In surface-to-surface missile series, 'Prithvi' has already been inducted. It is claimed that more than 90 percent of these missiles are indigenously developed with very little components bought from abroad. BDL's most famous production is related to three versions of ballistic missiles, named 'Agni'. The 'Agni' is wholly indigenous in terms of its design and its re-entry and propulsion systems. It has three versions so far—Agni I, Agni II, and Agni III. Details of this series of ballistic missiles are explained in the subsequent section.

Three DPSUs are engaged in defence production for naval forces. Mazagaon Dockyard Limited (MDL) is the largest and one of the oldest in the Indian defence industry. Along with Garden Reach Shipbuilders and Engineers, it has been engaged in both repair, maintenance of warships as well as production. Both DPSUs have constructed a series of specialised vessels such as frigates, destroyers and submarines. In the late 1970s, after the successful construction of a series of Leander class frigates through license manufacture, the MDL undertook a follow on class of 3,600 tonne frigate, called 'Godavari'. This class of frigate was produced mainly during the 1980s. Also during the same period, it produced two larger 6,500 tonne-'Delhi' class destroyers as well as two 1,500 tonne-Shalki class HDW – 209 Type submarines 35. Indigenously built submarine 'Shankul' was commissioned into the Indian Navy in 1994. In addition, both the DPSUs have built several patrol and coastal combatants for the Indian Navy and the Coast Guard. Production patterns during the 1980s and 1990s show that India has been able to initiate a number of projects for indigenous development in the defence sector. This has been partly possible due to increased allocation of funds for these projects as well as for R&D. Both the former and the latter have been given importance since the early 1980s. However, during the last two decades, funding was also cut or stopped many times, leading to a delay or abandonment of projects. This is common knowledge. For example, the project for LCA has been especially controversial as main reasons for its delay have been attributed to both funding and lack of access to technology. It is also expected that an increase in defence R&D (which is currently increasing and is expected to increase further) will boost indigenous production activities. However, the proportion of allocations for R&D still remains well under 10 percent.

Major R&D and Other Initiatives

As mentioned earlier, it was during the mid-and late 1980s, that the Indian defence industry got renewed attention. During this period, several projects were undertaken and carried out in the defence sector, many of which have been continued until today and are expected to continue in future. Many new projects have been added and are expected to be initiated in the near future. DRDO has been especially geared up to initiate and further R&D activities to boost and complement the defence industry in this regard. The DRDO, born out of the Defence Science Organisation during the 1950s, has contributed immensely to defence R&D in the country. With a network of nearly 50 laboratories/ establishments spread across the country, it has been considered as the main pillar of India's research activities.

Its achievements have been far and wide, most importantly including the IGMDP, MBT, LCA and other programmes. Under the IGMDP, it has been engaged in several series of missile programmes as explained earlier. Its latest endeavour includes the 'Agni' series of missiles with several tests conducted in recent years. The 2,500 km 'Agni II has been operationalised and is ready for induction in the armed forces. In addition to this, recent successful test of medium range Agni I (700-750 km range), single-stage and solid propelled, designed to fill the gap between Agni II and Prithvi, has been hailed as a major achievement.

It is also reported that the Agni I has been specially designed with Pakistan in mind. It is likely to be operational by the end of 2003 which will depend on the results of more tests this year. The Agni-III ballistic missile, with a strike range of 3,500 to 4,000 km, the technology not being too different from the earlier versions of Agni, is being developed and is likely to be tested by the end of this year. The solid-fuelled Agni-III will be both rail and road mobile to confer operational flexibility in deployment. It will be an entirely new vehicle, along with an inertial navigation system, to accord capabilities to deliver a one-tonne warhead. According to some analysts, a fourth version of the ballistic missile, named Agni-IV, in the range of beyond 5,000 km, is also underway. This would provide India with ICBM capability. If this was not enough, there are also reports that an ICBM programme, code named 'Surya' has also been started since the mid-1990s. This missile will probably be nuclear tipped and is likely to have a range of 8,000 to 12,000 km. It will be based on components developed from the Agni series and the Polar Satellite Launch Vehicle (PSLV) programme, the latter successfully initiated and undertaken by the Indian Space Research Organisation (ISRO). However, high ranking defence ministry officials and others responsible for such a kind of programme deny this. They argue that India does not need an ICBM programme as its security needs can be met effectively by IRBMs. Agni can act as a classic deterrent against any potential adversary, they say. According to a well-respected scientist, India is trying to develop a ballistic missile defence system like a hypersonic class of missiles and long-range detection and tracking radar with the objective of countering incoming missiles and other forms of offensive weapons. Hence, India has its eyes on developing defensive weapons systems development of weapons systems rest with DRDO, which in turn takes technical and other inputs from other scientific institutions like ISRO, the Indian Institute of Technology (IIT) and others, the production rests with the respective DPSUs and OFs. Missile production has been entrusted to BDL.

Apart from strategic weapons such as ballistic missiles, several tactical battle-field weapons systems have been developed and produced by India. The Prithvi, Trishul, and Nag fall under the latter category. Serial production of Prithvi missiles has been started by the BDL and delivered to the armed forces. Trishul and Nag have been periodically tested and serial production of these two missiles are expected shortly.

Another much publicised weapon system developed jointly by India and Russia, called Brahmos, a supersonic cruise missile, was tested recently. The first trial of Brahmos took place in 2001 and the second in 2002. The recent test of this missile took place from a naval vessel. High speed, stealth properties, advanced jamming protection and highly explosive warheads are some of the features of this missile which has a range of 290 km and a payload of up to 300 kg. This missile can be launched from multiple platforms – ship, land, submarine and air. The missile is expected, after a successful series of trials, to go into serial production by the end of 2003. Various versions will be developed, its air-to-ground version is configured to be fitted in the Su-30 MKI multi role fighter aircraft. All versions of this missile are also slated for sale on the international market.

Most recent developments in the fields of aerospace and other areas, in which India's defence industry is intricately involved, are many. They include the project on the Unmanned Aerial Vehicle (named 'Nishant'), which has cleared all tests. The Pilot-less Target Aircraft 'Lakshya', after a series of successful trials, is inducted into the IAF and Navy.

The LCA programme, which started during the 1980s and had faced a lot of troubles, both financial and mainly technological, has been accelerated again since the late 1990s. Despite these difficulties, already forty-eight test trials have been conducted and the second prototype is already on its way to have flight trials. According to the Secretary, DRDO, Dr. V. K. Atre, five more prototypes are intended to be built and the aircraft is planned to be inducted into the IAF after initial operational clearance. The Air Force is expected to have four operational squadrons of LCA between 2010 and 2015. The task of such a huge order is taken up by the HAL, which is quite hopeful of meeting the expectation. Kaveri aero-engine for the LCA, an indigenous project to replace the GE-404 for the LCA, is currently undergoing high altitude tests in Russia. A success of Kaveri, the first endeavour to produce an advanced aero-engine in India, is certainly going to boost the confidence of both the scientific and defence-industrial establishments manifold. This will also signal, along with LCA, a new era in the field of aerospace in India. As a spin-off project, its marine version is also contemplated.

India is also developing a twin-engine Medium-range Combat Aircraft (MCA). This was disclosed at the 54th Annual General Meeting of the Aeronautical Society of India (in Kolkata) by no other than the President of India, Dr. A P J Abdul Kalam, who is also considered as the father of missile and nuclear technology. He said that the MCA programme was in the design phase. He also said that India was working on the design of a hyper plane, a re-usable and cost-effective hypersonic space vehicle.

While reusable missile configuration and technology has not yet emerged in the world, Indian technologists have started working on a reusable hypersonic cruise missile system, an integrated design of multiple technologies derived from UAV, aircraft and missile systems 47. A new Intermediate Jet Trainer Aircraft (HJT–36), perceived as an interim arrangement to replace MIG trainers as well as to finally replace the indigenous Advanced Jet Trainers, was planned to be ready for production from 2003. Design and development of a Test Bed for Pegasus engines for the Navy, successful flight trials of Pilot-less Targeted Aircraft Engines (PTAE), up-gradation of Jaguar, modification of air to air re-fuelling of Mirage, up-gradation and modernisation of MIGs are some of the other programmes which have been undertaken by both the scientific establishments and defence industry. Successful trials of short range Battlefield Surveillance Radars (BESR), and the three dimensional Medium Range Radars (CAR) have demonstrated DRDO's breakthrough in radar technology. In the field of Navy equipment, one important development is the Advanced Technology Vessel project for indigenous submarines, which is expected to take some time, at least till early in the next decade. According to newspaper reports, major work on this project is still pending and its status has caused some concern. According to the Defence Minister, indigenous construction of an aircraft carrier will be soon begin at Cochin Shipyard, which may take a decade to be completed. Given the nature and extent of activities in the field of defence science and technology, it is obvious that the industry seems quite upbeat to do the follow-up job of serial production of a number of ambitious programmes.

From Licence to Co-Production

The 'self-sufficiency' model adopted during the first years, with massive industrialisation in all core sectors of the economy including defence, was replaced by what is known as the 'self-reliance' model, which roughly commenced during the late 1950s and early 1960s. The self-reliance model, with primary emphasis on indigenous production and development and secondary dependence on imports from reliable foreign sources, continues to guide policy. As explained earlier, the half–a-century of technology gap and a performance below all expectations in the defence industry, from the early 1960s to the mid-1980s, led to a renewed emphasis on indigenous production activities. The period since the late 1980s and early 1990s thus witnesses a change in nature of defence-industrial production activities. The earlier era, among others, witnessed an increase in license production, which reduced indigenous production to a considerable extent. The present times, however, have witnessed more emphasis on indigenous production, a major change in this regard being the increasing number of co-production activities coming from various sources. Although license production has been a stable form of production, it has not made India self-reliant in terms of upper-ends of defence production, especially in the field of design and development. With indigenous activities having its own weaknesses, especially financially and lack of or difficult access to foreign military technologies, other alternatives to fill the technology gap have been contemplated for some time. This is where the idea of joint design and development as well as co-production come in. Among other factors, trends in global defence industry have influenced this decision in many countries. On its quest for self-reliance in the 1990s and beyond, India has tried to follow this trend.

Several new projects in the Indian defence-industrial sector are planned to be jointly designed and developed, and India is keen on taking up this opportunity to the fullest possible extent. HAL has led the way in this. After the successful integration of several electronic components in the Su-30MKI by Indian scientists and technicians in recent times, the Russians are very interested in a partnership, initially in license production of the aircraft by HAL but incrementally substituted by joint production in future, which is unprecedented in this kind of fourth generation aircraft project. A new simulator which will make it possible to train pilots for the Su-30MKI is on the cards for India. HAL is going to produce this aircraft soon. Russia, in addition to this, has also proposed to become a partner in the ambitious fifth-generation combat aircraft project, of which details are not available. It has offered to design, develop and produce this project with India, thus sharing incurring costs.

Brahmos, as explained earlier, is a joint venture between India and Russia, which was expected to be ready for serial production. This cruise missile project started in 1998 and is said to be one of the major steps by India toward international collaboration. India's recent decision to initiate an Advanced Jet Trainer (AJT) project is also going to lead to the involvement of international collaboration partners.

The US aviation giant Lockheed Martin, which is interested in the AJT deal, is keen to offer technology transfer for this project. It has claimed that its model of an advanced trainer, the T-50 Golden Eagle, is the world's newest and only supersonic trainer. It has also shown an interest in close collaboration with defence companies in India, especially with HAL. Similarly, to get a share in the project, in which initially British Aerospace had been the front runner with its Hawk trainer aircraft, several British aerospace and defence companies are interested in joint ventures with their Indian counterparts.

This is the first time that, except for Russia, more and more front line arms producing countries are showing interest not in exports but, more importantly, in joint ventures and other forms of industrial participation. The Indian defence industry, especially since the last couple of years, has been experiencing noticeable changes. It is gearing up to take this opportunity which was previously quite limited. Industry watchers believe that the Indian defence industry is going to benefit from such swift changes in production policies in many ways.

Trends in Acquisitions

India's arms acquisitions, especially during the last decade, have been substantial. Two primary factors are attributed to this. First, the technology gap, which is either due to the long-lasting indigenous design and development activities during the 1960s to the 1980s and insufficient resources for R&D and production or the perception that arms acquisitions were only a short-term remedy (with an invitation for long-term difficulties, often ignored by decision-makers). Second, greater demands of security needs, where state-of-the-art weapons are necessary for national defence. A third factor, which is often cited by many analysts, is that of an inconsistency in arms purchases from abroad. While there have been arms imports throughout the time, the least active period was witnessed during the 1960s to the 1980s, in which an over emphasis on license production led to a situation in the defence-industrial sector where it was unable to provide requisite weapons at the right time, thus forcing the government to opt for immediate short term action in terms of imports.

The gap in the national arsenal became visible soon after the Gulf War, when India felt that it was way behind others in terms of overall defence preparedness. The most worrying aspect of India's defence preparedness was exposed when the Kargil conflict started in mid-1999. To its horror, it found out that it was ill prepared in terms of defence equipment as shortages of arms and ammunition were noticed. In brief, security needs were not matched by existing possession of weaponry and there was a need to fill the gap. India has imported several weapons systems from many countries. The main source of weapons for India's military is Russia, which accounts for nearly 70 percent of the total purchases. West European giants like France, the United Kingdom and Germany have also supplied several systems. Italy, the Netherlands and

Poland are some of the other European countries which have also supplied some weapons. New emerging suppliers include, among others, Israel and South Africa. The latter is considered to be a long-term reliable source of weaponry. The United States has recently also become an important supplier, despite the fact that there used to be times in which both countries had not got on well in the field of arms transfers. India imported a Mirage-2000 fighter aircraft from France. Recent reports also suggest that India is going to buy six 'Scorpene' submarines at an estimated cost of US $1.8 billion. There are also negotiations with the French on the purchase of 130 Mirage-2000H fighters amounting to an estimated cost of US $7 billion. Although such large-scale purchases often lead to procedural delays in India, it is quite hopeful of finalising the deals soon.

The Scorpene deal will also involve India in a different manner with the Mazagaon Dockyard Limited being responsible for the future transfer of technology for the building of the submarine in India. The French defence electronics company, Thales, has already signed an agreement with MDL in this regard. A contract (yet to be signed) regarding the purchase of Type-209 submarines from Germany is also in the pipeline. Also, a contract with Germany for SUT class Anti-submarine torpedoes for Type 209 ('Sishukumar' class) was supposed to be signed the status of which is not known yet. Italy has supplied 10 Seaguard TMX fire control radar and A244 ASW torpedos during the 2001/02 period for the Brahmaputra class frigates, produced by India.

Countries like the Netherlands, Poland, and Slovakia have supplied surveillance radar, armoured recovery vehicles and other systems. South Africa, considered a new partner in the military industrial cooperation, has supplied armoured personnel carriers (APC) in 2000. It is also involved in a new Ordnance Factory in India (40th OF at Nalanda). Israel, considered a potential future supplier and partner especially in the fields of defence electronics and aerospace, has supplied a number of items in the last half-a-decade.

These include, among others, Heron and Searcher class UAVs, EL/M variants of aircraft, combat battlefield and fir control radar. A deal to supply Barak class SAM is in the pipeline while there is also a rumour that anti-missile defence systems will be supplied for which negotiations are going on. Its proposed sale of airborne early warning systems (AWACS) to India has recently caused discomfort to many countries, primarily the United States which is opposing the sale as it involves some US technology. Russia, the most trusted friend in the field of military and industrial cooperation, has been the main source of defence equipment. In the last decade or so, it has supplied

Helix class AEW helicopters, MiG–29K aircraft, Su-30MKI (purchase worth more than US $5 billion in total) fighter aircraft, AA-11/12 class air to air missiles, naval and land versions of MRLs like BM-9A52/BM-23, T-90 MBTs, a wide variety of radar systems, SS-N-25 class anti-ship missiles, Krivak class frigates and others. The cumulative deal in the last five years (19972002) is estimated at US $6 billion. If this is not enough, Indo-Russian defence-industrial partnership has been gaining much momentum in recent times. India has recently been on the verge of finalising a deal to acquire the 45,000 tonne Kiev class aircraft carrier 'Admiral Gorshkov', Tu-22M3 (on lease) long-range strategic bombers, Akula class submarine and is expecting delivery of three Krivak class stealth frigates by March 2003.

In addition to these, both countries have signed an 'Inter-Governmental Commission for Military Technical Cooperation' recently to boost both military and industrial partnership. As the Indian defence industry is undertaking a series of joint ventures with Russia, both countries have also recently signed a protocol on arms exports under which exports of such systems are to be decided on a case-to-case basis.

One can witness a noticeable change in India's import of sophisticated weapons. During the 1990s, negotiations for arms purchases in many cases have involved discussion on joint industrial partnership. This is a clear diversion on the part of India as earlier it was based on outright purchase of complete weapons systems or license manufacture. In recent times, however, many formal and informal deals have included the willingness on both supplier and recipient's part to forge military technical and industrial ties. Informal understandings with major suppliers is paving the way for joint partnerships, which is benefiting Indian defence industry.

Civilian Production: Diversification as Key

It is often assumed that India's hitherto closed defence industry does not have much scope for civilian production. Similarly, conversion or diversion of military industry into civilian production has long been perceived as a non-starter in countries like India due to the obvious closed nature of its defence industry. During the Cold War period, the little conversion which was attempted in the West encountered a lot of problems. These ranged from technical issues of diverting military factories to civilian production to frequent changes in the political and security environments for military production during the 1960s and 1970s. Still, it was assumed that surplus arms production capacity could be quickly and successfully converted to suit civilian needs, once disarmament was decided upon.

The second phase of conversion, initiated by major arms producing countries in the West, started during and after the end of Cold War. Existing surplus defence-industrial capacities were tried to be converted through various means, including diversification, for civilian purposes. However, the process of conversion, considered a means to contribute to disarmament and peace, has faced many hindrances despite decisions to reduce military spending.

Still, conversion through diversification has been a major feature in India's defence industry which has not been discussed so far. In fact, many believe that India does not possess a sizeable industrial base to contemplate conversion – meaning that its facilities are still insufficient for conversion or diversion, which normally takes place in surplus capacities. But, on the other hand it is emphasised that enhancement of civilian production in the defence industry will benefit both the civilian and military sectors. Civilian production in the Indian defence industry had been encouraged since the late 1950s.

The primary goal of this attempt was to attain a greater degree of production efficiency and to maintain operational capacities during slack periods of demand. Mr V.K. Krishna Menon initiated this programme during his time (1958-62), which saw civilian products like coffee percolators, consumer electrical items, and engineering and construction equipment being produced by defence units. The war with China in the early 1960s, however, curtailed this activities as more emphasis was put on the establishment of a number of defence-industrial units. It is during this time that the aircraft producing company, HAL, was established, along with a number of OFs and DPSUs. It suffices to mention here that an initiative to begin civilian production in the defence industry was evident during the time when conversion was initiated in the West. Also, this initiative led to a similar process as was initiated in China where Lin Biao and other military political leaders initiated what is known as 'civil production during peace time and military production during wartime'.

Although the OFs had diversified into civilian production as early as in the 1950s, it received a major boost during the 1980s and 1990s. The diversification programme included a time-bound plan of action with strategies for each factory, and the appointment of professional consultants to identify products and potential markets.

This would enable the OFs to utilise their spare capacities. The former Minister of Defence, Sharad Pawar, had authorised the OFs to employ as much as 40 percent of their rated capacities for the production of goods for the civilian sector. Diversified products included a range of consumer goods for which quality certificates were awarded to five of the OFs. By the mid-1990s, the sale of civilian goods by the OFs had exceeded 10 million rupees. HAL, manufacturer of aerospace products for the defence sector, has also been involved in several products for the civilian market.

These include high technology products for space and other programmes. It was involved in several products for the PSLV programme undertaken by ISRO. Since the late 1980s, it has started supplying spare parts for civilian aircraft. In 1993, it joined an Asian consortium to co-produce medium and small passenger aircraft. It also has a tie co-operates with Boeing to take care of the maintenance of Boeing 737 passenger planes in India. The percentage ratio of civilian production to the military in the defence industry, including the OFs and the DPSUs. The Indian defence industry is optimistic about its civilian production. In a recent seminar on 'Current Trends in Embedded Technology and Applications', top defence scientists, including P. Rajkumar, Director of the Aeronautical Development Agency which has undertaken the LCA programme, are of the opinion that India's indigenous military systems are harnessing cutting edge technologies such as embedded systems, which, when allowed to trickle through into the civilian arena, could ignite huge markets.

Custom-built embedded units applied extensively to LCA and other aerospace systems have been in demand in the civilian sector, especially in information technology. National Aerospace Laboratory, a key unit of the HAL, has recently rolled out its first prototype of a 14-seater light transport aircraft, named 'Saras'. This aircraft is expected to enter into commercial production within the next two years. The market size of this category of aircraft is considerable. It is expected that production of this aircraft is going to benefit aircraft industry in India. DPSUs like Bharat Electronics have been engaged in civilian production in a big way.

In fact, BEL's production for the military sector is less than 50 percent. In the case of Bharat Earth Movers, it is less than 7 percent. Civilian production of two other DPSUs, Mazagaon Dockyard and Mishra Dhatu Nigam, lies at more than 50 percent. More than 350 items are produced by BEL for the civilian sector which are primarily meant for the communication market. Since 1992/93, it has also entered the cordless phone and cellular phone market.

Among others, it is now concentrating on the production of X-ray tubes for the world market. Other DPSUs are similarly producing a range of products for both domestic as well as international markets. The Indian defence industry has a huge potential for the civilian market. It is now entering into a phase of concentrated production. This means that industrial units are geared up to produce more and more dual-use items and at the same time concentrate on core areas of both military and civilian technologies. Spin-off and spin-on are both expected to constitute a major part in this strategy.

The opening up of the defence sector for private participation has not only created opportunities for the defence industry to venture more into the civilian market, the spin-on effect is also expected from the private civilian industries. The private industry in India is confident of contributing to this in future.

RISING DEFENCE EXPENDITURE IN INDIA

The Government of India has been investing heavily into its Defence industry due to strained relations with its neighboring countries and growth in international terrorism. The Defence budget for the year 2005 was $17.80 billion, a growth of 7.6 percent from the budget allocation of 2000. Typically 5.0 percent to 10.0 percent of the Defence budget is allocated for modernization and weapon induction. The larger share is allocated for payment, allowances, and for maintenance of aging military equipment. The Government of India expects its Defence expenditure to exceed $20.00 billion by 2008.

Private Investments on the Rise in the Indian Defence Industry

The Defence industry in the past has been dominated by the government-run public sector undertakings (PSU). This scenario has changed significantly with the Ministry of Defence providing license to private companies to manufacture select aerospace and Defence products.

In 2001, the country opened for up to 100 percent Indian private sector investments in the Defence industry and allowed foreign direct investment (FDI) of up to 26.0 percent in select areas of the Defence industry. Some of the key non-PSU industry participants supplying Defence equipment and services include Mahindra & Mahindra, Tata Group, Kirloskar Brothers, Larsen & Toubro, Ashok Leyland, Jindal, Max Aerospace & Aviation, and Ramoss India.

Increasing Public-Private Collaborations

The Defence industry is gradually liberalizing and the public sector is facilitating greater private sector participation in the area of Defence goods production. There are about 5,100 companies supplying around 20.0 percent to 25.0 percent of components and subassemblies to state-owned contractors and the market size is expected to be around $6.20 billion in 2005. Of India's current Defence procurement of capital items, more than 30 percent is imported, however, this is expected to change with the creation of more public-private partnerships.

The Indian Space Research Organization (ISRO) has a strong partnership with the Indian industrial sector for space programs execution. Over 500 small, medium, and large-scale enterprises work with ISRO, supplying hardware, undertaking fabrication jobs, and establishing fabrication and test facilities. The Indian industrial sector provides all raw materials and high-tech electronic items required by ISRO and has also contributed toward developing systems for launch vehicle spacecraft, remote sensing, and ground equipment. Around 231 technologies developed by ISRO were transferred to the Indian industrial sector for commercial use. ISRO also undertakes technical consultancy projects for industries.

INDIA'S OFFSET POLICY TO ENCOURAGE DOMESTIC PRODUCTION

India's offset policy for Defence goods has been designed to leverage the country's position as a large buyer and exporter. India's offset policy for the Defence industry states that any purchase from a foreign supplier in excess of $70.0 million will require a reinvestment of 30.0 percent of the total purchase amount in terms of components and services from India. The offset policy applies to imports by Defence PSU's, ordinance factories, and private participants of the industry.

The offset policy is also expected to act as a driver to create market-entry opportunities for mid-rung companies, which are looking at investing in research and development and manufacturing of Defence goods. The proposed offset policy is conducive for the private companies to have a larger presence.

Growth Opportunities in the Indian Defence Industry

The domestic capability of the Indian Defence industry is largely concentrated around the production of the PSUs and ordinance factories. This trend is expected to change with the recent selective liberalization of the Defence industry and a sound offset policy, which are expected to create greater private sector participation and facilitate bigger FDI inflows into the Indian Defence industry.

The Government of India has shown keenness in allowing international collaboration for the production of weapon systems, which are purely used for non-lethal purposes. The production of the following weapon systems are expected to be promoted in the future:

- Technologies/equipment for counter terrorism

- Surveillance, communication equipment, and sensors for border management
- Cyber security-synergies in the field of information technology
- Devices to neutralize improvised explosive devices (IEDs).

Suppliers and manufacturers of the above-mentioned weapon systems are expected to be some of the chief beneficiaries of the increased indigenization of the production process in the Indian Defence industry. Key areas of growth identified within the industry are expected to arise from the up gradation of the production capacity expansion, technology transfer, and modernization of Defence infrastructure.

DEPARTMENT OF DEFENCE PRODUCTION

The Department of Defence Production was set up in 1962, in the aftermath of the war with China, to create an indigenous defence production base which is self-reliant and self-sufficient. Indigenisation, particularly of armaments, proceeded apace in 1963. In November, 1965, Department of Defence Supplies was created to forge linkages between the civil industries and defence production units. The two departments were merged in December, 1984 to form the Department of Defence Production and Supplies.

Since 1962, 16 new ordnance factories have been set up and their capacities have been augmented and modernised selectively keeping in mind the emerging requirements of the Armed Forces. Presently, 39 Ordnance Factories and 8 Defence Public Sector Undertakings (DPSUs) are engaged in the task of manufacture of equipment and stores for Defence Services. In addition, capacities of civil sectors are also utilised for the purpose.

India maintains an extensive Defence industrial base principally owned by the government. At independence, industrialization was viewed to be the engine of growth and jobs for the rest of the economy, and since then the government has owned a large fraction of the industries and also tightly regulated the private sector. India believed that public ownership was necessary to insure developments that would benefit the entire country. India decided early that the Defence industries would be owned by the public sector, and the Indian penchant to establish a "socialist pattern of society" still dominates the Defence industrial base.

India's Defence industrial capacity lies in three main classes of enterprises: the Ordnance Factories (OF), the Defence Public Sector Undertakings (DPSU), and, to a much lesser extent, selected civilian public and private sector manufacturing establishments. The OFs, founded in 1801, are departmentally run government units. There are 39 OFs, grouped into five areas based on the type of armaments they produce: Ammunition and Explosives, Weapons, Vehicles and Equipment, Armoured Vehicles, and Ordnance Equipment.

There are eight publicy-owned DPSUs: Hindustan Aeronautics Limited; Bharat Electronics; Bharat Earth Movers; Mazagon Dock Ltd; Garden Reach Shipbuilders and Engineers Ltd; Boa Shipyard Ltd; Bharat Dynamics Ltd; and Mishra Dhatu Nigam Ltd. Both the OFs and the DPSU's are trying to move toward greater self-reliance. The government is also trying to promote greater civil sector participation in the armament process.

The indigenisation of defence equipment is an ongoing process and is achieved by transfer of technology and indigenous research. Indigenisation of spares of defence equipment has been undertaken in aircraft, warships, armament, tanks, vehicles and electronic as well as engineering equipment.

While the Ordnance Factories and Defence Public Sector Units (DPSUs) are manufacturing a wide range of products for the defence forces, the private sector has been involved in the supply of raw material, semi-finished products, parts and components of defence equipment. The combined value of the products of Ordnance Factories and Defence PSUs during 2000-2001 has been approximately Rs. 14000 crore as against approximately Rs. 1800 crore on import of stores (which excludes capital equipment) comprising components, spares, overhaul etc.

The Government has recently allowed private sector participation in the defence industry upto 100 per cent and with foreign direct investment permissible upto 26 per cent both subject to licensing, for manufacture of all types of defence equipment within the country. This is expected to add to the investment already made in the public sector.

The Defence industry sector has been opened for participation by Indian Private Sector upto 100 % of equity, with Foreign Direct Investment (FDI), component of it being permissible upto 26 %, both being subject to licensing permissions. This includes all types of defence equipment. Guidelines have been issued by the Department of Industrial Policy & Promotion (DIPP) in consultation with the Ministry of Defence regarding the modalities for consideration of applications for grant of licences. The private companies are allowed to apply either individually or by a partnership firm amongst themselves. The Chief Executive of the company/partnership will be a resident Indian. The company/partnership firm can have Foreign Direct Investment upto 26 % of the equity. Preference would be given to original equipment manufacturers or design establishments and those having a good track record of supplies. However, there would be a three years lock-in period for transfer of equity from one foreign investor to another foreign investor and such transfer would be subject to prior approval of Foreign Investment Promotion Board (FIPB) and the Government.

All applications from the private entrepreneurs will be considered by the Department of Industrial Policy & Promotion in consultation with the Ministry of Defence and the licenses would be granted by the DIPP. The licensees are required to put in place adequate safety and security procedures, which would be subject to verification by authorized Government agencies. The quality of the product will be assured by the Quality Assurance Agencies of the Ministry of Defence. The exports of manufactured items would be subject to policy and guidelines as applicable to Ordnance Factories and Defence Public Sector Undertakings.

DISPUTES TO INDIA'S CURRENT DEFENCE PRODUCTION

India's experience of developing its defence industry and research and development capability over the past decade has been mixed. The country's ordnance factories are capable of providing the Indian military with a significant proportion of their ammunition and low level material needs. In the period 1992/93-1997/98, for example, India only imported 11 per cent of its total ammunition needs. India is also planning to open a 40th Ordnance factory in the near future. Furthermore, speaking in the Indian Parliament, the *Lok Sabha*, on 4 July 2000, George Fernandes, the Indian Defence Minister, stated that the country's ordnance factories recorded a surplus of Rs 780 crores (a crore is ten million rupees) during the period 1999-2000. In addition to this, Fennandes stated that due to last year's Kargil conflict, output increased from 33 per cent to 900 per cent for ammunition items; 20 per cent to 108 per cent for clothing items; and 76 to 233 per cent for cables.

More generally, an overall increase in output value of 34.6 per cent in 1999-2000, as compared to the value of issue in 1998/99. The picture for the PSUs is similar. Output in the sector has been rising rapidly since the 1980s, and all the companies have started to move into profitability. According to the latest MOD, moreover, the value of production in 1998-1999 (Rs 7205.55 crore) registered growth of 15.57 per cent over that in 1997-1998 (Rs 6234.75 crore). In addition to this all the defence PSUs reportedly earned a profit in 1998-1999.

Set against that is the fact that these two elements of India's defence industrial base continue to receive large amounts of money from the government in the form of government loans. Between them they also employ in the region of 300000 people. The picture is further complicated by the fact that almost half the production of the PSUs goes to the civil sector; a small proportion of the Ordnance factory production also goes this way. (Put another way if is arguable that, certainly in the case of the PSUs, it is the production of equipment for civil use rather than for military use that is actually making money). Against this backdrop, questions have been raised about their efficiency and ability to meet production targets, as underscored by the fact that it has taken Garden Reach Shipbuilders 12 years to build the Indian Naval Ship (INS) Brhamaputra; three times longer than it would take Russia's cash strapped shipbuilders to do.

Traditionally, the price of purchasing systems and platforms from the PSUs has also worked out more expensive than purchasing them from abroad. For example, back in 1956 it was estimated that the cost of independently producing under license the HS-78 plane would be in the region of US$320000; come the end of the 1970s it stood at $1.5 million per unit.

Indigenous R&D

The success of India's indigenous R&D efforts is even more questionable: despite considerable investment through the 1990s nearly all major programmes implemented in the 1980s are experiencing time and cost over-runs.

The IGMDP: Covering the Prithvi and Agni short and medium/long range ballistic missiles, the Nag anti tank missile, and the Akash and Trishul surface to air missile, this programme has scored a number of notable and high profile successes. For example, the Prithvi has been tested regularly since 1988 and three versions of the missile (150km, 250km, and 350km ranges) are now believed to be in (or close to) production. The Agni was first tested in 1994 and in a 1998 missile test the missile flew close to 2500km. According to some reports, moreover, the missile is now operational. The Aksah, Nag and Trishul, meanwhile, are expected to enter service soon. However, none of these missiles are entirely indigenous. Some reports suggest, for instance, that five to ten per cent of the technologies used in the Prithvi are imported from abroad

The Arjun: India's experience of designing an indigenous tank has been less successful. Take the example of the Arjun tank. Originally, expected to be in operation service by 1985 the tank has suffered from continued problems, such as problems with the engine overheating. Limited production of the tank has now started; however the Indian Army has cut back on the number of tanks that it is ordering.

The LCA The story of the LCA is almost identical to that of the Arjun tank. The programme has experienced delays since its inception in 1983 for a variety of reasons. And the first flight-test, originally scheduled for 1996, is now not expected to take place until some time in 2002. The cost of the programme, in the meantime, has increased from Rs560 crores. This increased to Rs2188 crores in 1993, when approval was given to enter the Full Scale Engineering Development Phase-1.

Other Programmes: The picture is much the same for a number of other less high profile programmes, such as the Pinaka, MBRL. This was initiated in 1986 with a budget of Rs25.6 crores. This was subsequently increased to 49 crores. The system underwent troop trials in October 1999, moreover, but is still waiting for acceptance by the Army before entering full production.

A similar story emerges for products such as the Indian Small Arms System (ISAS). The only product deemed to have been a complete success is arguably the ALH. The failure of many of India's R&D programmes and its reliance on the outside world for key technologies is confirmed by a number of by external assessments, such as the United States government Military Critical Technologies List (MCTL). For example, India's capability to manufacture, gas turbine engines, and human crew systems (aeronautic systems technology) is not even considered worthy of a mention in the MCTL. Likewise, its ability to manufacture the systems necessary to ensure that a combat vehicle is superior to the technology that it is confronting. India scores a little better in the area of Marine Systems Technology, where it is rated to have limited Sub-surface and Deep Submergence Vehicle Capability. One area where India is deemed to have been successful is in the area of Means of Delivery Technology for nuclear and other non-conventional weapons, where it is rated as having a sufficient Theatre Ballistic Missile Capability (TBMC), some ICBM capability; and a sufficient Cruise Missile capability. By way of a comparison, outside the core-areas of competency that it has developed, India's defence production and R&D capabilities do not compare that favourably with other developing countries such as China, which has managed to develop its defence industry across a broader spectrum.

Consequences and Responses

India's inability to meet its top end defence needs have been compounded by the approaching obsolescence of a number of platform and systems; a problem that has been made even worse by the fact that Indian has not made any major defence purchases for the past ten years.

Last year's crisis in Kargil has also impressed the need to introduce new equipment on the armed forces-according to the reports, for example, the Indian military assessed Pakistan's Ukranian T-80s as being 'almost a generation ahead of what we had'. In response, as far as major systems and high-technology products are concerned, the government has reversed the pattern of the 1990s and shifted the balance of procurement funding away from its home grown programmes and back towards external procurement. This re-evaluation started in the late 1990s and has progressed since there.

Thus in 1996-97 and 1997-98 the DRDO's share of the defence budget decreased in real terms for the first time in that decade. At the same time, India announced its decision to purchase 40 SU-30MK fighter/bombers from Russia in India's largest ever defence deal.

Likewise, even though India announced that it would increase its defence budget by 28 per cent to $13.94 billion (2.5 per cent of GDP) in 2000-2001 this March, funding for domestic R&D was only raised by 5.2 per cent; the percentage of the defence budget allocated to defence R&D has also slipped to 4.4 per cent of the total budget. At the same time, while this year's defence budget has seen the amount of money for R&D fall in relative terms, the funds for the purchase of defence equipment from abroad have been steadily increased since 1998.

Reviving the Russian Link

Despite the challenge to their defence relationship that occurred following the end of the Cold War and the economic crisis in India, Russia and India still managed to maintain close defence ties throughout the latter part of the 1990s. For example, the two countries signed a long-term defence cooperation programme in 1994; a number of agreements for the upgradation of Indian defence equipment were initialled; India also agreed to buy 40 SU-30MKs in 1997; and according to the Russian Vice Premier Liya Klebarov, defence sales to India account for between 20 and 25 per cent of the annual total export of Russian military goods, making it India's largest arms supplier.

It comes as little surprise to find, therefore, that much of the money allocated for procurement will be spent in Russia. Although many of the deals have been under negotiation for some time, the October visit of the Russian president, Vladimir Putin, appears to have broken the logjam. Thus, although the details still have to be finalised, India and Russia officially agreed to extend their defence cooperation programme until 2010. Furthermore, India announced its intention to buy Russian arms worth more than $2 billion. Intended purchases include, additional Su-30 long range fighter bombers, a number of which will be made under license in India, more than 300 T-90 Main Battle Tanks (MBTS), one third of which will also be made in India, the ageing Soviet-era aircraft carrier, the Admiral Gorshkov, which will be provided for free but would cost $500 million to refurbish; an, as yet, unspecified number of MiG-29s for the ship; and a number of Smersh MRBLs.

European and Other Suppliers

India has also looked to solidify its links with European suppliers. For example, although the details of the deal have yet to be finalised the British based company BAE SYTEMS is also believed to have secured the deal to provide India with the Hawk advanced jet trainer aircraft. (India has been negotiating this purchase for over a decade). France has also been particularly successful, recently concluding an agreement to sell India additional Mirage 2000 fighters. Outside Europe, India has established a close defence procurement relationship with Israel, which is thought to have provided it, among other things, with equipment suitable for border surveillance. Furthermore, reliable sources have suggested that the Phalcon early warning plane (AEW) that Israel was building for China but recently agreed not to sell to Beijing after pressure from the United States will be delivered to India.

South African arms exports have also managed to carve out a small niche for themselves in the country. A number of Eastern European nations are also looking to provide India with new equipment and to help it upgrade its existing inventory. Quite simply, these purchases will fill those gaps that have appeared in India's armed forces in recent years.

INDIA'S DEFENCE INDUSTRY IN THE 21ST CENTURY

Major Policy Initiatives

India's defence industry entered a new phase of self-reliance on the eve of the 21st century. Since the mid-1990s, several initiatives have been undertaken by the government to effect changes in the defence industry. Soon after the liberalisation of the economy was announced in 1990/91, the defence industry started realising the importance of civil-military interaction in the industrial sector.

The private industries in India, which were thus far debarred from entering into defence production and whose role in the defence sector was limited to supplying spare parts and other minor contributions, started demanding a share in defence production.

In 1994, the then Defence Minister founded six Task Forces on major areas of defence modernisation, of which reforms in defence industry was an important part. This was carried out by the government in consultation with institutions like the Confederation of Indian Industries (CII). The CII, on its part was instrumental in bringing out a series of proposals in the broad field of private participation in the defence sector and armed forces–industry cooperation. Soon after this, the government initiated a programme called 'Army-Industry Partnership', under the auspices of CII which highlighted the importance of cooperative arrangements between the armed forces, defence industry and the government.

After India's nuclear tests, various sanctions were imposed on India, of which sanctions related to the import of military and dual-use goods and technologies were considered the most important.

Sanctions were imposed on more than 150 items, which affected the progress of many defence products. However, the impact of sanctions on military technology was taken up as a another phase of challenge for the defence scientists as they had faced similar sanctions after the test in 1974.

At that time they had faced more difficulties as the defence industry was not in a position to withstand such severe cuts which had resulted in delays in many major programmes. This time around, the defence industry had made significant progress to be able to withstand sanctions.

After the Kargil conflict in mid-1999, the government started looking into security gaps and founded a committee under Mr K. Subrahmanyam. He brought out a major report on this conflict, which is known as the 'Kargil Committee Report'. This report, among other recommendations, highlighted the importance of reforms in higher defence management and reforms in institutional processes in the security sector.

The Government also founded a Group of Ministers' committee to look into major aspects of the overall security management of the country. The committee submitted its report to the government, which is known as GoM Report on 'Reforming the National Security System.

This report highlighted the importance of self-reliance in India's defence industry and recommended several steps to introduce institutional changes into the system.

Coupled with changes at institutional and organisational levels, India's defence industry entered an entirely new era after the Government announced a major change in policy by outlining codes of conduct for and inviting private participation in the defence industry. This is seen as by far the most important policy shift in the defence-industrial sector in the last fifty years. By doing so, the Government, through an official notification No. 5(37)/2001-FCI, allowed private sector participation up to 100 percent and permitted foreign direct investment (FDI) up to 26 percent.

This decision has been hailed by both the private industry and the government-owned defence industry. Institutions like CII and FICCI, which represent interests and views of the private sector, have been instrumental in influencing such a marked change in policies. According to Mr Sushanto Sen, the Director General of CII, such a policy change is certainly going to benefit both the defence industry and the private sector.

In tune with the stated objectives of India's defence industry to achieve a higher degree of self-reliance and a desire to make its flagship units globally competitive, thus entering into competitive defence markets, the Government has also introduced some institutional changes that are expected to smoothen operations both at structural and organisational levels. Earlier, procurement procedures were considered cumbersome, and there were overlaps in organisational responsibilities of respective organs responsible for procurement. Under the new system, the Services Headquarters were integrated into the Ministry of Defence to provide closer interaction. The procurement structure is now a three-tier structure with the recent establishment of the Defence Acquisition Council (DAC) at the apex. Its primary role will be to accord in-principle-approval of long-term perspective plans (15-20 years), acceptance of necessity for the capital acquisition plan (5 years), identify 'Make', 'Buy' and 'Make and Buy' projects and monitor progress of the three Boards under it – the Defence Procurement Board, Defence Production Board and the Defence R&D Board. The Defence Procurement Board under the Defence Secretary will have the primary role of capital procurements and coordination. The Defence Production Board will be headed by the Secretary Defence Production and Supplies and will oversee all activities related to indigenous manufacture, progress in 'make' projects and will provide support to DAC.

The Defence R&D Board will be headed by the Secretary Defence R&D and will oversee progress, monitor and report on all R&D proposals in consultation with the user service and production board. Other measures at institutional level include direct linkages between the armed forces and the Ministry of Defence through integrated headquarters, which include respective perspective planning branches. In sum, organisational and institutional changes brought about recently seem to complement policy changes.

7

Rising Indian Defense Reforms and Modernization

For the past decade, pundits and commentators have showcased India as another rising Asian power like China. India's growing economy, larger international profile, and particularly its increased military spending, are seen as proof of India rising from being a regional power to perhaps a new Asian or even global power. Will India correspondingly move its military posture away from internal security and territorial defense, to emphasize power projection?

Many commentators have pointed to India's large military purchases as evidence that India is moving toward power projection and rivalry with China. Whether this is really happening is hotly debated in India. This chapter will look at the debate over defense and security reform in India and the establishment of India's first joint theatre command (for the Andaman and Nicobar Islands) as a test case.

India took an unprecedented step ten years ago by setting up a joint regional command for the Andaman and Nicobar Islands. The establishment of the Andaman and Nicobar Command (ANC) was perceived as evidence that India is starting to balance against a larger China by reforming its defence organization (Posen, The Sources of Military Doctrine; Rynning, Changing Military Doctrine). Although the ANC is a strategic location, India has historically avoided building up forces there and it has resisted building up power projection capabilities. Moreover, India has been reluctant to build jointness and joint operational commands, even though India's development of hard power capabilities are receiving increased attention. India provides an interesting case to examine different theories about how militaries learn.

Realism and internal balancing (Posen), constructivism (Kier), and organization theories (Nagl, Bickle) will be used to see if they can explain why some actors have proposed change and others have opposed it. This study will also look towards Michael Raska's framework of a Diffusion Dynamics Model to help structure its analysis.

INDIA AS A RISING MILITARY POWER

China has taken serious note of India's growing military power over the last decade. India, which has traditionally talked of the power of argument began to talk of the argument of power. In fact, the 1998 nuclear tests themselves were indicative of the fact that India had begun to realize the role of hard power in securing its national interests and also in making her voice heard in international politics.

India's growing military profile is especially evident in the maritime domain. The Indian navy has emerged as the net security provider in the Indian Ocean over the last decade. In 2004, it unveiled its first-ever naval doctrine that defined India's legitimate areas of interest stretching from the Persian Gulf to the Malacca Straits. It released its updated version in 2009, incorporating the rapid changes in the geo-strategic environment involving India. India's defense ties with the US have developed at a frenetic pace, which has played the central role in India's military modernization. For example, recent defense contracts signed with the US include US$ 1.1 billion for C-130J Super Hercules transport planes and US$2.4 billion for 10 Globemasters airlifters. In January 2009, the Indian Navy signed an agreement with the U. S. to buy eight P-8I planes worth nearly US$2.1 billion, so as to replace the aging long range aerial reconnaissance fleet of eight Russian-made Tu-142s and five IL-38 planes. The tests of its China-centric Agni series missile systems and the development of a Ballistic Missile Defense system. India's future military plans are even more ambitious, which further complicates China's strategic calculations. For example, the Indian Ministry of Defense in late 2011 announced its biggest expansion package to date, a US$13 billion military modernization plan. Under this plan within next five years, the Indian army is set to deploy 90,000 more soldiers and raise four new divisions along India's border with China, the largest such mobilization since the Sino-Indian border clashes of 1962.

India's Poly/Multi-aligned Diplomacy

The India that China defeated in 1962 was guided by a foreign policy doctrine called *non-alignment* vis-à-vis the superpower rivalry, and it remained the cornerstone of India's international diplomacy for more than four decades. However, this foreign policy paradigm underwent a U-turn when it metamorphosed into *poly/multi-alignment* under the new leadership in New Delhi in 1998. The new foreign policy outlook broadly had two components, namely, *improving relations with the US* and its *Look East Policy-II.*

The turnaround in India-US relations from being "estranged democracies" during the Cold War to "engaged democracies" in the 2000s has played a central role in bringing out a shift in China's India posture over the last decade.

The anti-China element in the dramatically improving Indo-US relations was not very difficult to discern. Chinese scholar Jing-Dong Yuan notes that the warming of US-Indian relations took place at a time when China-US relations were undergoing serious setbacks in the late 1990s.

In 1999, NATO bombed the Chinese embassy in the former Yugoslavia (the only embassy that it targeted); in May of that year, the Cox Report charged Chinese nationals with nuclear espionage and accused China of proliferation activities. hostile attitude toward the PRC further exacerbated tensions in early 2001. Also, the revised Nuclear Posture Review (NPR) included China as a nuclear target. Meanwhile, in a diametrically opposite turn of events, India-US relations suddenly displayed signs of dramatic improvement. US President Bill Clinton visited India in March 2000 (the first presidential visit since Carter's visit in 1978). The US' National Security Strategy Report of 2002 released by the White House redefined India-US relations, stating that because of "India's potential to become one of the great democratic powers of the twenty-first century," the United States would "invest time and resources [for] building strong bilateral relations with India," and "work hard to transform our relationship accordingly."

Consequently, the years 2002-03 witnessed a series of high-level meetings and substantial cooperation between the two democracies. Yet another contrast was the U.S.'s approval of Israel's sale of the Phalcon airborne warning and control systems to India in 2003 after the blockage of a similar sale to China in 2000.

Another Chinese security analyst Du Youkang argues that the US strategy of maintaining the balance of power in South Asia during the Cold War has gone beyond the balance of power and has tilted toward India. He cites the Clinton administration's pro-India attitude during the Kargil conflict, and his subsequent official tour to South Asia, where he spent six days in India compared to five hours in Pakistan. The growing strategic ties between the two countries provides a dangerous historical precedent for Beijing. During the Cold War, China perceived India-USSR relations in terms of an anti-China alliance in South Asia. So the strategic partnership between India and the US in the 2000s is, from China's perspective, the revival of the same anti-China alliance – the only difference being that the US has replaced the Soviet Union. Zhang Guihong compared the US-India Western Pacific.

The other pedestal of India's multi-aligned diplomacy included its *Look East Policy-II*. India's Look East Policy-I was officially initiated in 1992. Like most of the previous Indian policies it was reactionary and an outcome of ad hoc-ism.

The main driver behind this policy was the economic doldrums of early 1990s, and India saw Southeast Asia as a springboard to join unfolding globalization. However, India displayed an uncharacteristic proactiveness in projecting the Look East policy in its second incarnation in the first-ever India ASEAN summit in Phnom Penh, Cambodia in 2002. India added a politico-security dimension to this policy. It developed security ties with the ASEAN group. From ASEAN's perspective, developing such ties with India (apart from the US presence in the region) provided them a sense of strategic reassurance given their territorial disputes in the South China Sea with a rapidly growing, authoritarian China.

An important highlight of India's Look East Policy-II, from China's viewpoint, has been a transformational improvement in India-Japan relations. Although the ice between their relations was broken with the visit of Prime Minister Mori Yoshiro to India in August 2000, their relations broadened and deepened in the second phase.

The April 2005 joint statement issued during Koizumi Junichiro's visit to India introduced a "strategic" dimension to the partnership. The establishment of the Strategic and Global Partnership between India and Japan in December 2006 elevated relations to a new level. In 2006 Japan became only the second country with which India had a bilateral annual summit apart from Russia. When then Prime Minister Shinzo Abe visited India in August 2007, the joint statement sought to provide a roadmap for new dimensions to the strategic and global partnership. The October 2008 joint statement during Prime Minister Manmohan Singh's visit to Japan mentioned the advancement of the strategic and global partnership, making Japan the only country

Partnership Agreement (CEPA) which came into force in August of the same year. In late December 2011 India's External Affairs minister visited Japan in October 2011 for the Fifth round of the India-Japan Strategic Dialogue. Japanese PM Yoshihiko Noda visited India for the sixth annual meeting of the leaders of India and Japan. It was the success of India's Look East Policy-II (and not Look East Policy I) that made China remark that India's Look East Policy is "look to encircle China."

India Emerging as an Economic Giant

India and China had similar per capita income by 1974. However, China surged well ahead of India thanks to its deep economic engagement with the US after the Policy of Reform and Open Up (*gaige kaifang*) by Deng Xiaoping in 1978. While China's Open Door policy was a well-thought-out initiative, India, following its legacy of taking radical initiatives only while in crisis, embarked upon its own version of Open Door policy in 1991.

The much-needed reforms removed obstacles to economic freedom, and India began to play catch-up, steadily re-integrating into the global economy. A Goldman Sachs report from 2007 found another watermark in India's economic history since 1991 when it pointed out that since 2003 India has been one of the fastest growing major economies, leading to rapid increases in per capita income, demand, and integration with the global economy.

The story of India's economic success has captivated Chinese attention over the last decade. Among Chinese scholars a new discourse has begun over India's economic success story, especially in the IT and consensus that China is a great success in exports, inside China, focusing on China's lag in information technology, Chinese researchers ask why India has become so competitive in the international software market when India has many unattractive features."

Chinese scholars now debate an "Indian Model" as an alternative to the "Chinese model" for developing countries. The Indian model, as understood by Chinese scholars, is characterized by avoiding its weaknesses and exploiting its strengths.

For example, India leapfrogged from the primary sector (agriculture) to the tertiary sector (services) by exploiting its inherent advantages in the IT sector which includes a vast, young English-speaking population, the entrepreneurial genius of its private sector, computer literacy, a sound banking sector, and a culture that respects the rule of law.

Chinese analysts have especially taken notice of what they call "India New Economy" which is acting like an engine to the Indian Model. Ma Jiali argues that although India is a baby elephant in the manufacturing industry, it is a "doughty tiger" in the information sector.

Another set of scholars attributed India's success in this sector to its diaspora. It opined, "India's IT success is also attributed to the large cohort of educated overseas Indians who have good connections and invested heavily in their home country in recent years as a result of favourable government policies. The dynamism brought by the overseas Indians was comparable to the boost brought by the overseas Chinese since the 1978 economic reform in China."

India's Growing Soft Power

The drivers triggering a shift in China's India posture can be placed under the rubric of India's *hard power*. However, India's (re)rising *soft power* has also contributed to this shift in China's outlook a country's ability to alter the behavior of others through attraction rather than sticks or carrots. India has been a democracy right since its birth as a modern nation-state in 1947. However, its sluggish economic growth and weak military profile that led to its defeat in 1962 seriously tarnished this aspect of India's soft power. With the rising India story, its democracy as an important component of its soft power has again come into the global limelight.

India has more than 1 billion people. It is linguistically, culturally, racially, and religiously diverse, and it is growing economically at an enviable pace under democratic governmental institutions (except for the emergency period of 1975-77 when civil liberties were undermined). Its culture values peaceful coexistence, nonviolence, and religious tolerance. All of these factors, combined with the largest pool of English speakers outside the US, has increased India's power of attraction without need for coercion or persuasion, a fact not lost on an envious, hard power-minded China. The country to which India has projected most of its soft power is the US, through the export of highly skilled manpower, consisting mainly of software developers, engineers, and doctors. China has been keeping a close watch on the rising influence of the Indian community in the United States, especially over the last decade. In order to improve its own soft power in the United States, China has sent far more students to the United States than India. As per the Institute of International Education's annual report in the academic year 2009-10, out of 690,932 international students in the United States nearly 128,000 of them, or more than 18 percent, were from China while India sent only 107,897 students in the same academic year. However, with Oct 2011, educational exchanges between India and the US would rise much faster in the future.

THE ORIGIN OF THE RISING INDIA STORY

Admittedly, India shifted its foreign and economic policies soon after the end of the Cold War in 1991 when it started broadbasing its diplomacy, initiated economic reforms by dismantling the economic model based on *import substitution,* and went for market friendly policies. The economic reforms did give India economic stability in the sense that India started growing at 6% annually ever since the economic liberalization of early 1990s, however, political stability remained fragile. Once P. V. Narasimha Rao's government completed its five-year term in 1996, there was political chaos from 1996 to March 1998. From 1989 to 1999 8 governments came to power in New Delhi, six of them lasting less than a year and the shortest lasting for only 13 days. In fact, one of the reasons why India's candidature for the Asia Pacific Economic Cooperation (APEC) was rejected was its hung parliament in 1997.

The country got much-needed political stability at the centre when the BJP-led NDA (National Democratic Alliance) government came to office in March 1998 and took a series of radical initiatives in quick succession beginning with the nuclear tests in the Pokhran desert of Rajasthan on May 11th and 13th 1998, which, the author opines, was a *grand strategic masterstroke* (emphasis added) by independent India.

India initiated Multi-aligned/Great power diplomacy for the first time in its independent history when it developed strategic partnerships with all the great powers simultaneously, especially its relations with the its national security when it set up the National Security Advisory Board, National Security Council, Nuclear Command Authority, developed a nuclear doctrine, and so on.

More importantly, India developed a much-needed strategic vision whereby it redefined its geo-strategic construct well beyond the mainland of South Asia. The extended geo-strategic construct included the Indian Ocean, the Middle East, Central Asia and the Asia-Pacific.

The Chinese Perception of *Rising India*

China's perception of India has come full circle in that it started off treating India as a peer competitor, then it wrote off India as one, and again China has begun to treat India as a main strategic threat in its regional grand strategy. To illustrate this, despite all the rhetoric of *Asian Solidarity, Hindi-Chini Bhai-Bhai, civilizational dialogue* and so on in the 1950s or even earlier, the *realpolitik*-minded Chinese security planners had realized in their long term calculations that India, given its political, geographic, cultural, diplomatic, and demographic attributes, is going to be their main rival in constructing Asia as the *neo-Middle Kingdom.*

This apprehension was justified as India, despite the partition, was on a natural course to emerge as the predominant power in Asia due to its centrality in the British Empire, its geostrategic location in the Indian Ocean, its competent navy, and its diplomatic and cultural links with the Middle East, Southeast, and Africa. Not surprisingly, the first Asian Relations Conference was held in New Delhi in Mar-Apr 1947 and not in Beijing.

While China, in a sharp contrast, was ostracized by the international community, India's democracy and its non-alignment policy was a far more acceptable political and diplomatic model for the fledgling Third Finally Nehru's reconciliatory policy of acting as a bridge between East and West enjoyed far greater international legitimacy in a world that was trying to recover from two World Wars in a short period, than the Maoist Agenda of deepening the polarization between the two super powers by exporting revolutionary violence and intensifying the class struggle.

What was more troublesome for Maoist China was that India was destined be the main intermediary in the US-Soviet strategic game. After 1949, democratic India began to be seen as the main interlocutor by the USSR under Stalin because he had come to the conclusion that the US could not be militarily defeated, and so the next best option was negotiations. At the same time Stalin had mistrusted Mao since 1927. Similarly, the US shared its core political value with India, which was democracy. In short, communist China was becoming increasingly edgy and even jealous of India's growing *soft power* in this phase. The net result of these internal and external Indian positives was that China singled out India as its main competitor to the top of the Asian mountain.

With its military victory over India in 1962, China grabbed the initiative from India and projected itself as *primus inter pares* in the developing world. A hard power-minded China institutionalized this victory with its policy to use Pakistan as a strategic spoiler against India in South Asia soon after the 1962 war and openly sided with Pakistan in the 1965 war, as argued by Subhash Kapila .

The second shift in China's perception of India started when China entered the super power rivalry following Henry Kissinger's secret visit to China to see Chairman Mao Zedong in July 1971, which was followed by U.S. President Richard Nixon's visit to China in Feb 1972. China accepted the US offer to ally with permanent seat in the U.N. Security Council in 1971 replacing the Republic of China on Taiwan.

This strategic partnership further deepened under President Jimmy Carter and his anti-Soviet advisor Zbigniew Brzezinski. Brzezinski rewrote the rules of China-U.S. rapprochement and offered all advantages to China in return for its promise to confront the Soviets in the East. Under the Reagan administration their relations followed Carter's policies. In the early 1990s under President Bill Clinton, FDI flows to China increased from about US$5 billion a year in 1989 to US$20 billion by the late 1990's. The huge inflow of FDI converted China into a manufacturing giant.

The high point in the U.S.-China relationship was the signing of a nuclear deal in 1997. It was Clinton's welcome gift to Chinese President Jiang Zemin. This agreement further strengthened a 1985 U.S.-China nuclear cooperation agreement, which allowed exports worth billions of dollars of nuclear technology into China without hindrance. China, as an original member of the Nuclear-5 or "nuclear weapons states," could import everything for the commercial exploitation of nuclear technology.

Meanwhile India, in sharp contrast, was facing a reversal in fortune. Just as China was an international pariah until 1971, India was ostracized from international nuclear commerce after its nuclear detonation in 1974. Washington tailored new rules to punish India economically and diplomatically too. The new rules, enacted in 1978, denied India economic aid and nuclear technology.

It was in this context, in which India was subjected to international sanctions and also was grappling with its internal issues, while China remarkably enhanced its political, diplomatic, economic, and military clout that the latter no longer treated India as a strategic rival in Asia.

However, things took a turn a third time and China had to again reorient its India stance. After its military victory over India in 1962 and the subsequent South Asia and never think of challenging China's predominant role in Asia. However, India undertook an array of path-breaking initiatives in quick succession in late 1990s (and beyond) to herald its arrival as a great power in the unfolding 21st century that removed this Chinese (mis)perception.

The year 1998 was an eventful year in terms of China rediscovering the Indian threat. India's annual 6% GDP growth in the 1990s and *de facto* nuclear power status made China review its traditional perception of India. What really stunned the Chinese, however, was India's first-ever *Multi-aligned diplomacy,* or what the Chinese defense analysts call *Great power diplomacy,* under which it developed strategic partnerships with all the major powers of the world concurrently, especially with the United States and later with Japan. When an economically better-off and nuclear-armed India ventured into the South China Sea (with possibly the United States' support) in October-November 2000 and conducted naval exercises with Vietnam and South Korea , China could no longer afford to rely solely on its proxy Pakistan to keep India confined within South Asia. China's strategic attention which was traditionally focused on the Asia-Pacific suddenly found an emerging security nightmare in the growing Indo-United States strategic partnership in South Asia, somewhat similar to the one during the Cold War between India and then Soviet Union.

Why did the traditional Chinese strategic posture of India shift?

Jing-dong Yuan opines that China used to dismiss India as a peer competitor, citing India's handicaps, like poverty, poor infrastructure, and sluggish bureaucracy. However Beijing is now paying increasing attention to India's drive for great-power status through robust diplomatic initiatives, a military buildup, Indo-US relations, and new regional initiatives. Based on similar Chinese writings on India, the author argues that the interplay of four factors led China to reorient its strategic perspective on India. They included, India's rising military profile, its poly/multi-aligned diplomacy, growing economic clout, and rising soft power.

COMPETING THEORETICAL PERSPECTIVES

The traditional explanation makes the case that military innovation will likely come from an external threat or problem that will cause the civilian leadership to force change on a reluctant military that will resist efforts to change them. According to Posen, "In general, only civilian intervention can shake loose these inter-service treaties and jealousies to produce an integrated grand strategy." In contrast, there are other approaches that stress intervening factors that limit the effects of external threats to translate into coherent defence reforms. Kier stresses how the political-military culture of a country will place limits on how civilian and military planners "imagine" what the next war will be like and what changes are possible. So even though Britain, France and Germany all had similar experiences with the horrors of trench warfare in WWI and were experimenting with new military technology in the inter-war years, they would not all respond with the same reforms and military innovation. Others, like Nagl, have applied this to why some militaries can learn and adapt to the demands of counter-insurgency warfare and others cannot.

Lastly, another group stresses that military change and innovation is not always forced on militaries from above but can from below. These analysts take the position that militaries can develop informal and formal doctrine "by doing" and that innovation inside the services is also possible. Bickel uses this framework to explain how the US Marine Corps developed their Small Wars Manual in the 1930s by learning from their experience in the Banana Wars.

Recently, Michael Raska, at RSIS, has been working on operationalizing these different theories of military change into a comprehensive framework that can examine different cases/countries. One is termed the Diffusion Dynamic Model, which has proven useful when looking at India's defense reform. The place of India's defense reforms is at the "modernization" phase, given the intersections of experimentation (pattern of diffusion) and adaptation (diffusion path). The limited experimentation of new, but limited reforms -- like the ANC -- are good examples of this.

INDIA'S GROWING SOFT POWER

The drivers triggering a shift in China's India posture can be placed under the rubric of India's *hard power*. However, India's (re)rising *soft power* has also contributed to this shift in China's outlook a country's ability to alter the behavior of others through attraction rather than sticks or carrots. India has been a democracy right since its birth as a modern nation-state in 1947. However, its sluggish economic growth and weak military profile that led to its defeat in 1962 seriously tarnished this aspect of India's soft power. With the rising India story, its democracy as an important component of its soft power has again come into the global limelight. India has more than 1 billion people. It is linguistically, culturally, racially, and religiously diverse, and it is growing economically at an enviable pace under democratic governmental institutions (except for the emergency period of 1975-77 when civil liberties were undermined). Its culture values peaceful coexistence, nonviolence, and religious tolerance. All of these factors, combined with the largest pool of English speakers outside the US, has increased India's power of attraction without need for coercion or persuasion, a fact not lost on an envious, hard power-minded China.

The country to which India has projected most of its soft power is the US, through the export of highly skilled manpower, consisting mainly of software developers, engineers, and doctors. China has been keeping a close watch on the rising influence of the Indian community in the United States, especially over the last decade. In order to improve its own soft power in the United States, China has sent far more students to the United States than India. As per the Institute of International Education's annual report in the academic year 2009-10, out of 690,932 international students in the United States nearly 128,000 of them, or more than 18 percent, were from China while India sent only 107,897 students in the same academic year. However, with Oct 2011, educational exchanges between India and the US would rise much faster in the future.

INDIA'S RISE AS A GREAT POWER

In considering India's rise as a great power, this chapter focuses specifically on India's relations with its strategically significant neighbours, Pakistan and China. Though India's increasing projection of influence may change the regional dynamics, the fundamental balance of power among India and its neighbours will not change dramatically in the near future. Pakistan is already overwhelmed by the military strength of India, thus its strategic outlook will remain unchanged, while China and India have increasingly intertwined relations and evenly-matched conventional and nuclear forces, ensuring relative regional stability.

Analysis

The Problem of Pakistan

India's geographically closest and most frequently problematic relationship is with its neighbour and prodigal twin, Pakistan. India's rise as a great power will have its most immediate impact on the extremely dangerous stalemate which exists between the two states. Many security concerns converge in Pakistan, as: the state has been a key supporter of the Taliban in Afghanistan, factions of which the Pakistani Army is now fighting in a de facto civil war; elements within the state support Islamic terrorist organisations that periodically attack India, provoking regional crises; and, the Pakistani Army has a growing nuclear arsenal, which could be vulnerable to misuse by malicious elements within the state. India and Pakistan engaged in wars in 1965 and 1971, with crises about continuing Pakistani support for insurgents in the disputed Indian state of Jammu and Kashmir erupting periodically, and threatening war in 1990. Following Indian and Pakistani nuclear tests in May 1998, Pakistani incursions across the Line of Control in the Kargil region of Kashmir led to another limited war, and the veiled nuclear threat by Pakistani Foreign Secretary Shamshad Ahmed that, 'We will not hesitate to use any weapon in our arsenal to defend our territorial integrity.' Major terrorist attacks in Jammu and Kashmir on 1 October 2001 and in the Indian capital Delhi on 13 December 2001 again threatened war, though merely resulted in major military manoeuvres by India, code-named *Operation Parakram*. The lack of military retaliation by India despite grave provocation seems to suggest that India is successfully deterred by Pakistan's nuclear capability, and this in turn only fuels the eagerness of some elements within Pakistan to provoke India. Pakistan has adopted an "asymmetric nuclear escalation posture", which has deterred Indian conventional military power and thus enabled

Pakistan's 'aggressive strategy of bleeding India by a "thousand cuts" with little fear of significant retaliation.'

India is four times larger and seven times more populated than Pakistan. As Pakistan averages only 300 miles in width, it is susceptible to a central assault that would split the country in two. A number of important Pakistani cities also lie close to the international border in the Indus River basin. As Pakistan is thus extremely vulnerable to conventional attack by India's larger military, it defines such an attack as an existential threat to the Pakistani state. Pakistani Lt. Gen. Khalid Kidwai thus outlined that Pakistan would use its nuclear weapons if: India attacks Pakistan and conquers a large part of its territory; India destroys a large part of Pakistan's land or air forces; India blockades Pakistan in an effort to strangle it economically; or, India pushes Pakistan into a state of political destabilisation. This asymmetric escalation posture is designed for a rapid first use of nuclear weapons against conventional attacks, thus leaving India without the ability to punish terrorist attacks through conventional retaliation. As elements within Pakistan continue to provoke India, this creates an extremely dangerous imbalance reliant on India's restraint to maintain peace.

India and Pakistan escalating to the use of nuclear weapons within the first 12 days. New analyses of this eventuality reveal that a conflict between India and Pakistan, in which 100 nuclear bombs were dropped on cities and industrial areas within the two countries, would kill more than 20 million people from the blasts, fires and radioactivity. In addition, the explosions could produce enough smoke to cripple global agriculture. Smoke generated by burning cities could create a climatic response that immediately reduces sunlight, cools the planet, and reduces precipitation worldwide. This "nuclear winter" would reduce or eliminate agricultural production over vast areas, simultaneously decreasing crop yields nearly everywhere. Approximately one billion people worldwide today live on marginal food supplies and would be directly threatened with starvation. While some analysts maintain that nuclear weapons would be used in only a measured way, the chaos, fear and interruption of communications that would follow nuclear war's commencement leads some to doubt that attacks would be limited in any rational manner. Additionally, Pakistan could face a decision to use its entire nuclear arsenal quickly or lose it to Indian forces which seize its military bases. Thus, unrestrained nuclear war in South Asia potentially has cataclysmic regional and global consequences.

Following the terrorist attack by Kashmiri militants in December 2001 and the subsequent military standoff with Pakistan in *Operation Parakram*, the

Indian Army announced a new limited war doctrine in April 2004 called the Cold Start doctrine, which aims to allow conventional retaliation without posing an existential threat to Pakistan. Under Cold Start, the Indian army would avoid delivering a catastrophic blow to Pakistan, and instead make shallow territorial gains, 50-80 kilometres deep, that could be used in post-conflict negotiations. This doctrine aims to deny Pakistan the justification of "regime survival" for employing nuclear weapons in response to a conventional Indian attack. However, Walter C. Ladwig III foresees that, 'An operational Cold Start capability could lead Pakistan to lower its nuclear red line, put its nuclear weapons on a higher state of readiness, develop tactical nuclear weapons, or undertake some equally destabilising course of action.' The danger of escalation is further compounded by the relatively immature "command and control" and early warning systems of both the Indian and Pakistani nuclear arsenals. There also remains the danger of nuclear accident as, if one nation accidentally detonates a nuclear warhead on one of its own military bases, it probably will not have adequate surveillance intelligence to know that it has not been attacked by its enemy, and thus may falsely "retaliate" against the other country.

Meanwhile, in the context of the continuing conflict in Afghanistan, Pakistan believes that the United States would intervene to prevent war, as it relies on Pakistani troops along the Afghan border and supplies for American forces are transported through Pakistan. Thus, Pakistan believes the only potential military action available to India is air-strikes against Islamist training camps, which itself is not a serious problem, and may actually help Islamabad by killing destabilising jihadists while generating massive support among Pakistanis for their government. The dual problems of nuclear escalation and American reliance on Pakistan for counter-insurgency meant that following terrorist attacks in Mumbai by Pakistani group Lashkar-e-Taiba on 26 November 2008, which killed 163 people, India was unable to respond with conventional military strikes. Any attack by India might either destabilise the Pakistani Government, or escalate the conflict to nuclear exchange. In the event of state disintegration, Pakistani nuclear weapons could fall into the hands of militant elements who would attempt to use those weapons against India or the West.

Unfortunately, there is no easy path to stabilising reform within Pakistan. Pakistan essentially has a feudal political establishment, run by a civilian aristocracy of wealthy agricultural landowners and industrialists, and the Army. The civilian political parties primarily function as patronage networks, without deep-seated ideological differences, and merely struggle to control state resources. As a key aim of the agricultural and industrial élites is to avoiding paying income taxes, the Pakistani Government is also chronically in debt. The Army is seen by most Pakistanis as the primary defender of the nation and the ultimate guarantor of domestic stability. The ever-present threat of India is used to justify the Army's disproportionate share of national resources, and the Army itself also owns and manages a large agricultural and industrial empire. Domestically, the Army is the ultimate power-broker between the political parties, and has acted on several occasions to remove the party in power. As successive governments have received bailouts from international financial institutions, neither the civilian political élites nor the Army have felt any real incentive to institute fundamental change.

For the time-being, the Army is objectively the most stable and responsible force to control the country. The Pakistani military is the only state institution that works effectively, and without it Pakistan would probably have disintegrated long ago. The dire alternatives are representatives of the rising wave of radical Islam who arose from the madrassas under the patronage of General Zia ul-Haq, and gained their training in the US-backed *mujahedeen* struggle against the Soviet occupation of Afghanistan. These elements, and more recent jihadist recruits, are currently involved in Kashmiri terrorist organisations like Jaysh-e-Mohammad, and Lashkar-e-Taiba, as well as in the Afghani and Pakistani Taliban which occupy Pakistan's border provinces. While the Pakistani Army and intelligence services are often unwilling to directly challenge these forces (and, indeed, currently cultivate relations with the Kashmiri groups and the Afghani Taliban), and external (and, particularly, American) attempts to move forces into Pakistani territory would almost certainly make things worse, this unstable situation is likely to continue.

As India's power increases, so will its ability to strategically encircle Pakistan, through relations with Iran and Afghanistan, and via naval power. At the same time, India's patience for Pakistan's continuing terrorist provocations will probably lessen. Nevertheless, Pakistan's deterrent capabilities remain, as attacks on the Pakistani state – either unsuccessful or successful – are likely to result in either nuclear exchange or widespread chaos and bloodshed. If India continues restraint, however, and reaches out to more moderate elements within the military and civilian political parties, it could leverage its growing economic strength to gradually help a more moderate Pakistani state develop.

The Challenge of China

On a grander strategic level, relations between India and China will be highly significant as India emerges as a great power. There is a growing interdependence between the two Asian giants, as China is now India's number-one trading partner, with more than $52 billion in bilateral trade, and estimates are that China-India trade will surpass US-China trade by 2020. China's powerful manufacturing sector complements India's combination of a raw materials and cutting-edge technology economy. Strategically, a strong and influential India helps to create a more multipolar world, consistent with Chinese interests, although China increasingly regards India as its main Asian rival.

China is thus involved in a complex game of encirclement with India. China has armed Pakistan with nuclear weapons and ballistic missile technology, and has built 'strong military-to-military ties with Burma, Pakistan, Nepal, Bangladesh, and Sri Lanka as part of what Indians see as a strategy to tie India down, Gulliver-like, in its region.' China is also developing deep-water ports throughout the Indian Ocean to support its projected blue-water naval capacity.

Meanwhile, on the border, China continues to press its claims to vast tracts of Indian territory. Over the past years, increased friction in the border area between India and China has led to incursions by Chinese troops, the wounding of several Indian border police, and a build-up of military forces on both sides, as Beijing has been uncharacteristically assertive in its claims to sections of India's Arunachal Pradesh state. The Indians responded by moving 30,000 troops and their latest warplanes into the area, leading some analysts to predict a China-India war within five years.

China rejects the McMahon Line that forms the border, and places the traditional Sino-Indian border at the base of the Himalayan foothills. Stratfor's George Friedman argues that, for China, control of Tibet is of vital strategic importance, providing a barrier against its populous and economically and militarily-advancing neighbour.

The high mountain passes of Tibet provide virtually impenetrable terrain which is easy to protect militarily. Along the frontier directly south of this border, in India, is one of the largest population concentrations in the world. If China were to withdraw, Beijing fears that this population could migrate into Tibet, and Tibet could gradually turn into a beachhead for Indian power that would directly abut Sichuan and Yunnan provinces. The Chinese thus see control of Tibet as a matter of fundamental national security. They also see the 1959 decision by Indian Prime Minister Jawaharlal Nehru to give asylum to the Dalai Lama, and the continuing support for the Tibetan government-in-exile, as perpetuating this threat. Thus, 'Beijing's price for a border settlement and for normalisation of ties with India, appears to be that

India dismantle the Tibetan settlement in Dharamshala and request the Dalai Lama take up residence in another country.'

On a broader front, 80 per cent of China's oil and gas supplies transit the Indian Ocean and South China Sea, so the Chinese navy is increasingly making its presence felt in the area in order to secure its lines of supply. For China, like India, the steady flow of imported resources is not just an issue of economic growth, but also of the longevity of the Chinese Communist Party. Chinese leaders increasingly fear that adversaries could blockade sea lanes and strategic bottlenecks such as the Strait of Malacca, and are thus moving to an offshore defence policy that will include "distant ocean defence". China's actions, however, may impinge upon India's interests and destabilise relations.

Jason Blazevic argues that, following "defensive realist" strategies, each nation will attempt to gain power for self-preservation and other nations will see this move as a strategic threat, thus decreasing collective security. As part of this competition, China has been developing a so-called "string-of-pearls" strategy, expanding influence into ports in Burma, Sri Lanka and Pakistan.

According to a report by US defence contractor Booz Allen Hamilton, 'China is building strategic relationships along the sea lanes from the Middle East to the South China Sea in a way that suggests defensive and offensive positioning to protect China's energy interests.' China emerged as the biggest military spender in the Asia-Pacific in 2006, and now has the fourth-largest defence expenditure in the world. Its navy is also considered the third-largest in the world behind only the US and Russia, and is superior to the Indian Navy. In this context, India perceives Chinese actions as power maximisation, and fears that China's forward-basing strategy will be used to contain India and rapidly achieve hegemony in the Indian Ocean.

Meanwhile, China and India have adopted nuclear "assured retaliation" postures (what they sometimes refer to as "credible minimum deterrence"), which rely on a small but secure and survivable nuclear force that assures a retaliatory strike against a primary opponent. In many ways, this seems like the most stable aspect of the competition between India and China, though it is yet to be seen what reaction a new generation of *Surya* missiles might provoke in China. Meanwhile, analysts like Stephen Walt expect that China will follow a consistent but non-provocative build-up of its military capabilities and diplomatic alliances over the long-term, aiming to gradually edge the United States out of a hegemonic position. India is likely to mirror this build-up and thus tension, and possible low-level confrontation, may result on the India-China border and in the Indian Ocean region.

RISE OF MILITARY POWER PROJECTION IN INDIA

The range of foreign policy tools employed by independent India, military power projection may not come readily to mind. Indeed, the conventional wisdom is that India's traditional foreign policy orientation all but precludes projection of military power beyond its territory. Such a belief not only fails to appreciate India's past and likely future use of military power abroad, it also ignores the fungibility of military tools for projecting both "hard" and "soft" power.

In the past five years, all three branches of the Indian armed forces have articulated the need to be able to operate beyond India's borders. The navy's 2007 maritime strategy speaks repeatedly about the need to "project power" as a means of supporting foreign policy objectives and achieving national aims. In particular, the Indian Navy is keen to boost its ability to decisively influence military operations on land. For his part, when Air Chief Marshal S. P. Tyagi was chief of the Air Staff, he argued that India needed "a strategic reach to safeguard our national interests," while official statements note that the Indian Air Force "is increasingly used for power projection beyond South Asia."

Similarly, a local defense analyst reports, "[T]he Indian Air Force's revised war doctrine envisages its transformation into an aerospace power capable of conducting full-spectrum operations and extending its strategic reach from the Persian Gulf to the Strait of Malacca."

Even the traditionally inward-looking army is reportedly focusing on expeditionary warfare, with discussions at a recent infantry commanders' conference focused on transforming the infantry into an "expeditionary force" for use in an "out of area contingency." Unsurprisingly, a number of analysts both inside and outside of India look at recent military acquisitions and perceive that

India has begun inducting power-projection platforms, such as aircraft carriers, nuclear-powered submarines, long-range combat aircraft with mid-air refueling capability and landing platform dock ships for expeditionary warfare and humanitarian missions and is also developing an intercontinental ballistic missile with a strike range in excess of 5,000 km—all with the collective aim of influencing events far from home.

Similarly, external observers such as Ashley Tellis contend that "India is slowly maturing into a conventional great power," while the *New York Times* has run headlines proclaiming the "Land of Gandhi Asserts Itself as Global Military Power."

Such language and actions certainly run counter to the traditional view of India's early leaders, who profoundly believed that "power, especially military power, was the cause of evil," as well as contemporary civil and military leaders who believe that India has little need to develop the capacity to project military force far beyond its borders. As one former joint secretary in the Ministry of Defence bluntly remarked to the author, "India does not believe in power projection." Similarly, a former cabinet minister discounted the notion that India would ever militarily intervene in another nation's internal affairs, with the remark that "India would never do a Grenada." Even some retired flag officers believe that India will never undertake out of area power projection, claiming the concept is "not in the Indian psyche."

Instead, it is often suggested that India seeks only to project "soft power"—the attractive qualities of its culture and society—abroad to gain influence without resorting to military force. The idea of projecting India's culture, religions, art, and political morality abroad has traction within the Indian government, and some officials go so far as to suggest that India will seek to become a "soft power superpower." In that vein, several recent academic studies of Indian "power projection" have tended to focus largely, or even exclusively, on the non-military aspects of India's efforts to influence neighboring regions.

Is India poised to become a "global military power" with the ability to forcibly "influen[ce] events far from home," or will it retain its well-documented allergy toward military power projection? As with many things in life, the truth lies somewhere between these two extremes. This article argues that, in the medium term, the limitations of political will and military capacity will prevent India from achieving some of the more ambitious power projection goals discussed by defense analysts and members of the strategic community.

On the other hand, this article demonstrates that the idea that India has rejected and will continue to reject military power projection is untenable. This latter view appears to be based on an incorrect understanding of both the concept of military power projection and the fungibility of military tools for the projection of both hard and soft power, as well as India's needs in a changing geopolitical environment. Moreover, the notion that power projection is alien to India's strategic thinking overlooks the fact that India has not hesitated to "sort out" its neighbours when New Delhi felt that its interests were threatened. In comparison to a superpower such as the U.S., India's power projection needs are limited, but they are nonetheless real. This article seeks to bring analytical clarity to the concept of military power projection in the Indian context and to explore the potential range of power projection capabilities India may possess in the coming years. To accomplish this goal, the article proceeds in three parts. First, the concept of military power projection is defined, and nine types of power projection missions are identified. Second, India's past use of power projection and future needs are briefly discussed in the light of contemporary strategic priorities.

The final section discusses the utility of each of the three components of conventional military power (sea, air, and land) to fulfil the nine missions and examines India's potential power projection capability in these three areas. Given the previously noted focus by other scholars on Indian soft power projection, this article focuses solely on the use of military tools to shape political events abroad.

EXAMINING MILITARY POWER PROJECTION

To some, the phrase "power projection" suggests imposing regime change on a state far away from home for strategic gain. In this view, a prototypical example might be Operation Iraqi Freedom, the 2003 U.S.-led invasion of Iraq. While such a conceptualization captures some key elements of power projection, it is far too narrow. The U.S. Department of Defense (DoD) defines power projection much more broadly as being "[t]he ability of a nation to apply all or some of its elements of national power—political, economic, informational, or military—to rapidly and effectively deploy and sustain forces in and from multiple dispersed locations to respond to crises, to contribute to deterrence, and to enhance regional stability."

Focusing specifically on the final element of national power in the DoD's definition—the use of military tools—it is possible to disaggregate military power projection into nine different aspects based on the political goals being sought and the level of force employed. Four of these relate to the employment of "soft" military power (securing sea lanes of communication, non-combatant evacuation operations, humanitarian relief, and peacekeeping), and five are primarily concerned with "hard" military power (showing the flag, compellence/deterrence, punishment, armed intervention, and conquest).

Soft Military Power Projection

Securing Sea Lanes of Communication. The protection of shipping lanes from attack by hostile states or irregular threats. As the Indian Navy's maritime doctrine notes, trade is increasingly critical to the Indian economy, which makes the protection of the sea lanes transiting the Indian Ocean a significant priority. Following the attacks of September 11, 2001, the Indian Navy played a high-profile role in escorting U.S. shipping through the Straits of Malacca.

More recently, Indian naval vessels have been deployed to the Gulf of Aden, where they have thwarted several attempted hijackings by pirates.

Non-combatant Evacuation Operations. The evacuation of Indian or friendly third country civilians from a foreign country when they are endangered by war or civil unrest. For example, during Operation Sukoon (Urdu: Relief) the navy evacuated 2,280 Indian, Sri Lankan, and Nepalese civilians from Lebanon ahead of the 2006 Israeli-Hizbollah War. Several orders of magnitude larger was the airlift of over 100,000 Indians from Iraq and Kuwait ahead of the 1991 Gulf War.

Humanitarian Relief. The use of military forces abroad to assist in the aftermath of a natural disaster. Following the 2004 Asian tsunami, the Indian Navy mobilized 32 ships and over 20,000 naval personnel to evacuate casualties, as well as provide emergency sources of power and water to the peoples of Sri Lanka, the Maldives, Indonesia, Thailand, and Malaysia.

Peacekeeping. Military operations designed to support diplomatic efforts to reach a long-term political settlement to an ongoing dispute. India has been one of the most significant contributors to U.N. peacekeeping missions. As of 2009, the Indian Army had roughly 8,000 personnel deployed in the Democratic Republic of Congo, Lebanon, East Timor, the Ivory Coast, and the Golan Heights.

Hard Military Power Projection

Showing the Flag. The symbolic deployment of military forces to a region to demonstrate political interest, resolve, or willingness to take more forceful military action. For example, in June 1987 the Indian Air Force violated Sri Lankan airspace when it undertook Operation Poomalai (Tamil: Garland), the forced airdrop of relief supplies to ethnic Tamils during the siege of Jaffna.

This action sent a clear message to the government in Colombo about New Delhi's desire to see a negotiated end to the conflict and helped lead to the signing of the Indo-Sri Lankan accord. More recently, the Indian Navy has undertaken several high-profile deployments to the South China Sea and the Persian Gulf, which have been interpreted as important signals of Indian interest in these regions.

Compellence and Deterrence. The use or the threat of military force against another state to induce it into or dissuade it from pursuing a given policy. In this form, power projection acts as a diplomatic tool, attempting to influence the decision-making process and calculus of foreign actors. For example, the governor of East Pakistan's decision to surrender to India in 1971 has been attributed to the compellence effect of well-timed air strikes on his residence in Dhaka at the very moment he was conducting a crisis response meeting. In the same conflict, the destruction of East Pakistani airfields after the air force in the territory had been attritted was an exercise in deterrence by denial that sought to preclude intervention by an outside power.

Punishment. The punitive use of force against another state in response to its pursuit of a given policy. Aside from limited punitive strikes on Pakistani posts across the Line of Control in Kashmir in response to militant activity (not an expeditionary use of force), punishment has not been widely employed by the Indian military.

Armed Intervention. The forcible movement of military units into another nation's territory to influence the internal affairs of the target country, short of outright conquest. Historical examples in India's immediate neighborhood range in size from the 1988 deployment of a parachute battalion to the Maldives (Operation Cactus) to put down a coup to the 1971 intervention in East Pakistan by three corps of the Indian Army to assist guerillas fighting for independence.

Conquest. The offensive use of military assets to forcibly occupy non-contiguous territory controlled or claimed by another state.

This has not been an aspect of power projection pursued by independent India, although at the time some observers believed that the use of military forces in Hyderabad (Operation Polo), Goa (Operation Vijay), and elsewhere as part of the post-Independence consolidation of the Indian Union was "an act of military aggression and conquest."

Given this disaggregation, it is clear that power projection is a much broader concept than mere invasion seeking regime change. Military assets, depending on how they are employed, can advance a state's foreign policy goals by facilitating the projection of either hard or soft forms of military power. Moreover, since Independence, India has employed at least seven, and perhaps eight, of the nine aspects of military power projection.

INDIA'S CONVENTIONAL MILITARY AND POWER PROJECTION

The three varieties of conventional military power—sea power, air power, and land power—all contribute to power projection in different ways. As Table 1 indicates, sea power has a high degree of fungibility across various power projection missions and will likely form the foundation of India's global reach in coming years. This is particularly true in India's "extended neighborhood," since the region stretching "across [Asia's] sub-regions—be it East Asia, West Asia, Central Asia, South Asia or Southeast Asia" is largely a maritime domain. In contrast, air and land power play more limited, but nonetheless important, roles in India's power projection capabilities.

Sea Power

In light of the fact that roughly 90% of India's external trade by volume and 77% by value is seaborne, Indian maritime power has a role to play in sustaining domestic economic development. Indeed, a host of observers dating back to the pre-Independence period has argued that India's economy is "at the mercy of the power which controls the sea." In the northern Indian Ocean, securing sea lanes of communication will be facilitated by the Indian Navy's ability to exercise "sea denial" (negating an enemy's ability to use the sea but at the same time making no attempt to control the sea itself) in a region stretching from the Arabian Sea in the west to the Straits of Malacca in the east. Moreover, as India looks farther away for energy resources, its political and military leaders are explicitly linking this effort with the need for the Indian military, particularly the navy, to be able to "protect the country's economic and energy interests" in key parts of the Indian Ocean.

Aircraft carriers, surface ships and submarines equipped with land-attack cruise missiles, and amphibious landing ships—the latter of which are discussed with land power below—are the key maritime power projection platforms that can influence events on land from the sea. While submarines can rely on stealth to approach an enemy coastline, task forces of cruisemissile-armed surface platforms, amphibious assault ships, and aircraft carriers require the assistance of attack submarines, maritime patrol aircraft, and modern destroyers to protect them from hostile submarines, aircraft, and anti-ship cruise missiles. Tankers and supply ships sustain maritime forces with food, fuel, and ammunition when operating a significant distance from friendly ports.

In 2008, then-Chief of Naval Staff Admiral Sureesh Mehta foresaw that the navy of 2020 would be "capable of influencing the outcome of land battles and performing a constabulary role in the Indian Ocean region." Achieving this will require a significant upgrade in capabilities. Naval planners envision a three-carrier fleet as the cornerstone of India's future blue-water navy: the 44,500-ton, Russian-built INS *Vikramaditya* (Sanskrit: Brave as the Sun) which is expected to join the fleet after 2012, and two domestically built aircraft carriers of the Vikrant class weighing in at 40,000 tons (INS *Vikrant*) (Sanskrit: Powerful) and 64,000 tons (INS *Vishal*) (Sanskrit: Great), scheduled to enter service in 2015 and 2018, respectively. At the same time, the introduction of the fourth-generation supersonic MiG-29K Fulcrum provides India with the most powerful naval strike aircraft in the region and increases its force projection capacity by an order of magnitude.

However, these optimistic projections mask a dark reality: at present India's existing 28,000-ton aircraft carrier, launched in 1953, is on its last legs. Should the induction of the *Vikramaditya* or the *Vikrant* be delayed beyond the middle of the decade, as some informed observers speculate, the navy could find itself without a carrier for several years. At the same time, only 11 of the 30 Mk. 51 Sea Harrier fighters that were in service in the 1980s remain, and at the time of this writing, there is yet to be a test flight of the naval version of Hindustan Aeronautics Limited's domestically designed Tejas lightweight fighter, which is supposed to replace the Harriers in providing air defense to the carriers.

Furthermore, the *Vikramaditya* and the *Vikrant* will carry only 16 fighters each. Assuming that the bigger *Vishal* will accommodate a larger complement of aircraft (50–60), analysts say it would have to operate in tandem with one of the 40,000-ton carriers to produce "as much striking power as a single U.S. Nimitz-class carrier. Even armed with precision-guided munitions, a contingent of this size could sustain only a modest land bombardment, and only for a modest time."

Moreover, a three-carrier fleet will only ensure that the navy has at least one carrier at sea at all times, given the repair, training, and deployment cycles for modern naval vessels. To be able to implement Admiral Mehta's constabulary role in the Indian Ocean, the navy would need to have the ability to maintain two carriers at sea at all times, which would suggest a need for twice as many flattops. With an estimated unit cost of $1.5 billion, against an annual naval procurement budget of $2.3 billion, building each additional carrier over six or seven years could easily tie up 9% to 11% of the acquisition budget per platform, making a rapid expansion of the fleet unlikely.

The Indian Navy's surface-strike capability centers on the 290-kilometerrange supersonic BraMos cruise missile. A joint venture between Russia and India, the BraMos can achieve Mach 2.5 speed, which is three times faster than the U.S. Tomahawk cruise missile. While highly effective in an anti-shipping role, the BraMos is less useful as a land-attack weapon because it possesses only one-tenth the range of the U.S. Tomahawk.

This latter characteristic is also true of the land-attack variants of the Russian-designed 3M-54 Klub cruise missile (275 kilometer range) also in service with the Indian Navy. The relatively short range of these missiles would render surface-launched cruise missile strikes against a state with even modest anti-access capability (attack submarines, anti-ship missiles, or supporting surveillance systems) a risky proposition. According to published reports, the Defence Research and Development Organization is currently developing a subsonic cruise missile with a reported range of 1,000 kilometres. Code named *Nirbhay* (Sanskrit: Fearless), it could fill an important gap in the navy's land-attack capability. However, test flights of the missile have been repeatedly delayed.

Finally, the Indian Navy's ability to project maritime power in the Indian Ocean and beyond is constrained by the fact that it is currently decommissioning surface ships faster than it is adding them. At present, large portions of India's fleet of 57 surface combatants, including five of its eight destroyers and seven of its 11 frigates, are approaching the end of their service life. The navy requires these types of platforms, equipped with advanced anti-aircraft and anti-submarine systems, to operate in hostile littorals. Moreover, to achieve a real power projection capability, the navy will require several additional fleet replenishment tankers and modern replacements for its cadre of Soviet-era minesweepers.

Air Power

Air power projection comes mainly in two forms: strikes against ground-based targets and the transport of ground troops. Since the latter role is primarily a supporting one, it is taken up in the discussion of land power below. As a tool for power projection, the use or threat of air power is primarily used for compellence/deterrence or to punish another state, should the initial efforts fail to bring about a desired policy change. Affecting targets at a range beyond a few hundred miles requires advanced strike aircraft (typically operating in conjunction with refueling tanker aircraft) capable of penetrating enemy air defenses, longer-range cruise missiles, or ballistic missiles.

The chief of the Air Staff, Air Chief Marshal F. H. Major, has argued that Indian air power needs "a strategic reach to safeguard our national interests," which requires a "long-range presence, persistence and 'forward-basing arrangements'." In this vein, the IAF's revised war doctrine is reportedly structured around "both pre-emptive action and swift retaliation" across a region stretching from the Persian Gulf to the Straits of Malacca. However, the air force has long suffered from the piecemeal acquisition of aircraft, and much of its fleet is facing obsolescence—raising questions about future combat power.

Nonetheless, the IAF has pushed for an independent strategic role in future conflict, arguing that air power can influence the battle space through deep-strike missions. The air force "aims to achieve this objective by operating advanced, long-range platforms with air-to-air refueling capability" and "must be equipped for long-reach, persistence, all-weather, precision, air dominance, networked, and space-enabled force capabilities." Most notable in this regard are efforts to induct long-range strike aircraft—particularly 272 fourth-generation Sukhoi Su-30s.

The combination of SU-30s with precision-guided munitions, such as the AS-14 air-to-surface missile, would produce a significant ability to strike targets across the immediate neighborhood. Even though long-range strike Sukhoi aircraft are quite capable, their ability to operate at a significant distance depends on the IAF's in-flight refueling capability. Although the IAF does have six IL-78MKI Midas tanker aircraft (which doubles the Sukhoi's range to 6,000 kilometres), this only amounts to, in the words of one retired air marshal, "baby steps towards acquiring the capability of projecting combat power in the region.

At this point in time, the capability is limited to a token force and cannot be described as significant." In this regard, the IAF's hope to acquire an additional six new Airbus Military A330 Multi-Role Tanker Transports is a positive step. However, to support an expeditionary strike package of 60 aircraft, which would provide a modest ground-attack capability against multiple targets, at least 15 IL-78/A330 tankers would be required, notwithstanding the need for reserves or simultaneous capability in other areas. If the entire fleet of Sukhois were to be so supported, the IAF would require nearly 60 tanker aircraft. Beyond existing procurement plans, achieving the capability to support 60 Sukhois with tankers would require an additional \$1.13 billion, while equipping the entire fleet would cost \$11.7 billion, against an annual IAF procurement budget of \$4.19 billion.

Strike aircraft are not the only way that offensive air power can contribute to compellence/deterrence or punishment type power projection missions. Given the simultaneously increasing lethality of air defense systems and the cost of combat aircraft, India may instead increasingly rely on surface-tosurface missiles for "deep strike against heavily defended targets in depth, such as airfields." This could presage an increased role for India's ballistic missile forces, which just saw the 3,000-kilometer range Agni III approved for induction into the army. The follow-on 6,000-kilometer range Agni V intercontinental ballistic missile is expected to be tested in 2011. While these missiles are commonly associated with India's strategic nuclear program, they could be employed in a conventional role if necessary, thus having potentially coercive effects on neighboring powers.

Land Power

The employment of expeditionary land power requires the facilitation of airlift or sealift capabilities, as well as specially trained forces (such as airborne troops or marines), long-range command and control capabilities, and a significant logistical ability to support and sustain troops once an initial landing has been made.

The chief of Army Staff, General Deepak Kapoor, had argued that "in keeping with our growing regional aspirations," the army needed to develop the capability to deploy ground forces for an out of area operation. In that vein, at a 2009 infantry commanders' conference, the army's senior leadership explored the idea of transforming into an "expeditionary force" capable of responding to an overseas contingency on short notice.

Although such capability may be required to fulfil U.N. peacekeeping obligations, there is some evidence that senior army leaders have been pressing for an increased overseas presence, "even outside the U.N. banner." "Given its emerging regional power status," one former Indian flag officer contends, "India may be called upon to project power in the region, which may involve airlift of large military forces to areas of interest . . . outside of our borders and [the capability] to provide sustained logistic support."

This would, in turn, require a substantial expansion of the country's strategic airlift capability, which some argue is virtually nonexistent. Lacking sufficient assets to suppress air defenses, some analysts believe that India's transports lack the ability to operate in hostile air environments. However, other observers contend that India has sufficient civilian airlift capacity to move and sustain up to a brigade of troops in a permissive environment—provided there is access to secure airfields.

The strategic reach provided by heavy airlift also has utility in noncombatant evacuation operations and humanitarian relief missions. In 1991 the IAF, along with civil air assets, played a key role in evacuating 100,000 Indian nationals from the Persian Gulf ahead of the Gulf War. More recently, India's airlift capabilities have reached across the extended neighborhood to ferry supplies and humanitarian aid during crises in venues from Lebanon to China.

For future power projection, Brigadier Gurmeet Kanwal (Retd.), the head of the Indian Army's principal think tank, the Centre for Land Warfare Studies, argues that India requires a dedicated air assault brigade by early 2012. The

Agra-based 50th (Independent) Parachute Brigade might form the core of an air assault capability. But such a unit would require extensive organic fire support in the form of Lancer and Hind attack helicopters, to compensate for the lack of artillery possessed by such highly mobile troops. Moreover, the ability to move such a force in a rapid reaction scenario would require a significant increase of airlift capability. The IAF is rumored to be interested in buying 10 Boeing C-17s for heavy lift. However, moving a single battalion 2,000 kilometres in one day to respond to a crisis in the immediate neighborhood, as was done during the 1988 coup in the Maldives, would necessitate a lift capacity of 19 C-17 equivalents. Furthermore, the ability to do so with an entire brigade would require 55 C-17 equivalents. Although the former is notionally within the capacity of present airlift assets, questions persist about the condition of these aircraft, raising doubts about the military's capacity in an emergency. Achieving the latter target by 2012 appears unrealistic because acquiring the equivalent of 55 C-17s would cost an estimated $9.1 billion, not including spare parts and maintenance. Against an IAF procurement budget of $4.19 billion, even if these aircraft were phased in over the next decade, it would still tie up 20% of the IAF's annual budget for new transport aircraft for the period.

In terms of amphibious lift, the navy's present ability to move 3,000 troops plus vehicles and equipment is centered on the INS *Jalashva* (Sanskrit: Sea Horse), a 16,900-ton, American-built Landing Platform Dock (LPD) that can transport nearly 1,000 soldiers and six medium helicopters. Acquired in 2007, the *Jalashva* addresses India's lack of heavy sea-lift and mass-landing capability, while also providing a potential command-and control platform for fleet operations in an amphibious landing or emergency response scenario. There is great interest in acquiring more LPDs through a combination of foreign acquisition and indigenous development. The present complement of Magar-class Landing Ship Tanks—which can transport 500 men or 15 armored vehicles—will be supplemented by four new amphibious assault ships.

In line with these developments, a joint doctrine for amphibious warfare was developed by the tri-service Integrated Defence Staff and tested in exercises in 2005 and 2007. Earlier this year, the army formally stood up a dedicated amphibious brigade, the 3,000-man 91 Infantry Brigade based at Thiruvananthapuram, which is expected to form the core of a larger amphibious force in the future. The navy has expressed a desire to double the size of its own Marine Commando Force, which focuses on maritime counterterrorism operations and offshore raids, from its present strength of 2,000. Yet, such efforts will likely be hindered by budgetary constraints.

The *Jalashva,* operating together with one of the new carriers and a pair of Landing Ship Tanks, provides roughly the same size amphibious force as a typical U.S. Marine Expeditionary Unit in terms of deployable troops, armored vehicles, fighter aircraft, and helicopters. With proper logistical support and training, this force could provide India with an expeditionary intervention force that could respond to contingencies or crises of limited scope or duration in its "extended neighborhood." As with the carrier battle groups, the ability to operate close to hostile shores requires assistance from surface vessels with advanced anti-submarine and anti-aircraft capabilities. Should the Indian military reach its target amphibious lift capacity of 10,000 personnel, which would require both new amphibious platforms and more amphibious-ready troops, New Delhi would notionally be able to mount an operation like the 1983 U.S. intervention in Grenada. Similarly, it could respond to a major humanitarian crisis or non-combatant evacuation mission. This would go a long way toward Admiral Mehta's stated goal of playing a constabulary role in the Indian Ocean littoral region.

The army's ability to conduct expeditionary operations is no doubt enhanced by its long history of involvement in U.N. peacekeeping missions, which provides practical experience in small-unit operations as well as support functions: intelligence, medical, logistics, transportation, and engineering. However, one should not take the parallel too far because traditional peacekeeping operations are conducted in more-benign environments— which makes deployment, logistical support, and intelligence gathering significantly easier.

WILL INDIA PROJECT MILITARY POWER IN THE FUTURE?

There is good reason to believe that India will have at least as great a need for military power projection in the future as it has in the past. New Delhi's primary strategic priority over the next decade—deepening internal consolidation— requires sustained economic development and enhanced internal security. This, in turn, is at least partially dependent on developments in the country's immediate neighborhood. As current National Security Advisor Shivshankar Menon has argued, "[U]nless we have a peaceful and prosperous periphery, we will not be able to focus on our primary tasks of socioeconomic development." Furthermore, the achievement of regional peace and stability in South Asia will be a necessary precondition for India to claim great-power status.

Unfortunately, many of the countries on India's periphery are weak or fragile states. For example, *Foreign Policy* magazine's 2010 index of failed states included five of India's neighbours (Afghanistan, Pakistan, Bangladesh, Burma, and Sri Lanka) in the top 25. Although many of the challenges plaguing India's immediate neighborhood are political and economic in nature, and therefore not necessarily directly amenable to solutions based on the application of conventional military power, New Delhi may periodically require the ability to shape events in these countries that military power projection provides.

Further afield, successive political leaders in India have identified the arc from the Persian Gulf to the Straits of Malacca as "a legitimate area of interest . . . for the first quarter of the 21st century." As a result, the Indian Navy's maritime strategy states that "whatever happens in the [Indian Ocean littoral region] can affect our national security and is of interest to us." India's interests in this region are largely economic in nature, with energy access and growing regional economic engagement meshing with concerns about the safety of ships transiting the entire Indian Ocean littoral. In recent years, official statements have been increasingly blunt about the importance India attaches to energy security, which is deemed "vital for an assured high rate of [economic] growth." At present India imports over half of its natural gas and 70% of its oil, the vast majority of which comes from the Persian Gulf. Over the next 20 years, India's oil consumption is expected to grow at an annual rate of 5% to 7%—more than three times the global average rate of increase—which will more than double present day consumption by 2025. To sustain its high rates of economic growth, India must secure access to new sources of hydrocarbon energy.

The ability to influence events in this broader region may take on increasing importance as India's comprehensive national power grows. Scholars of international relations argue that as a state's wealth and material power increase, it "will select a larger bundle of security and welfare goals than a less wealthy and less powerful state." In terms of foreign policy preferences, scholars also argue that rising powers have generally sought to expand their spheres of influence— as state power increases, so do political interests abroad. This expanded material capacity and broadening of political interests are expected to translate into an increased interest in favourably shaping the state's strategic environment. Therefore, it is reasonable to assume that India will have at least the same level of need for power projection missions going forward as it has in the past. It will, in fact, most likely make increased use of such tools in the future.

The New Delhi has already employed its power projection assets to provide regional public goods (e.g., humanitarian relief, non-combatant evacuation operations, and securing sea lanes of communication) in parts of the Indian Ocean littoral in a manner befitting a regional hegemon. One key difference between great powers and other states is that great powers create external security for their region beyond merely protecting their own borders. Any country can have regional interests, but great powers also have regional responsibilities. As the dominant regional power in South Asia and an aspirant to a seat on the U.N. Security Council, India is likely to be called on in the future to take an increased role in ensuring international peace and security, either under U.N. auspices or as a part of various multilateral coalitions. While some in New Delhi may hope India can free-ride to great-power status, including ducking hard decisions and avoiding shouldering a burden, this status is unlikely to be achieved without bearing more responsibility. It is not possible to precisely identify in advance the specific contingencies that could compel India to project hard military power abroad, but, beyond the historical instances already noted, India may find several additional reasons to send its armed forces beyond its borders.

Future Military Roles

Support Forces Deployed on Peacekeeping Missions. It is hardly inconceivable that Indian peacekeepers (or those of friendly nations) could be targeted by belligerent parties during the course of their duties, thus potentially requiring a forcible extraction or rescue operations along the lines of Operation Khukri in Sierra Leone, where Indian forces rescued 230 U.N. peacekeepers who had been held hostage for over 75 days by the rebels of the Revolutionary United Front. Because India's local U.N. partners in the region were too weak to respond effectively, the success of this operation depended in large part on the rapid introduction of a battalion of Indian grenadiers and para-commandos airlifted directly from the Kashmir Valley, as well as a flight of Indian Air Force (IAF) attack helicopters.

Protecting Indians Abroad. Several recent events highlight the increasing salience of this issue. Following the 2000 coup in Fiji that ousted Prime Minister Mahendra Chaudhry, an ethnic Indian, there was significant pressure on the Indian government to take steps to protect Fiji's large Indian community. However, the lack of naval capacity rendered such an operation impossible. Of even more concern are the five million Indians employed in the Persian Gulf. A contingency in this region is hardly unthinkable, given the 1991 and 2006 emergencies that required major evacuations of Indian nationals from conflict zones.

Prevent Open Hostility from Immediate Neighbours. Aside from the domestic pressure brought by ethnic Tamils within India, the geopolitical imperative behind India's 1987 intervention in Sri Lanka was to preempt intervention in the conflict by an extra-regional power. Although the Sri Lankan conflict has ended, the imperative remains. If, for example, a neighboring country such as Burma were poised to emerge as a full-fledged satellite of China, New Delhi might feel compelled to act to protect its own interests.

Recognizing that India will likely have an increased need and desire for power projection in the future is not the same as arguing it will employ these capabilities indiscriminately around the globe. Such operations will still have to be in response to a threat to a vital national interest and have significant support from the population, if not, ideally, the international community. Nonetheless, these instances are likely to increase as India gains in international stature.

ALTERNATIVE REGIONAL STRATEGY FOR INDIA: EXPLORING SOFT POWER OPTIONS

In the SAARC summit held in October 2011 at Maldives the members of the SAARC unequivocally agreed to focus their effort on building connectivity across the region in order to enhance regional cooperation on energy and economic development. Although the Summit emphasised various issues, what it projects for India is the prospect for a leadership role in the region. For this, India needs to develop an alternative strategy that would accommodate its neighbour's politico-security concerns while building consensus on vital issues affecting the regional stability.

As an epicentre of South Asia, in terms of economic prosperity and political stability, India can play a pivotal role through building bridges across the region, which will not only benefit the region's economy but also enhance its "benign power" image. Building such an image requires soft power skills. India shares strong cultural, religious, historical, and ethnic linkages with many countries in the region. But, these linkages have only been adversely revived so far by the vested interest groups in order to reinforce the discord with its neighbours.

Much of its foreign policy strategy which is focused on its neighbours for safeguarding territorial integrity and national sovereignty is also dependent upon its hard power potentials such as military assets. It is only in the recent times, perhaps after the 9/11 that India has realized the significance of soft power in diplomacy, which is essential to win the hearts and minds of the people.

In the South Asian context, the concept of soft power per se operates very intricately. For instance, countries of this region share the so-called soft power resources of culture and values but they hardly harness such resources for shared prosperity and stability. One reason could be the animosity created out of shared historical experiences and cross ethno-political cleavages that ripped apart the region geographically. However, the process of globalization and information revolution has dramatically changed the politico-security environment of South Asia where the cost of attractiveness outweighs the cost of coercion in the big power's diplomacy.

VISION 2020

Modernising for an Era of Strategic Uncertainty

In the prevailing era of strategic uncertainty, while terrorism is gradually becoming the primary threat, the external and internal threats and challenges faced by India are such that a large army is still required to be maintained. Also, a high degree of preparation and operational readiness are still necessary as conventional war, though improbable, cannot be categorically ruled out due to unresolved territorial and boundary disputes with China and Pakistan. At the same time, heavy capital investments in modern defence equipment are undoubtedly a drain on a developing economy that is ill equipped to handle the burgeoning defence expenditure. Several eminent analysts have recommended that qualitative upgradation should be accompanied by quantitative downsizing of personnel strength of the army to generate funds for modernisation. However, given its responsibilities for border management and the manpower-intensive sub-conventional operations that the army is involved in—this is easier said than done.

Future conventional conflict on the Indian sub-continent will in all probability result from the ongoing low-intensity limited war on the Line of Control (LoC) with Pakistan or the unresolved territorial and boundary dispute with China and will be predominantly a land conflict. The Indian Army lacks a potent firepower punch, especially in the mountain sector. Precision-guided munitions (PGMs) have still to enter service in numbers large enough to make a real difference.

The reconnaissance, surveillance and target acquisition (RSTA) assets necessary for the optimum exploitation of even the existing firepower assets are grossly inadequate. Automated command and control and decision support systems have been on the drawing boards for several decades but are yet to mature. According to former Vice Chief of Army Staff Lieutenant General (Retd.) Noble Thamburaj, the modernization focus of the 11th Defence Plan is on "precision fire power, air defence, aviation, Future Infantry Soldier as a System, infrastructure development, network centricity and achieving battlefield transparency through improved surveillance, night vision and target acquisition.... Considering the receding span of technological cycle, (the) right balance has to be maintained between state-of-art, current and obsolescent technologies."

Main Battle Tanks: T-90S replaces Arjun

On Army Day 2010, Chief of the Army Staff General Deepak Kapoor admitted that a large number of India's battle tanks are 'night blind'. The indigenously designed Arjun main battle tank (MBT) has been in the pipeline for over two decades. Though the tank has many good features, it has consistently failed to meet the army's General Staff Qualitative Requirements for an MBT and orders have been placed for only 124 tanks to be manufactured.

The Defence Research and Development Organization (DRDO) had been repeatedly pressing for comparative trials of the Arjun with the T-72M1 and the T-90S. Success in these trials has led to orders being placed for another 124 Arjun MBTs. Since the lack of progress on the Arjun MBT had significantly slowed down the pace of armour modernization, in 2000, India signed a deal with Russia to acquire 310 T-90S tanks and assemble 1,000 in India.

In 2008, the Ministry of Defence (MoD) decided to acquire another 347 T-90S tanks. The first India assembled T-90S (Bhishma) rolled off the production line on January 8, 2004. Ultimately, "The army's future armour profile could comprise approximately 1,700 T-90S, 1,800 upgraded T-72M1 and 250 to 500 Arjuns." Almost 1,800 T-72M1 (Ajeya) tanks are still awaiting modernisation. The lack of a suitable fire control system and night fighting capability are major handicaps. The upgradation of 500 to 600 of these has now commenced "at the rate of 200 tanks per year". The upgrade package includes a new fire control system comprising a TISAS (thermal imaging stand alone systems) night sight and TIFCS (tank integrated fire control system), new TADIRAN radios, a gyro-based navigation system and a Laser warning system. The ability to fire on the move is being improved with a better stabilization system. An add-on ERA (explosive reactive armour) package will enhance protection against APFSDS and HEAT rounds. Eventually, the T-90S 1,000 hp power pack, de-rated to 850 hp, will be retro-fitted.

The problem of defective indigenous ammunition is still to be resolved. The DRDO has commenced conceptual stage development of Future Main battle Tank and Future Infantry Combat vehicle for the 2020-25 time-frame. T-90S Russian tanks have provided new teeth to India's strike formations in the plains and corrected the imbalance that had resulted from Pakistan's acquisition of T-80 UD from Ukraine and the Al Khalid tanks jointly designed with China. Hence, armour modernization is proceeding apace but cannot yet be classified as a success story.

Generating firepower asymmetries

In a future conventional war that will be fought under the nuclear shadow, manoeuvre will be extremely limited. This restriction will lead to much greater emphasis being placed on firepower to achieve the laid down military aim. Hence, it is imperative that artillery modernization is undertaken with alacrity so as to generate firepower asymmetries on the future battlefield. After a long spell of keeping the powder dry, action on modernization of the Indian Artillery is livening up once again.

Beginning in January 2008, the MOD issued three global tenders for 155 mm guns and howitzers for the mountains, the plains and self-propelled guns for the deserts. Summer and winter trials were expected to be held over the next one year and it was anticipated that contracts would be awarded as early as in the first half of 2010. However, none of the manufacturers have as yet been invited for trials. It is a well-established fact that potent artillery firepower had turned the tide and eventually paved the way for victory during the Kargil conflict. Despite the lessons learnt in Kargil, modernization of the artillery has continued to lag behind. The last major acquisition of towed gunhowitzers was that of about 400 pieces of 39-calibre 155 mm FH-77B howitzers with a range of 30 km from Bofors of Sweden in the mid-1980s.

This gun had proved its mettle in the Kargil conflict. After two decades of neglect during which the 100 mm and 122 mm field guns of Russian origin and the indigenously developed and manufactured 75/24 Indian Mountain Gun joined the long list of equipment bordering on obsolescence but still in service with the army, tenders were floated and trials were held for a 52-calibre 155 mm gun to replace all field and medium guns. Just when a contract for 120 tracked and 180 wheeled self-propelled (SP) 155 mm guns was about to be concluded after years of protracted trials, South African arms manufacturer Denel, a leading contender for the contract, was alleged to have been involved in a corruption scam in an earlier deal for antimaterial rifles (AMRs).

The other two howitzers in contention, from Soltam of Israel and BAE (Bofors) of Sweden reportedly did not meet the laid down criteria and Army HQ recommended fresh trials, setting the programme back at least three to four years. Another bone of contention was that the howitzers that had been offered were technology demonstration models and not guns that were in actual service with the home country armies.

MODERNISING THE INDIAN INFANTRY

Why has it taken the Army so long to conceive an upgrade package for the oldest, most potent and intensely employed fighting arm, the Infantry, even after the so-called revolution in military affairs?

The foot soldier, the original and most versatile weapon system that is always taken for granted, has emerged from the dubious shock and awe strategy of recent campaigns as its ultimate arbiter. India has paid dearly for the neglect of its infantry in terms of cost, casualties and over-stretch of battle. But the Infantry has never let us down. Kargil was its finest hour. Gen VP Malik, the Army Chief of the time, wryly noted: "We will fight with what we have."

So when for the first time an international conference of Army and defence industry was launched last week to put the forgotten soldier centre-stage, some misgivings were natural. While Army Chief Gen JJ Singh outlined his vision for the soldier system of the future, the conspicuous and total absence of Government - MoD - robbed the conference of any sanctity. In sharp contrast, for a MoD-sponsored defence finance seminar earlier in the month, Government officials and ministers were stepping over each other at Vigyan Bhavan.

Free India's Army came into being in 1947 and within weeks, the Infantry soldiers landed in Srinagar to save J&K from being gobbled up by Pakistani tribal raiders. Since then, the Infantry has not ceased fighting proxy wars there and later, elsewhere too. A former Army Chief, Gen SR Choudhury, who was not from the Infantry, described the Infantry as the Army and vice versa. Field Marshal Montgomery said: An army is considered only as good as its Infantry.

The experience of four wars, several border skirmishes, two out-of-area missions, the ceaseless campaign to counter cross-border terrorism in Kashmir, numerous other insurgencies in the North-East, internal stability operations elsewhere in the country and UN peace keeping operations make the Indian Infantry the most battle-hardened and combat rich force in the world.

The simple and uncomplaining infantryman has given so much to so many for so little. The modernisation of the infantry was first attempted - halfheartedly - in the mid-1980s by the Perspective Planning branch of the Army Headquarters. The bias for mechanised warfare, zealously pursued by Gen Sundarji, was so pronounced that the Infantry modernisation plan was skipped altogether. Guns, tanks, APCs were the weapons in demand. The Infantry was ignored. Had a modest upgrade package been undertaken at that time, infantry would have been more combat contemporary and effective.

Instead, till recently, some soldiers were still using World War II equipment and clothing. Shameful as it was, soldiers had to buy rucksacks and other accoutrements from the market. DRDO is still to come out with a light bulletproof vest. The Army failed to accurately visualize the nature of combat it would fight in the future. Pakistan-sponsored insurgency in Punjab did not alert the nation and the Army to the proxy war brewing in J&K. We defaulted on both counts - anticipating low intensity conflict and cross border terrorism and preparing the Infantry for it.

Despite the sustained counter-insurgency and counter-terrorism campaign in J&K and the North-East since the 1990s, the Army was sluggish in investing in the infantry. The first Gulf War reintroduced the fiction that wars could be won from the air.

The air campaigns in Bosnia and Kosovo temporarily turned fiction into reality. But 9/11 broke the myth of supremacy of air power. Operation Enduring Freedom in Afghanistan lasted 76 days; 65 of these were air operations.

The 11-day land offensive secured a temporary and incomplete victory against the Taliban. Operation Iraqi Freedom on the other hand, fought for 20 days was bereft of any preparatory air campaign though a secret air war preceded it. Unhappily for the US/NATO-led coalition forces, despite their pyrrhic military victories, low intensity wars in Afghanistan and Iraq are continuing in full blaze.

The recent 34-day war in Lebanon and the ongoing campaign in Gaza demonstrate the limits of Israel's military power. Used to decisive victories in less than 10 days, Israeli Defence Forces (IDF) were badgered by Hassan Nasrallah's jihadi militia. Reliance on air power, tanks and guns in Lebanon as substitute for ground troops - infantry - was motivated by casualty aversion. We too have to be sensitive to casualties.

The wars in Lebanon, Iraq and Afghanistan spurred by the growing cult of Osama bin Laden and Hassan Nasrallah require a redefinition of the concept of power and military success. Success would necessarily be an inclusive military victory encompassing post-conflict stability and reconstruction.

For this we need Infantry. The Indian Army should not get overly seduced by high-sounding warfare like 'netcentric' that the West is being diverted into. This is not to suggest we ignore the strides in high-tech warfare. But as a former US NATO Commander noted recently: "This netcentric stuff is great but our men in Baghdad are being blown up with their Humvees by IEDs." He suggested that we address the battle we are fighting before switching to the one we will fight in the future.

India's supreme operational challenge is and will be the maintenance of internal security. Just last month, Prime Minister Manmohan Singh stated this ground reality. The Infantry is at the heart of counterinsurgency and counter-terrorism operations and may well get sucked into anti-Naxal operations as well. Keeping the Army operationally ready for both conventional and unconventional missions is imperative but the emphasis has to be on the business of the day: CI and CT.

The Indian Infantry is belatedly embarking on a modernisation programme to enhance its combat skills through increased lethality, communications, surveillance, mobility and suvivability. These force multipliers will enable the soldier to fight all-weather, 24x7 and on any terrain in the right battle-configuration albeit with the accent on LIC.

The GSQR for the Future-Infantry-Soldier-As a System (F-INSAS) must empower not encumber the soldier. DRDO must compete with domestic and international industry. DRDO has one more chance to make amends for its omissions and commissions. F-INSAS must strike the right balance between the surge of technology and sensibility of the soldier keeping the battle of the future in mind. Defence Minister AK Antony should accord F-INSAS the highest strategic priority.

2020: DEFENDING INDIAN FORCE

The Flashpoint. NATO's Allied Force saw induction of more than 400 planes into the Balkan skies. Phase-I witnessed cruise missiles, F-117 Nighthawks, B-2 bombers, F-15/16 Eagles, F-16 Falcons and B-52 bombers which rolled in from as the diverse directions and places as Adriatic Sea, Missouri, Italy and England. With that Kosovo moved to a new level of misery.

The largest air attacks since WWII commenced on a country which does not threaten the global equilibrium nor its neighbours. And none know the precise exit strategy nor the endgame. However, this much is clear that the resultant giagantic refugee problem will heavily eat into the NATO manpower and resources for a long time to come.

Of late, unfortunately, the American foreign policy has been driven by ultimatums. Whenever, a disagreement occurs, the lone super power needs to deliver on such threats. But the air attacks without ground troops support cannot always win. So Osama bin Laden remains where he was. Saddam continues to visit his mistresses. And now NATO's credibility is up for grabs. The Balkans is likely to be the graveyard of air-attacks-alone theory. For history argues that a determined infantry cannot be evicted by massive air attacks. The Kosovo spillover will not only impact on the health of the EU, but also put a question mark on the American global dominance.

However, Americans are likely to continue with such ill-advised actions on a variety of flashpoints worldwide in a desperate attempt to disallow emerging new power equations. This will further tie down in knots the NATO credibility. Let's try to visualise how India can re-organise internally to meet the new challenges arising out of the deteriorating international scenario.

The Indian Faultline. This faultline can be traced back to the Mauryan empire's unwise decision of renouncing war. Like corporate graphs, the military power graph of a nation either gradually creeps upwards or if not in use, the law of gravity pulls it downwards! Thus unwittingly, in subsequent centuries the neglect of the military component resulted in unprecedented foreign invasions.

Incomprehension of the dynamics of military power by the subsequent rulers and the attempts to absorb, appease and amalgamate the invading armies put the foreign rulers at the seat of power in Delhi with ease. This is akin to allowing an adversary in a soccer match to dominate your half of the field.

Obviously goals will be scored. The other aspect of the Indian Faultline rests on the fact that majority of the Indian rulers employed the military power ruthlessly internally to pacify the outlying provinces (instead of attempting economic development) while refusing to correctly posture it to meet the threats from invasion.

This short sighted approach continued on India's attaining independence. Many elders (product of a similar mindset) tend to defend the actions of Indian political leadership of 1947 on singular ground of inexperience. One tends to disagree because all it needed was to review the historical evidence of foreign subjugation and the leadership would automatically have deduced the reasons. And initiated corrective measures. This small exercise really did not require a very high caliber in leadership either.

On one hand, the international stability appears to be in a tail spin. Because the lone super power is determined to rise and shine at every flashpoint despite the time tested principle of never jump into somebody else's civil war. On the other hand, India is finally waking up to the fact that the world does not feed on morals! India needs to re-look and re-fashion its internal factors to meet the prevailing new external lawlessness.

The Have-Nots. Indians over the centuries have done to the Untouchables, what the Americans did to the Blacks. Suppression. The Blacks even today cannot easily rise in the American society because of one simple fear that they will return the favour in ample measures. Fortunately for India, the Untouchables retain their levels of tolerance like the rest of the Indians. Therefore, rapid education and economic development of the backward/rural areas needs to be implemented on a war footing. Time lost in this respect will be directly proportionate to heightened levels of social disharmony which India can ill-afford as an emerging power.

Unity-in-Diversity. The Indian tragedy is that this slogan since 1947 has only harped on the aspect concerning *diversity,* encouraging divisive tendencies from Kashmir to Kanyakumari! For aspirations towards building a modem nation-state, the buzz word has to be integration and not disintegration. Give spin to integration by merging the MoD with Service Headquarters and right down the line to the Theatre Command. More efficiency at a much lesser cost with availability of a larger fire power. A unique functional role model of unity in diversity for India is its military. Be it the Sikhs, Rajputs, Jats or the Madras Regiments, the cultural diversity is adequately maintained at the lower end of the spectrum. Uniformity through training is achieved at the higher end of the spectrum.

The social scientist and the economist must sit together with the military analyst to understand, innovate and devise methods to integrate the society accordingly.

Bibliography

Ajey Lele: *Strategic Technologies for the Military : Breaking New Frontiers*, Sage, Delhi, 2009.

Alperovitz, Gar. *The Decision to Use the Atomic Bomb*. New York: Vintage Books, 1996.

Anil, K.C.: *Military and Democracy in India: Challenges, Politics and Power*, Sumit Enterprises, Delhi, 2009.

Banerjee, Sumanta: *In the Wake of Naxalbari: A History of the Naxalite Movement in India*, Calcutta: Subarnarekha, 1980.

Bellamy, C.: *Knights in White Armour: The New Art of War and Peace*, London, Random House, 1997.

Benjamin, Joseph : *China-Pak Relations : Prospect and Retrospect*, Reference Press, Delhi, 2004.

Bhat, T.P. : *India and China : Trade Complementarities and Competitiveness*, Bookwell, Delhi, 2008.

Budge I: *The New Challenge of Direct Democracy*, Oxford, Polity Press, 1996.

Chitkara, M.G. : *Indo-Pak Relations Challenges Before New Millennium*, APH, Delhi, 2001.

Clinton, William J. *A National Security Strategy for a New Century*. Washington, DC: Government Printing Office, 1998.

Damrosch, L.F.: *Law and Force in the New International Order*, Boulder, Westview Press, 1991.

Daniel J.: *Bandits on the Information Superhighway*. O'Reilly & Associates, Inc.: Sebastopol, 1996.

Dasgupta, B.: *The Naxalite Movement*, Bombay: Allied Publishers, 1974.

David Post : *The Rise of Law in Cyberspace*, 48 Stan, L. Rev. 1367, 1996.

Dixit, Prabla: *Defence Economics: A Struggle for Power*, New Delhi, Orient Longman, 1981.

Fletcher, Arnold: *Afghanistan, Highway of Conquest*, Ithaca, New York, Cornell University, 1965.

Frederick B.: *Protection and Security on the Information Superhighway*. John Wiley & Sons, Inc.: New York, 1995.

Friedman, G.: *The Future of War of Cyber Crimes*, N.Y., Random House, 1996.

Gaur, Mahendra : *Indian Policy of Neighbour*, Delhi, Kalpaz Pub., 2006.

Ghosh, Ajoy : *China-Pak Conflict : Threat to South Asian Security*, Reference Press, Delhi, 2003.

Gupta, A., & Laliberte, S. : *Security by Example Defend I.T.* New York, Addison Wesley, 2004.

Hahn, Harley: *Harley Hahn's Internet InSecurity*. Prentice Hall: Upper Saddle River, 2002.

Hays, Peter L. and others: *Countering the Proliferation and Use of Weapons of Mass Destruction*, New York, NY: McGraw-Hill, 1998.

Hoffman, Bruce: *Inside Terrorism and Internet Crime*, New York: Columbia University Press, 1998.

Huntington, P. : *The Soldier and the State : The Theory and Politics of Civil-Military Relations*, Natraj Pub, Delhi, 2005.

Huntington, S.P.: *The China Modernisation Military and the State*, N.Y., Vintage Books, 1964.

Joel Moses: *The Computer Age, A Twenty-Year View*.Cambridge, MA, The MIT Press, 1979.

John M. Seidl: *Politics American Style: Race, Environment and Central Cities*, New York, Prentice-Hall, 1972.

Juvale, R.P. : *Military Strategy and Diplomacy*, Cyber Tech Publications, Delhi, 2010.

Karanjit Siyan: *Internet Firewalls and Network Security*. New Riders Publishing: Indianapolis, 1996.

Keane J.: *Democracy and Cyber Crimes*, London, Verso, 1988.

Kumar, Raj : *Weapons and Military Technology*, Sumit Enterprises, Delhi, 2009.

Laliberte, S. : *Security by Example Defend I.T.* New York, Addison Wesley, 2004.

Martin H. Greenberg: *Studies in Nuclear Terrorism*, Boston: G.K. Hall & Co., 1979.

Mary, W.: *Asian Power and Politics: the Cultural Dimensions of Authority*, Cambridge, Belknap Press, 1985.

Peter G. Tsouras: *Dictionary of Military Quotations*, Manas, Delhi, 2006.

Posen, B.R.: *The Sources of Indian Military Doctrine*, Ithaca, 1984, Cornell Univ. Press.

Radhakrishna: *Handbook of Military and Defence Services*, Sumit Enterprises, Delhi, 2009.

Rosen, P.: *Societies and Military Power: India and its Armies*, Ithaca, Cornell University Press, 1996.

Rudolph, Heimanson: *Dictionary of Military*, N.Y.: Oceana Publications, 1967.

Singhal, D. P.: *India and Afghanistan: 1876-1907. A Study in Diplomatic Relations*, St. Lucia, University of Queensland, 1963.

Strange, Susan: *The Retreat of the State: The Diffusion of Power in the World Economy*, Cambridge: Cambridge University, 1996.

Sutton, J., *Technology and Defence Market Structure*, MIT Press, Delhi, 1998.

Index

G

I

L

M

N

P

R

S

T

V

❑❑❑